FIFTEEN SERMONS

PREACHED BEFORE

the University of Oxford

BETWEEN A.D. 1826 AND 1843

NOTRE DAME SERIES IN THE GREAT BOOKS

John Henry Newman, *The Idea of a University* (1982)
St. Thomas Aquinas, *Treatise on Happiness* (1983)
William James, *Psychology: The Briefer Course* (1985)
John Henry Newman, *An Essay on the Development of
Christian Doctrine* (1989)

FIFTEEN SERMONS

PREACHED BEFORE

The University of Oxford

BETWEEN A.D. 1826 AND 1843
IN THE DEFINITIVE THIRD EDITION OF 1872

By JOHN HENRY NEWMAN

INTRODUCTION BY

MARY KATHERINE TILLMAN

University of Notre Dame Press
Notre Dame, Indiana

University of Notre Dame Press
Notre Dame, Indiana 46556
www.undpress.nd.edu

Library of Congress Cataloging-in-Publication Data

Newman, John Henry, 1801–1890.
  [Sermons. Selections]
  Fifteen sermons preached before the University of Oxford between
A.D. 1826 and 1843 / John Henry Newman ; introduction by Mary
Katherine Tillman.
    p.   cm. — (Notre Dame series in the great books)
  ISBN 0-268-00996-1 (alk. paper)
  1. Church of England—Sermons.   2. Angelican Communion—
Sermons.   3. Sermons, English.   I. Title.   II. Series.
BX5133.N4F5   1997
252'.03—dc20   96-26441

∞ *This book is printed on acid-free paper.*

CONTENTS

Contents

THE DEFINITIVE
THIRD EDITION OF 1872

An Introduction

MARY KATHERINE TILLMAN

THIS series of Anglican sermons on faith and reason was preached by John Henry Newman (1801–1890) in the University Church of St. Mary the Virgin, Oxford. Occasionally alluded to by Newman as "Discourses," being more like lectures than anything today called *sermons,* the volume is now commonly referred to as the *Oxford University Sermons (OUS),* or as, simply, the *University Sermons (US).* The first of the series was written in Newman's evangelical youth (Sermon I, 1826), but most are from the intellectually formative, more rationalist period when he was Tutor of Oriel College (Sermons II–IX, 1830–1833). The last six were preached during his later Anglo-Catholic years (Sermons X–XV, 1839–43).

The volume's first edition of 1843, *Sermons, Chiefly on the Theory of Religious Belief, Preached before the University of Oxford,* sold out immediately and, in "little more than a fortnight," was followed by a second edition "with not above a page difference between them"—this in striking contrast to Newman's previous volumes of sermons, which had taken a year to exhaust their first editions.[1] By 1843 there was heightened interest in this already controversial leader of the Oxford (Tractarian) Movement, who had just resigned his position as vicar of St. Mary's, and who, it was now broadly (and correctly) rumored, was on the verge of becoming a Roman Catholic, thereby occasioning the same move by countless others.[2] The hundreds who flocked to the university church to hear Newman preach were attracted mainly, however, by the depth of his spiritual insight, his arresting psychological discernment, the originality and freshness of his ideas, and his stirring, plain-spoken eloquence.

From the high pulpit of the fifteenth-century university church a formal University Sermon was given ten times a year by a clergyman especially chosen for the occasion, "the select preacher." Although the vice-chancellor had honored Newman with the exceptional invitation to preach before the university when he was but twenty-three and still a deacon, it was not until two years later, on July 2nd, 1826, that he delivered his first University Sermon.

My emphasis in this introduction will be on the essential unity of the series of fifteen sermons taken "as a whole." As Newman wrote to his sister just before the volume came out, he had "been working out a theory" during the twelve years between the second sermon, preached in April of 1830, and his publication of the entire series of fifteen in early 1843.[3] The best recommendation for the volume, he continued in the same letter, was that "it is consistent," for he had "kept to the same views and arguments for twelve years." Though, at the time, Newman worried that the University Sermons would be thought "sad, dull affairs," and that some of them would be "very hard," Jemima Newman Mozley responded a month or so later: "I do not know any volume I have ever read that was so attractive and satisfying to the mind except Butler's 'Analogy.' It makes deep things so very simple."[4] Newman replied gratefully: "I certainly thought it, though incomplete and imperfect, yet my best volume."[5] Newman and his sister were not alone in their high estimate of the work. Early biographer Wilfrid Ward notes: "By the more speculative minds in Oxford, as W. G. Ward and the students of [S. T.] Coleridge, [the University Sermons] were regarded, as by Newman himself, as containing his best and most valuable thoughts."[6]

Often unwittingly assumed to be but one more among Newman's many collections of sermons, sometimes hidden in the shadow of his widely celebrated *Parochial and Plain Sermons* of the same period, the volume of *Oxford University Sermons* is, in its own right, an integral, cohering and unique work. It contains, in what might be called "serial" arrangement, the most ingenious and philosophically fertile of all Newman's sermons, perhaps even of all his writings. More intellectually investigative in content than his doctrinal, ethical, and devotional sermons, this early volume is accessible (more so than his challenging late work, *An Essay in Aid of a Grammar of Assent*) to students of philosophy, theology and religion, and to anyone interested in a truly "contemporary," attractive, and helpful understanding of faith's relation to ordinary everyday thinking. The sermons "are not theological or ecclesiastical," Newman said, "though they bear immediately upon the most intimate and practical religious questions."[7]

Shortly after his 1870 publication of the *Grammar of Assent,* Newman returned to the 1843 volume of University Sermons and expanded it by inserting, in proper chronological sequence, an additional unaltered sermon (now the third) from the same early years. He added bracketed notes of clarification from his now Catholic perspective, a dedication to Dean R. W. Church, an Advertisment dated late 1871, and a new title, *Fifteen Sermons Preached before the University of Oxford between* A.D. *1826 and 1843.* Most importantly, he inserted a comprehensive, condensed preface of nine pages. This third edition, published early in 1872, is here returned to print in its entirety.

A preface for the *University Sermons* had originally been conceived of in 1847, when Newman was studying theology in Rome shortly after his 1845 reception into the Catholic Church. At this time his *Essay on the Development of Christian Doctrine,* rumored in America to be "half Catholicism, half infidelity," was already being translated into French. Because of the ecclesiastical circumstances of the day, Newman feared the worst from the Roman censors, who, he knew, would be more able and inclined to read the French than the English. Though in the end he need not have worried, he drew up in Latin twelve *Theses de Fide* clarifying his position on the relation of faith and reason in order to secure the *imprimatur* of Jesuit theologian Giovanni Perrone.[8] As Newman wrote to J. D. Dalgairns, his Oxford associate (and, soon, fellow Oratorian) who was overseeing the French translations of both the *Essay on Development* and a selection of the University Sermons: "I shall put before [Perrone] as clearly as I can my opinions about Faith and Reason. If he approves, of which I don't despair, I might put what I draw up as a Preface to the *Sermons.* . . ."[9] He meant a Latin preface, which Dalgairns would then translate into French.

Although Newman thought the earlier sermons were "much better written . . . than the last,"[10] he understood the later ones to be "more precise, as well as more accurate, in their doctrine."[11] And the crucial point at this particular moment, "as the essay on Devt lags in translation," was to make haste in publishing a supportive "set" of the University Sermons in French, namely, the last six sermons (X–XV), precisely

> as *bearing upon* my Essay viz The question of Probability, evidence etc etc. . . . What I wish to say is, "I am not maintaining what I say is all true, but I wish to *assist in investigating* and bringing to light *great principles* necessary for the day—and the only way to bring them out is *freely* to investigate, with the

inward habitual intention (which I trust I have) always to be submitting what I say to the judgment of the Church." COULD NOT THIS FEELING BE EXPRESSED IN THE PREFACE? I will put down here, as I read thro' the *Sermons,* any thoughts which strike me *(which will make the preface).*[12]

By means of the French translation of that particular, highly relevant "set" of the University Sermons, together with their new, clarifying preface, Newman hoped to smooth the way for the coming French translation of the *Essay on Development.*

> The truth is, I think people want *preparing* for the Essay by laying down principles which have long been familiar to our minds. . . . These [last six] *Sermons* take in the *two* principles which are so prominent in the Essay, that no real idea can be comprehended in all its bearings at once—that the main instrument of proof in matters of life is 'antecedent probability.'[13]

The lengthy 1847 correspondence with Dalgairns on the French translation, together with Henry Tristram's 1937 publication of the Latin *Theses de Fide,* provide valuable notes and comments on the last six sermons individually and on the volume as a whole, and also present some of Newman's views as a newcomer to the Roman church of that day. This concentrated review of the *University Sermons,* in particular of the last six, provided Newman with the main materials for his English Preface to the third edition of 1872.

Sometimes the Oxford University Sermons are divided into two groupings (Sermons I–IX and X–XV), because of Newman's temporary preoccupation with the French translation of the final six as preparatory for the *Essay on Development* and because of the six-year hiatus between Sermons IX and X, during which time Newman traveled in the Mediterranean then became completely involved in the leadership of the

Oxford Movement. There was a similarly formative hiatus of four years between Sermons I and II. Furthermore, the final six sermons (or, sometimes, the "final six but one," excluding XV) may appear to be the only ones on the faith-reason relation, for most of them have one or both words in their titles. Every one of the fifteen sermons, however, contributes significantly to establishing Newman's broad and full understanding of the workings of the human mind, in clear contrast to the more truncated views of human reason and belief brought forth in the centuries immediately preceding his own. Newman's was an enlarged and rich understanding of reason and faith, one that makes sense to and is serviceable for ordinary people today; and it is an understanding which is much more akin to the views of Aristotle, the Greek tragedians, Cicero, and of the early Fathers of the Church, than to the skeptical and rationalist views of modern philosophy and of "post-Christian" critiques of religion.

The fifteen University Sermons belong together as Newman himself published them in the third edition. Only taken altogether do they have their full impact and accomplish their purpose, to illuminate and persuade. In his 1843 Advertisement for the original edition, Newman refers to the sermons as a "series,"[14] by which he means a developing round of views on various aspects of faith, reason, and their multiple relations of distinctness, compatibility, and opposition. Not only because Newman was "working out a theory" in them but also because all of them are, in his words, "discussing portions of one and the same subject,"[15] each of these fifteen views stands in need of and is inextricably linked to the others and without them easily narrows and even distorts Newman's position. Only when all fifteen are taken together as a whole, do they powerfully proclaim the radical disjunction between the mentality of faith and the mentality of the secular world and, at the same time, the proper and mutually beneficial conjunction of natural reason and religious faith.

Newman's consternation, when he and Dalgairns were corresponding in 1847 about which among the fifteen sermons to select for the French translation, arose in part because the translator apparently was not respecting the interrelations and unity of the sermons. "That on the 'Usurpations of Reason' is indeed one of the *set,* and I should be glad to have it published—but it cannot be published without the next to it, 'Personal Influence.' . . ."[16] Toward the end of the same long letter to Dalgairns, again emphasizing the unity and integrity of the volume as such, Newman wrote: "After [re]reading these Sermons I must say I think they are, *as a whole,* the best things I have written, and I cannot believe that they are not Catholic, and will not be useful."[17] He would sketch a preface for them, he said, realizing that "a great deal depends on a clear explanation [of] *what I mean* by reason and by faith—and the *drift* of the whole."[18]

While Newman makes no pretense that his circle of views on the faith-reason relation is exhaustive or final, he presents a developing series of closely interrelated approaches to carefully selected aspects of the subject. By means of continuous, imaginative variation and shifts in perspective, by means of argument, especially from analogy, and by example and illustration, these distinct views work together even as a kind of *system* of integrated ideas. Newman's investigative and tentatively analytical approach to the experienced mystery of the mind's movements, a highly original approach written "with no aid from Anglican, and no knowledge of Catholic theologians,"[19] provides an early glimpse of, and invaluable insights into, the fundamental issues and ideas, the methodological approaches, and the centering vision that would, with remarkable consistency and continuity, further unfold in Newman's Roman Catholic writings from 1845 until his death in 1890.

In particular, Newman's efforts to perfect his understanding of the faith-reason relation found immediate expression in the 1845 *Essay on the Development of Christian Doctrine,* and then later expansion in his educational writings of the 1850s. The tension and the reinforcement of faith and reason, each to the other, occurs again in the passionate tour de force of the final chapter of his 1864 *Apologia pro Vita Sua,* and finally, the relation finds its fullest unfolding in his 1870 magnum opus specifically devoted to this subject, *An Essay in Aid of a Grammar of Assent.*

Not once did Newman impugn or repudiate his Oxford University Sermons—as too youthful, too imperfect, too Anglican, or too inquiring. In his mind they remained of a piece, among themselves and in direct continuity with his other writings: initiating, exploratory, seminal. In 1853 he wrote, "I stand by my (Oxford) University Discourses . . . and am almost a zealot for their substantial truth."[20] And in 1872 he proudly reissued them in their third edition.

2

One autumn weekend, I traveled from the University of Notre Dame's London Program, where I was teaching a course called "Newman on Faith and Reason," to see an extraordinary exhibition in Rouen, France. Nineteen of the thirty paintings in the serial masterpiece *Les Cathédrales* by Newman's younger French contemporary, Claude Monet (1840–1926), had been brought home from their dispersion throughout the world for a 1990s centenary celebration. Taken in its visual fecundity as an authoritative whole, *Les Cathédrales* is considered one of the principal sources of twentieth century art, for it introduced the temporal dimension and a new kind of transcendence into the universe of painting, advancing by what Monet termed the *series* a new notion of artistic form, development and system.[21]

Severely limiting his motif and restricting his compositional options, Monet had systematically articulated variation upon variation of Rouen's great Gothic cathedral. The multiple views approach their single subject gradually, circle around it and fan across its statue-pocked face, as the canvases strain to hold its swelling volume, intensity, and grandeur. Still more varied in coloration and in technique than in point of view, the paintings conjugate the tenses of the sun's passage in brilliant inflections of light and shadow and in changing moods of atmosphere and effect.

To select the precise vantage points from which he might approximate in paint the vision he beheld, Monet had walked around and around the cathedral, studying it from this angle and that and in this light and that. He would stop and squint, move back and forth, a little to the left and then to the right, hastily jot and sketch on his notepads, then resume his walking again. "He contemplates the panorama stretching before his eyes, by framing off with his hands the space he intends to reproduce, so as to judge it better by isolating it."[22] After occasional visits to Rouen, Monet began to paint *en plein air*, then moved into rented rooms along the shop-lined Place de la cathédrale in the old medieval sector of the city.

First, from the east, Monet painted a prefatory *Vue générale de Rouen*, the distant cathedral framed in a hazy sea of sky and city: a great, tactile harmony of colors in motion, dabs of paint and swirls of dabs, the three towers ascending in somber, rupturing verticals against a background of vibrant sunset in which all details are lost—just as I last glimpsed it through the window of my departing train. Next, much closer now, from a side street in the direction of its south flank, Monet painted the cathedral in blue-gray silhouette against a clear pale-orange sky. Then in muted mauves and blues he composed two views of the thick base of the cathedral's medieval tower, paintings nearly identical to one another but for details of shading and texture. Attached to the stolid, stunted tower are small dwellings with shimmering, multicolored windows pulsing with life, in contrast to a dark passageway leading westward through which Monet surely walked, hurriedly, out into the brilliant afternoon sun.

Here at last he found the full face of his centering motif, the great western façade, which was to completely occupy his imagination, his visual field, and his canvases for over two years to come. He painted at an almost frenetic pace, working on site at the same hours of successive days and on the same dates in successive years in order to capture with empirical precision the same seasonal illuminations, moods, and effects.

"Everything changes, even stone," Monet wrote home to his wife at Giverny.[23] The play of mottled light and shadow on the crenelated façade, portal, and towers seemed to change too quickly, he said; he could not keep apace. Often he developed several canvases at a time—a record fourteen one day in March 1893—moving from one to another about half-hourly as the sun arched above. Or, when the light was more suddenly modified, as by the passage of a large cloud or the dissipation of a morning haze, he would dart his brush, stroke by stroke, from one canvas to the next and the next. Guy de Maupassant observed Monet in the mid-80s when his new serial method was beginning to emerge: "Off he went, followed by children carrying his canvases. . . . He picked them up and put them down in turn, according to the changing weather."[24]

Finally, in his studio at Giverny, Monet edited and reworked the cathedral canvases one by one, framed and grouped them, excluded some of them, exhibited others, and rearranged them again and again. At last the series was finished, the intention realized: *Les Cathédrales*—a single, unfolding, organically related whole—bespeaking with incomparable eloquence, and comprehensible on many levels, transcendent issues far more immense than the colossal object of the artist's gaze: timelessness and change, appearance and reality, tradition and modernity, urbanity and nature, matter and spirit, the labor of toiling bodies and the work of creative minds, the human and the divine.

Now regarded by art historians as the apogée of his mature serial paintings, *Les Cathédrales* was exhibited by Monet in varieties of sequences and groupings. Even though reviewers kept describing the series as moving from dawn to dusk, Monet insisted that it not be interpreted as "a collective chronometer" or, for that matter, as a sequence of "topographical notations."[25] Perhaps partly to disabuse viewers of such facile interpretations, Monet chose canvases of different sizes, diverse types of frames, and quite varied subtitles for his multiple views of the cathedral.

Monet's letters reveal that his unprecedented, technical usage of the term *série* dates from around 1890, the idea having germinated in him during the decade of the 1880s, though earlier glimpsed in his more experimental works.[26] His serial method became firmly established, "an intentional and systematic procedure," in his hundreds of serial paintings of the 1890s and beyond.[27] Most simply, what Monet meant by a *series* of views was the spatio-temporal development of a single motif by means of formal variations. This in no way depended upon a programmatic or consecutive ordering of the pictures or on any other mechanical or simply deducible feature. The "formal factors" which, for Monet, constituted the variants in his serial method included point of view, design and layout, the tubes

and tools of his palette, the strokes and layerings of his paint—
in short, the techniques and the materials of the master artist.
But the key to the composition of a series was the particular
interrelationships and the manner of coherence among these
formal factors in a tightly integrated group of paintings. A
single motif gradually made its appearance to the viewer by
means of multiple views carefully selected according to spatial
and temporal, atmospheric and seasonal requirements. Monet's
fidelity to perceptual experience and to nature, together with
his gift for creative transformation, issued in a poetic equilib-
rium of all of these rigorously balanced elements. Systematic
unity pervades the gradually articulated whole effected by
the artist's intentionality, discriminating choices, and creative
genius. It was this coherence of the whole that was so highly
praised by his contemporaries Pissarro, Degas, Renoir, and
Cézanne. As Pissarro commented about *Les Cathédrales*, "in the
ensemble, I have found that superb unity which I have so much
sought."[28]

Writer and critic Gustave Geffroy, who watched Monet
at work, called him an "alchemist" who had acquired the
"singular ability to see the disposition and influence of tones
immediately":

> All of these forms and these glimmers of light speak to one an-
> other, collide with each other, influence one another, saturate
> each other with color and reflections. . . . Quickly, he covers his
> canvas with the dominant values, studying their gradations, con-
> trasting [and] harmonizing them. This procedure [is what] gives
> the paintings their unity.[29]

Monet himself said that painting multiple views of a single
subject was the only way he could "get to know its life" and
that such "cumulative understanding" was "gained by the jux-
taposing of successive instants."[30] As he told a visitor to one of

his exhibits: the paintings "acquire their full value by the comparison and the succession of the whole series."[31] And yet their full value would never be their complete or final value. Monet realized that even an entire series of paintings, because they are spatial portrayals, could render but limited views, "only approximations," he said; still, their variations, cumulation and exhibition, he hoped, might be able to convey "an idea" of the living reality he wished to make visible.[32]

Even though some critics saw Monet as preeminently faithful to the tradition of the French masters,[33] others labeled his work mere "impressionism." These latter accused him of subverting the canons of objectivity and abandoning methodological rigor in favor of a chaotic subjectivism. But Monet did not go about his work in haphazard fashion at all. He proceeded "according to a methodical, rational plan, of inflexible rigor, in some ways mathematical. . . ."[34] Monet was systematic in a way that could never be closed or final. As he himself wrote, "anyone who claims to have finished a picture is terribly conceited."[35] The artist alone judges, by means of internal and external factors, perhaps even unconsciously, just when the series is, not completed, but finished.

Marcel Proust wondered whether the same methodological principles of serial painting as those employed by Monet might not be applied, analogically, to the art of the great writer; for, after all, "the work of the writer is but a kind of optical instrument offered to the reader enabling him to discern what, without this book, he would perhaps not have been able to view by himself."[36] Proust muses:

> Let us imagine today a *littérateur* to whom the idea might have come of treating twenty times, in diverse lights, the same theme, and who would have the sensibility to do something as profound, as subtle, as powerful, as overwhelming, as original, as compelling, as the *Cathédrales* . . . of Monet.[37]

3

Just such a *littérateur,* I am suggesting, was John Henry New-man, whose serial artistry in the Oxford University Sermons was begun nearly a full century before the above, forward-looking comment of Marcel Proust. Newman's modes of perceiving and representing the objects of our thought and devotion are not unlike those of Monet. In layers of paint on canvas, fine artist Monet created magnificent views of the Gothic cathedral in the variegated light of the sun and its shift-ing shadows; in strata of words on paper, liberal artist Newman created enduring views of the temple of the mind illuminated by Kindly Light, even as in a glass darkly. For both artists, the unifying principle of a serial system of interrelated artworks may be said to be the object at its center *as present to* the ener-gized mind and imagination of the artist. But one might also say that, for both artists, the object or motif is, in a way, sec-ondary to the atmosphere or light suffusing the object. "In Thy Light, we see light," Newman prayed: "Christians are said to be 'called into His marvelous light,' to 'walk as children of light,' to 'abide in the light,' to 'put on the armour of light.'"[38]

For Newman, as for Monet, change saturates the very atmosphere in which we live, perceive, and think. It is the ambiance of the visible world. "In a higher world it is otherwise, but here below to live is to change, and to be perfect is to have changed often," Newman wrote in his *Essay on Development,* shortly after concluding the University Sermons with his re-markable sermon on development.[39]

Words, whole sermons, or an entire volume of sermons, like the artist's dabs of paint, whole canvases, and entire series of painting, are employed by Newman to portray a multi-faceted subject from a particular point of view. Each sermon takes a view on the relation of faith to learning or to reasoning under only one of its aspects, and each sermon anticipates additional disclosures in other sermons and still other works. The wholeness of truth and the mind's relation to and within it exceed human words and notions. Truth is beyond the single view and the abstract system, and it ultimately eludes the best that limited human portrayals, even taken altogether, can ever represent. Naturally speaking, the human mind ever approximates truth in its perceptions, images, and ideas.

For Newman, the limitations of human understanding are writ large in every theoretical position and every science, in every philosophical and theological system of thought. Each view can indeed be a glimpse of the whole—that is, of the whole considered under this or that partial aspect and from this or that limited perspective. But human language in all of its families, even the language of sacred scripture and of sacred doctrine, remains ever the human attempt to give color and shape to realities that exceed and reach beyond it.

> This vast and intricate scene of things cannot be generalized or represented through or to the human mind. . . . Who shall give method to what is infinitely complex and measure to the unfathomable? . . . Almighty God has condescended to speak to us so far as human thought and language will admit, by approximations.[40]

One of Newman's pervasive representations of thinking is that of a circling or centering activity. Roman man of letters Cicero, whom Newman claimed as his only master of style,[41] wrote about the orator's method of verbally walking around his subject, and describing it from all angles, as one might circle a great sculpture in order to better grasp its integral form and beauty. As Newman puts it:

> Truth of whatever kind is the proper object of the intellect. . . . Now the intellect in its present state . . . does not discern truth

intuitively, or as a whole. We know, not by a direct and simple vision, not at a glance, but as it were, by piecemeal and accumulation, by a mental process, by going round an object, by the comparison, the combination, the mutual correction, the continual adaptation of many partial notions, by the employment, concentration, and joint action of many faculties and exercises of mind.[42]

Just like the artist's horizon, his position in the cathedral square, his "school" of painting, so the context or horizon of any view, according to Newman, is a particular (dis)position and orientation. A particular tradition or a particular "circle of ideas" serves as a kind of antecedent atmosphere in which an individual's thinking originates. As a passing cloud can diffuse the artist's light of the moment, so, for Newman, an insight can curl itself up like a hedgehog and roll away, or a skein of ideas can unravel and splay. Ideas themselves have a drift, a bearing, or an upshot, he says, and great ideas need elbow room and open air for full exploration, and the large field of history for germination and maturation. Thinking presents itself in a variety of shades and hues amid multiple prejudices and predispositions. Thinking is always already interpretive.[43]

Above all, though amenable to the disciplinary fixatives of logic and science, thinking is dynamic movement, perhaps closest to music in its flow, impermanence, and fragility. The stock notions that Newman calls "the furniture of the mind" are brought home to the mind by language and education; they become ingrained by habit and culture. Isolated facts simply take up floor space in a room without a view, as it were, unless and until they are claimed, arranged and situated by the vigorous activity of a healthy mind. Only by the mind's activity can information and orientation together produce a *view* and, perhaps, by accumulation and judgment even produce knowledge.

For Newman, the living mind that is undisciplined by education and training is like a whirlwind. It changes like a chameleon, veiling itself in any and every view rather than in no view at all. Just as the senses of an animal are activated naturally by its proper food or by an enemy or its offspring, so too the human mind is energized and enlivened by its proper object, truth. Newman conceives of "the wild, living intellect" as a great inward center of ceaseless activity exploring, discarding, balancing, economizing, and appropriating views, making progress by saying and unsaying, as it connaturally senses its way toward truth. It is "not the mere addition to our knowledge that is the illumination; but the locomotion, the movement onwards, of that mental centre, to which both what we know, and what we are learning, the accumulating mass of our acquirements, gravitates."[44] No wonder a new organon that goes beyond those of Aristotle and Bacon, an *organum investigandi,* is considered necessary by Newman. What is wanting, especially in matters of morality and religion, is a method more like the calculus, like Pascal's *esprit de finesse,* or the flexible ruler of the mason of Lesbos in Aristotle's *Nicomachean Ethics.* A method more delicate and accurate than that offered by the canons of formal logic or the rules of empirical science is needed in order that the representations of living thought are brought closer to concrete reality. This ordinary inductive method, informally logical to be sure, is the accumulation of probabilities by the prudently judging mind until certitude can be reached and concrete action taken.[45]

A particular view, considered only in and of itself, can make its object appear distorted—that is, as expanded or contracted, enlarged or economized, magnified or telescoped—according to the antecedents and predisposition of the viewer. Many views help correct the distortions of the single view, for no one viewer can see simultaneously all the sides and angles, all the layers and relations of any single object.

> [I]n proportion to the variety of aspects under which it presents itself to various minds is its force and depth, and the argument for its reality. Ordinarily an idea is not brought home to the intellect as objective except through this variety; like bodily substances, which are not apprehended except under the clothing of their properties and results, and which admit of being walked round, and surveyed on opposite sides, and in different perspectives, and in contrary lights, in evidence of their reality. . . . [T]he *primâ facie* dissimilitude of its aspects becomes, when explained, an argument for its substantiveness and integrity, and their multiplicity for its originality and power.[46]

A single view is always partial for it abstracts but an aspect of that which it views. Without the object, the many views of the thing would not exist; without the views, the object itself would be inaccessible. Considered from without, views frame aspects of their object; considered from within, views belong to persons and are, accordingly, as varied as persons are. As Newman wrote in an early letter to his brother Charles, "We survey moral and religious subjects through the glass of previous habits; and scarcely two persons use a glass of the same magnifying power."[47]

Views gradually disclose their object by circling around it as, for example, the liturgical seasons turn again and again about the great events held sacred in the memory of the Church. Or again, the views can gradually draw out their object in temporal continuity and development, as, for example, Holy Week does, day by day leading the Christian through each of the works of salvation. As Monet did by painting the cathedral in a distant cityscape, then ever more closely, and as he also painted the cathedral façade as its appearance changed with the times of the day, so too did Newman write "abstractly" about the varied aspects of a circle of ideas, but also "concretely" about the idea's spatio-temporal unfolding through the phases of its historical development.

Such is Newman's treatment of the idea "University" and of the idea "Church," as he circles each of these leading ideas and also develops it, pausing at each critical juncture in its forward career.[48] While Newman walked around his subject—as he does, say, in *The Idea of a University* when he considers theology (and each of the disciplines) as an essential, inextricable part of "the complete circle of learning"—he could not *simultaneously* include the historical development of the subject, which, however, he soon thereafter imaginatively unfolds in his series of essays on the *Rise and Progress of Universities*.[49] Nor can a historical view, such as that taken of the idea of Church in *An Essay on the Development of Christian Doctrine*, simultaneously lay out theologically a single aspect of that doctrine, such as the ecclesiology of the laity, the subject of his later work *On Consulting the Faithful in Matters of Doctrine*.[50]

The academic disciplines, to Newman, are abstracted, partial views of reality, each presenting from its unique standpoint and by means of its singular methodology but one aspect of the entire field of knowledge. Each view or discipline is in need of the insights and balancing factors provided by the others. "[T]he Sciences, into which our knowledge may be said to be cast, have multiplied bearings one on another, and an internal sympathy, and admit, or rather demand, comparison and adjustment."[51] Without these always unfinished conversations and transactions among the disciplines, the imperialist tendencies of any one discipline or group of disciplines would not be checked. With these ongoing negotiations of discipline and method, more stable, justified views are formed, the boundaries of disciplines are secured or enlarged, and the idea "University" continues to be realized. Newman, like Monet, knew that:

> In the combination of colours, very different effects are pro-
> duced by a difference in their selection and juxta-position; red,
> green, and white, change their shades, according to the contrast
> to which they are submitted. And, in like manner, the drift and
> meaning of a branch of knowledge varies with the company in
> which it is introduced to the student. . . . There is no science but
> tells a different tale, when viewed as a portion of a whole, from
> what it is likely to suggest when taken by itself, without the safe-
> guard, as I may call it, of others.[52]

The opposite of developing a large and philosophical habit
of mind, which is the goal of liberal education, is the assumption of a stance Newman calls "viewiness," which consists of
"extempore philosophy," a simulation of various unconnected
views and opinions, name-dropping, "nutshell truths for the
breakfast table."[53] Here one takes on and lays down notions at
whim, as if they were one's own to bandy about and had no
referent, as if truth did not matter. This is the easy outcome of
an overly broad or too general education, one which is neither
disciplined nor deep. Overspecialization, on the other hand,
can be equally problematic, for here one can develop a narrow,
unphilosophical mind that is stuck in one view forever, like the
inflexible bigot rigidly riding but one hobbyhorse and riding
the beast to death.

The best partial views, be they expressed in words or notes,
in symbols, sounds, or colors, be they poems or paintings, sym-
phonies or sciences, are distant reflections of aspects of the
eternal Logos, Truth Itself. To view even a single aspect of
the way things are, not in the order of logic, but, really, in what
Newman called "the order of chronology,"[54] is a remarkable gift
that can permeate the whole of one's thought and life. In fact,
Newman says, "this is what is meant by originality in thinking:
it is the discovery of an aspect of a subject-matter, simpler, it
may be, and more intelligible than any hitherto taken."[55]

But distortion becomes fixed when a single view is mistaken for the whole. Taking one abstracted aspect for the whole concrete reality or one method of approach as the only correct one is like worshipping the tabernacle or icon as the god. And yet, consistently throughout the University Sermons, Newman refused to reject popular views of faith and reason. Whether commenting on the superstitious acts of belief of ordinary people or the stubborn single-mindedness of the bigot or heretic, he preferred to elicit the inherent albeit partial truth to which each view gives testimony. He denounced only those who exalt human reason as the ultimate arbiter and judge in all things, the proud and unyielding philosophers who do not approach truth on their knees. The oblivious systematizers and rationalists who engage in unreal abstractions and in endless argumentation inappropriate to a given subject receive only slightly less remonstrance than the cynic in matters of religious belief.

Essential to understanding Newman's writing is awareness, on the part of the reader, of Newman's lifelong endeavor to explore and articulate views and coherences of views. He multiplied them indefinitely, especially in tensile relation to one another, in order to discover as many aspects of his subject as possible. For example, in sermons X and XI, the true centerpiece of this volume, Newman *contrasts* faith and reason, then, the following Sunday, he *relates* faith and reason. Sermon I presents faith and reason from a distance on the large field of history: the antiquity of religion in relation to the modernity of his day with its enlightened critiques, scientific advancements, and social progress; and sermon IX presents the same issues up close in the heart of the individual: religious submission of will vs. the self-sufficiency of stubborn willfulness. Sermon II contrasts the God of philosophy, an abstraction of reason, with the incarnate, personal God of revelation. Sermon III takes the same antagonism, but views it specifically in relation to moral life. Sermon V further develops the Christian "principle of personation" from sermon II, presenting personal influence and good example as the true teachers of Christianity. The relation of sight and faith in sermons VI and VII is yet another variation on the central motif of the book; as is the tension between the worldly theories of freedom and progress and the inward rule of conscience and personal responsibility, which is the subject of sermon VIII. And so forth.

In reading any work or part of a work by Newman, one must grasp the view from within which he is writing and the likelihood that there is at least one other place in his writings, and probably several others, where he takes a different tack or view of the very same subject or issues. One can, correctly, read all of Newman's works as views on the subject of education and as themselves pedagogical. One can just as legitimately, however, read all of Newman's works as centered upon the phenomenon of conscience: its foundational function for all moral and religious life, its natural endowment in every human being, its instrumentality in the divine pedagogy, its freedom, its relation to authority, and so forth. One can also validly view the relation of reason and faith as Newman's pervasive motif, cathedral-like, at the center of all of his works and, in particular, these Oxford University Sermons.

This volume, then, may be seen as a developing, circling series of sermons, each a unique though partial view upon an aspect of its ever-elusive object, namely, the actual reason-faith relation as experienced personally by this individual or that, and as experienced communally by the entire church catholic. Taken altogether, the sermons present a more encompassing view than any single sermon by itself. They effectively offer the reader an enlarged understanding of the most noble activities of which human beings are capable. But the offering, Newman fully realizes, is not exhaustive or complete, for there are many aspects of the subject still to be discovered, disclosed, and contemplated. The faith-reason relation will be developed again and again in Newman's writings, from other vantage points and in other lights and seasons.

Illuminated in the University Sermons are large contemporary issues which concern not only reason and faith but also science and religion, nature and grace, modern secularism and Christianity, as well as the natural formation of mind, character, and conscience that is so necessary for the full realization of religious faith in the individual and community. Investigating the uses and the limitations, for faith, of evidences and miracles, of linguistic expression and argument, of formal proof and implicit reasoning, of entire systems of thought and tradition, Newman is perhaps most attentive of all to the grounds of religious faith in the lives of ordinary people, children, and the uneducated. Taking into account antecedent desires, presumptions, and probabilities, he convincingly uncovers the significance for faith of a right moral disposition. He emphasizes, too, the indispensability for faith (as well as for learning) of the personal influence, witness, and example of others. All of these elements, especially when conjoined and compounded, contribute to the unequivocal reasonableness of religious faith.

4

It has often been said that Newman is not a "systematic" thinker, there being no single work among his eighty-some volumes in which to find his leading ideas defined and methodically organized, nor in fact to find any one of them neatly constructed, exhaustively explored, or comprehensively related to the others. Nor can his writings taken altogether be seen as systematically arranged, so multiple and varied are they in subject, style, and genre. He did not wish to be called a theologian, much less a metaphysician, both terms more properly reserved for thinkers committed to complete and unchanging arrangements of axioms and their logical deductions.

Moreover, it is said, Newman's habit was to write and publish in a rather piecemeal and occasional fashion, "not without a call," as he put it—that is, in response to invitation or duty, or from the emergency of some compelling issue of the day.[56] Furthermore, how could someone who took as seriously as did Newman ordinary, concrete experience—the developmental nature of the human person, as well as of knowledge, ideas, and institutions—abstractly categorize that living experience within a formal system of thought; for is it not true that growth is the evidence of life and that the real is the measure of the notional? Surely the unique genius of the essayist and the controversialist, the teacher, preacher, poet and novelist, all of which Newman indeed was, is not the same genius as that of the great philosophical and theological system builders of the past, thinkers such as Aristotle, St. Thomas Aquinas, René Descartes, Immanuel Kant, and G. W. F. Hegel.

Why, then, does Newman insist that the most important and enduring lesson a young student must learn is *to think systematically?*

> . . . I hold very strongly that the first step in intellectual training is to impress upon a boy's mind the idea of science, method, order, principle, and system; of rule and exception, of richness and harmony. . . . Let him once gain this habit of method, of starting from fixed points, of making his ground good as he goes, of distinguishing what he knows from what he does not know, and I conceive he will be gradually initiated into the largest and truest philosophical views, and will feel nothing but impatience and disgust at the random theories and imposing sophistries and dashing paradoxes, which carry away half-formed and superficial intellects.[57]

Surely this was the case in Newman's own education, from school days at Ealing through undergraduate and fellowship years at Oxford.

Method and system, like sketches and maps, outline pathways of thought and inventory its content. They tame and discipline its freedom into art and science, pushing it back to first principles and securing each step of its progress. The ordering and systematizing of thought are necessary to the full development of any view that is more than mere opinion or hearsay. But to map and systematize the workings of the mind is in itself to freeze them, as a photograph or a painting freezes a view. While true in some sense to what it pictures, a representation is "unreal" in that it never captures the living person in one portrait or even in many. In a series of portraits, however, of a cathedral, say, or of an individual as infant, child, adolescent, adult, and aged, one is able to see more truly and objectively, and thus can better discern and approximate what it is that is represented.

> [A]s views of a material object may be taken from points so remote or so opposed, that they seem at first sight incompatible, and especially as their shadows will be disproportionate, or even monstrous, . . . yet all these anomalies will disappear and all these contrarieties be adjusted, on ascertaining the point of vision or the surface of projection in each case; so also all the aspects of an idea are capable of coalition, and of a resolution into the object to which it belongs. . . .[58]

Throughout his life, Newman's writings reflect explicitly his use of and reflection upon the principle of system. In 1825, shortly before he delivered his first University Sermon, Newman wrote in his *Journal:* "The necessity of composing sermons has obliged me to systematize and complete my ideas on many subjects."[59] In 1832, Newman writes in the fifth University Sermon: "Truth is vast and far-stretching, viewed as a system; and, viewed in its separate doctrines, it depends on the combination of a number of various, delicate, and scattered evidences; hence it can scarcely be exhibited in a given number of sentences."[60] In his first book, *The Arians of the Fourth Century* (1833), Newman discusses "the Apostolical Tradition, that is, the Creed," in contrast to sacred scripture, as "systematic knowledge [that] was withheld" from the unbaptized.[61]

When he was fully engaged in the Oxford Movement, Newman assumed the enormous task of constructing a systematic theology for Anglicanism, a *"corpus theologicum et ecclesiasticum."*

> [T]he chief work he ["the Author," i.e., Newman] took upon himself [in writing his 1837 *Lectures on the Prophetical Office of the Church* was] that of systematizing what they [the Anglican divines] had variously put forth. . . . We have a vast inheritance, but no inventory of our treasures. All is given us in profusion; it remains for us to catalogue, sort, distribute, select, harmonize and complete. . . ."[62]

His 1838 *Lectures on Justification*, he hoped, would be a contribution to "the consolidation of a theological system, which . . . may tend to inform, persuade, and absorb into itself religious minds. . . ."[63]

Here it may well be objected that Newman's theory of the *via media*, the leading idea of the projected Anglican system, balanced midway between Catholicism and Protestantism, ultimately failed; that he himself came to see that theory and system pulverized before his eyes as mere "paper logic"; and that he thereby came to realize the impossibility of ever providing a systematic framework for such an unwieldly inheritance. In truth, however, one of the things Newman came to realize through that devastating experience was the inadequacy of an abstract theological inventory that in no way embodied the developing reality or fact of the Church as a whole, in all of its lived, complex, internal relations, part with part. To be sure, the revered texts of the past and their interpretations were an essential part of tradition, but not without their experienced incorporation into the faith, worship, and everyday lives of the people of God. This ample embodiment he would gradually come to find in what he called "the Catholic system," which he embraced as a whole in 1845. In 1850 he illuminated his enriched understanding in this way:

> A convert comes to learn, and not to pick and choose . . . and it does not occur to him to weigh and measure every proceeding, every practice which he meets with among those whom he has joined. He comes to Catholicism as to a living system, with a living teaching, and not to a mere collection of decrees and canons, which by themselves are of course but the framework, not the body and substance of the Church.[64]

Much later, in his 1877 preface to the third edition of the *Prophetical Office,* Newman proposed his final and most developed model of the Church, a living *corpus ecclesiasticum,* explaining how it is that: "Theology is the fundamental and regulating principle of the whole Church *system.*" . . . "Again, a religion is not a proposition, but a *system;* it is a rite, a creed, a philosophy, a rule of duty, all at once. . . ."[65]

In the fifteenth of his Oxford University Sermons, delivered in 1843, it can be seen that Newman's entire, influential "Theory of Developments in Religious Doctrine," both here and in the 1845 *Essay on Development,* depends ultimately upon the interlocking notions of *series* and *system:*

> One proposition necessarily leads to another, and a second to a third; then some limitation is required; and the combination of these opposites occasions some fresh evolutions from the original idea, which indeed can never be said to be entirely ex-

hausted. This process is its development, and results in a series, or rather a body of dogmatic statements, till what was at first an impression on the Imagination has become a system or creed in the Reason.[66]

Newman often wrote of "the great system of things," of "the system of nature," and of "the providential system of the world." In the *Grammar of Assent,* he acknowledged his main source for this understanding of the interdependence of all of creation:

> [Bishop Joseph] Butler . . . is the great master of this doctrine, as it is brought out in the system of nature. . . . [H]e observes that "the world is a constitution or system, whose parts have a mutual reference to each other; and that there is a scheme of things gradually carrying on, called the course of nature, to the carrying on of which God has appointed us, in various ways, to contribute."[67]

Newman proceeded according to a notion of system that is perhaps more in tune with ordinary people's experience, with their at least implicit awareness of being time-bound and limited in understanding, of apprehending, serially, one thing at a time from one point of view at a time—a notion that bespeaks modernity's sense of the temporality of human consciousness and the historicity of the world.

To say, then, that Newman is not a systematic thinker, or that his writings are not systematic, cannot possibly mean there is no method, no arrangement, no logical coherence in his thinking, no principles or patterns in the content of his thought, no part-whole relationships and organic development of both structure and content in his vision of "the great providential system of the world" as it comes forth in ordered unity from the generous hand of the Creator. Insight into this reality, Newman says, is like a "vision, analogous to eye-sight, which my intellectual nature has of things as they are, arising from the original, elementary sympathy or harmony between myself and what is external to myself, I and it being portions of one whole, and, in a certain sense, existing for each other."[68]

There could hardly be a thinker more aware of and concerned to communicate the integral wholeness of the visible world in its analogical relation to the invisible world and thus of the at least implicit intentionality of human beings coming to understand themselves as situated in the circle of creation and historically, providentially, destined for eternity.

Are there then, for Newman, any limitations of system and of systematic thinking? Indeed there are, particularly in matters of religion and morality. Systematization can result in artificial constructions, which may erroneously be taken as real.

> Now the great practical evil of method and form in matters of religion,—nay in all moral matters,—is obviously this:—their promising more than they can effect. At best the science of divinity is very imperfect and inaccurate, yet the very name of science is a profession of accuracy. . . . [It can lead] the mind to mistake system for truth, and to suppose that an hypothesis is real because it is consistent: but all such objections, though important, rather lead us to a cautious use of science than to a distrust of it in religious matters. . . .[69]

Even though Newman ultimately offers no categorical or finished edifice of ideas for perusal, he does indeed both think and write on the principle of system, that is, Monet-like, according to ordered coherences of ideas circulating around and developing from a common center. Abstracted from this systematic context, each sermon and each volume—indeed each aspect of a writer's body of thought—presents but a partial and isolated view and, as such, is subject to the many misinterpretations and distortions by critics and commentators who see only that single aspect. As Newman perceptively writes in the *Grammar of Assent:*

> The same doctrines, as held in different religions, may be and often are held very differently, as belonging to distinct wholes or *forms,* as they are called, and exposed to the influence and the bias of the teaching, perhaps false, with which they are associated. Thus, for instance, whatever be the resemblance between St. Augustine's doctrine of Predestination and the tenet of Calvin upon it, the two really differ from each other *toto cælo* in significance and effect, in consequence of the place they hold in the systems in which they are respectively incorporated, just as shades and tints show so differently in a painting according to the masses of colour to which they are attached.[70]

As Newman verbally circles his subject matter in the fifteen Oxford University Sermons, considering now one now another aspect of the complex relationship of faith and reason, one can see emerge from them the structuring form of three broad and general views—like the more distant cityscapes of Rouen that Monet painted before he moved in to focus upon the cathedral up close.[71]

First there is the *popular* view, one which always has some truth in it, but which is too limited a perspective to encompass very much—say, a tourist's passing view of the cathedral of Rouen on a dark and rainy day. Secondly, there is the *counterfeit* or *false* view, which also sees something real but short-sightedly takes itself alone as the entire truth—as would, say, a gallery-goer, who, upon seeing Monet's isolated canvas of the cathedral viewed at six in the evening, would stubbornly insist: "But the cathedral of Rouen is not yellow; I've seen it with my own eyes." And thirdly, the *proper* view of the matter, as far as we can see—say, Renoir's trained and sympathetic judgment of his friend Monet's cathedral series taken as a whole.

The first view. The popular view of reason, the tourist's view, true as far as it goes but limited, is that reason consists in explicit and convincing arguments and proof. In the popular view, reason is *contrasted* with faith, which is seen to hold, on weak grounds, private opinions concerning religious matters. Reason, an extension of common sense and more or less synonymous with "the mind," is understood to be based on strong, explicit evidence; faith, a feeling or sentiment, more or less synonymous with "the heart," is based on conjecture and presumption. Reason is objective and difficult to convince; faith is subjective and personal and accepts things easily. This is the popular view.

The second view. The erroneous or counterfeit view of reason, that of the stubbornly myopic gallery-goer, who would, after wagering all he had on the fact, accompany you to Rouen to show you that the cathedral is truly not yellow—this view sees reason as not merely contrasted with faith, but *opposed* to faith. Reason, based on sense experience and logic alone, is sole judge of what counts as true; it is the faculty of seeking out evidences, framing proofs, investigating and arguing about all things, including the silent and the sacred; the mythic, the miraculous, and the mysterious. All things are to be analyzed and clarified in the glare of day; nothing else is objective, true, or real; nothing else counts as knowledge. This dominating, *secular* reason, as Newman calls it, encroaches, usurps, and reaches beyond its own limits when it presumes to deal with religious and moral matters. The fatal error of secular reason, Newman says, is to think itself judge of religious truth without preparation of heart, to think "that Truth can be approached without homage." Beginning in doubt and suspicion, worldly reason is ever skeptical and critical, will argue forever and always find objections.

Faith too is misunderstood by the gallery-goer, for it is seen as the opposite of secular reason; that is, as credulity, superstition, fanaticism, and bigotry. This specious view of faith takes religion to be private and basically illogical, exclusively a matter of ardor and enthusiasm, a matter solely of the heart. False faith is ready to believe anything and everything, dismissing as "too heady" and rationalistic all intellectual content and inquiry, and thus all creeds and doctrines, all confirmation and intellectual defense of its subjective inclinations. Interestingly, although they may seem like opposites in their bogus dichotomizing of head and heart, these false substitutes for reason and for faith are really alike, according to Newman. They are the two sides of the same counterfeit coinage, the one arising in reactionary response to the other. They both rely on the private judgment of the individual, making the self both sanctuary and object of worship.

In *The Idea of a University,* Newman calls this devotion to argumentative, encroaching reason by the names of "the religion of philosophy" or "the religion of civilization." It is the more than likely, though not the necessary, outcome of the cultivation of the intellect for its own sake. The deification of reason is the real danger of the liberal education he advocates, warns Newman in the tradition of St. Augustine, Dante, and St. Thomas, for it can lead to pride of intellect and faith in secular reason alone as the unfailing instrument of all truth. The aggrandized rationalism of the captious critic often leads to the absolutizing of one's own private judgment, or of the private judgment of so-called experts, of science, of professionals, of philosophers, or even of secular society as a whole, and accordingly leads to "Liberalism" with respect to religion.

The inoperative reason of the gullible and the fanatical, on the other hand, often results in "dogmatism" in religion. And so religion, too, can readily range beyond its boundaries. It does so, according to Newman, when it leads people "to apply such Scripture communications as are intended for religious purposes to the determination of physical questions," or "in the usurpation of the schools of theology in former ages" when they issued decrees on the subjects of the senses and the intellect.[72] In writing to friends, Newman defended Darwin against the charge of atheism. "It does not seem to me to follow that creation is denied because the Creator, millions of years ago, gave laws to matter." And to the convert biologist St. George Jackson Mivart, who had been attacked by W. G. Ward, Newman remarked: "Those who would not allow Galileo to reason 300 years ago, will not allow any one else to now."[73] Newman wryly comments in *The Idea of a University,* that "those who accuse us of wishing, in accordance with Scripture language, to make the sun go round the earth, are not the men to deny that a science which exceeds its limits falls into error."[74]

The second or erroneous view of reason and of faith, and of their relation to one another, then, sees the two as not just contrasted, but as outrightly opposed to one another, and it takes a stand on which of the two must blot out the other and reign supreme.

The third view. How, then, does Newman describe the proper or true views of reason and faith, once they come into focus and color in the partial and kindly light we are granted as humans? What is "the large and true sense"? Reasoning, says Newman following Aristotle, is a faculty of the mind by which we gain knowledge upon grounds given; that is, it is a mediated, temporal process by which, from the knowledge of one thing, we advance to the knowledge of another. Reasoning is not the same as arguing: one may reason well but argue poorly; or someone may have a reason without being able to give it. Importantly, in the University Sermons Newman is distinguishing what he will develop again decades later, with only slight variation, in the *Grammar of Assent,* namely, what he here calls implicit reasoning, explicit reasoning, and the analysis of our reasoning, all of which are the act of one and the same reasoning person. The process of reasoning is complete in itself. Only a fragment of it can be exhibited for analysis; logic is reason's ordered, retrospective account of itself, its reasoning on or analysis of reasoning. Though reason is one and the same faculty in all, it varies in the concrete. Its results differ according to its subject matter, according to the person who is reasoning, according to its success in bringing the mind from premises to conclusion. Although it can be cultivated by training, reasoning remains as much a mystery as remembering, for there is always something which is incapable of proof. Newman often uses such words as "lines" and "drifts" and "upshots" of thought, its "enlargements" and "contractions," its "hues," "postures," and "skeins,"—indicating both the richly textured integrity and the indeterminateness of ordinary, concrete reasoning. In one of the most quoted passages from the University Sermons, he describes the concrete, implicit reasoning processes that are going on in our everyday lives all the time.

> The mind ranges to and fro, and spreads out, and advances forward with a quickness which has become a proverb, and a subtlety and versatility which baffle investigation. It passes on from point to point, gaining one by some indication; another on a probability; then availing itself of an association; then falling back on some received law; next seizing on testimony then committing itself to some popular impression, or some inward instinct, or some obscure memory; and thus it makes progress not unlike a clamberer on a steep cliff, who, by quick eye, prompt hand, and firm foot, ascends how he knows not himself, by personal endowments and by practice, rather than by rule, leaving no track behind him, and unable to teach another. . . .

And such mainly is the way in which all men, gifted or not, commonly reason,—not by rule, but by an inward faculty.

Reasoning, then, or the exercise of Reason, is a living spontaneous energy within us, not an art.[75]

This, then, is how faith is rational. "I have been engaged in proving the following points," Newman concludes in the same sermon: "that the reasonings and opinions which are involved in the act of Faith are latent and implicit; that the mind reflecting on itself is able to bring them out into some definite and methodical form; that Faith, however, is complete without this reflective faculty, which, in matter of fact, often does interfere with it, and must be used cautiously."[76]

Faith "in the true and large sense" is an acceptance of things as real, an acceptance of testimony. (I believe what you tell me because it is you telling me, and you have never deceived me.) The act of faith is complete in itself, independent of what is *popularly* called reason, that is, explicit reason (or else, how could it be that children and the unlearned savingly believe?) Yet because faith includes within it the implicit reasoning process which is its antecedent, though not its cause, it is itself an exercise of reason. Faith, Newman says with St. Thomas Aquinas, "is the reasoning of the religious mind." Of the *religious* mind. Faith is kept from abuse not by inquiry and investigation, but by a preparation of heart and a right moral and religious disposition. The eye of faith, its regulating principle, is love: the love of its "Great Object."

Some safeguard of faith is needed, some corrective principle which will secure it from its counterfeits and direct it toward its object. For Newman, it is not the mind that ultimately safeguards faith, but the rightly disposed heart. He writes: "Love *forms* faith into the image of Christ." Love will cause the mind to recoil from cruelty, impurity, and idolatry.

"The direction, firmness, consistency, and precision of [faith's] acts, it gains from Love." We believe because we love, and we understand because we believe: thus speaks the venerable Christian tradition. The divinely enlightened mind sees in Christ the Object that corresponds to its own affections and longings; and it trusts Him, or believes Him, from loving Him. For Newman a moral state, a right state of heart, is made the very means of gaining Truth. "I believe in order that I may understand," chorus those Fathers of the Church so familiar to Newman. And so he says, "Faith is the condition of general knowledge." Faith is a moral, as well as an intellectual, principle created by antecedent grounds which are themselves its main evidence. "I believe because I love and trust the One who speaks the words of eternal life. To whom else shall I go?" Here, then, are mighty reasons for the faith and the hope within.[77]

One decides according to one's state of heart, that is, by the principles that are habitual to one's moral self. These not only decide a person one way or another, but they actually color and interpret the evidence. Unbelief considers itself especially rational, or critical of evidence, but it too (like belief) relies on presumptions and prejudices as much as faith does. Opposite presumptions, to be sure: antecedent *im*probability as a sufficient refutation of the evidence. Thus, Newman speaks of "the plausibility of atheism," when the heart is not rightly disposed. How immensely important then is a loving and faith-filled upbringing and education for the young, and the development in them of a sense of mystery and wonder, of early prayers and devotions, of good example and strong moral models. These form the lifelong predispositions by which love begets love.

So the grounds on which the assent of faith is based are antecedent grounds, by which Newman means presumptions, prepossessions, and prejudices; inclinations and wishes; hopes, fears, and desires; our interests and the residue of traditions; existing opinions, views, and habits of mind—in short, the sum total of being a real, living person. Each of these grounds taken individually is indeed weak evidence, as the popular view of faith rightly holds. But accumulating and convergent in their drift, these implicit reasons taken altogether can sway the rightly disposed mind to personal certitude strong enough to act on. A creative and originating principle, faith comes into play when there is no time to think, when investigation would blunt the practical energy of the mind. Even when there is time to think, evidence is not called for until antecedent probabilities are insufficient. Desire and hope are faith's main evidence.

Newman illustrates the relation of faith and reason in a wonderful concatenation of analogies, a favorite mode of inference for him.[78] Human beings have additional faculties that are analogous to sense, namely reason and faith. The senses give direct acquaintance with external things in proximate relation. Reason supplies the deficiency of the senses in that it allows one to know things beyond the reach of sense. It proceeds from things that are known and assumed to be true to things that are not known. Reasoning is a process of gaining knowledge upon grounds given, of asserting this because of that. Faith too is an instrument of knowledge concerning things external and unseen, an acceptance of things as real or true upon previous grounds. Therefore faith is an exercise of reason, an act of the intellect, and a way of knowing. As reason is a higher instrument than the senses, so faith rises above reason. It is but "agreeable to analogy," Newman concludes, that Divine Truth should be attained by the highest and most subtle method— one less tangible than the senses and less open to analysis than reason, a way that is irreducible to explicit processes of reasoning.

Again, Newman draws an apt analogy between the claim that faith is "weak" and so should not be trusted and the claim that other faculties of the mind are also "weak," and yet are used with confidence. Sense, memory, and even reason often make mistakes, yet one still basically trusts and relies on them; so why not trust the venture of faith and "launch out into the deep"? The cumulative effect of these chains of analogies, like that of Monet's series of cathedrals, is meant to engage the properly disposed viewer by means of their compelling form.

The large and true view of reason's relation to faith is, then, that if one possesses the habit of faith, that is, if one's heart is alive to its Great Object and predisposed to trust what is revealed (if thus the seed falls on good ground), then thoughtful exercises of reasoning and reflection can provide encouragement, a stay, and sure support for faith. But faith is not only for the reflective and the educated; it is for the ordinary person, for everyone. Even if I cannot give explicit reasons for the hope within me, this does not necessarily mean that I am acting irrationally, that I do not have implicit grounds for what I hold. If I do not know or cannot give the reasons, I can take comfort in Newman's assurance that the teaching Church can and does.

Furthermore, reasoning can sanction without being the origin or cause of faith. Explicit reason as questioning, investigative, and defending, can minister to faith, just as faith serves reason by both enlarging its horizon and setting its boundaries. Finally and importantly, even critical reason has a service and responsibility to faith: while the eye of one's heart is on its Great Object, reason staves off intellectual abuse, the influences of a malformed conscience, or the intrusions of unwarranted authority.

The Oxford University Sermons are themselves written from within a larger view, which one might call the "humanly speaking" view. In other words, Newman's intention is not as explicitly spiritual or religious on the subject of faith as it is, say, in his *Parochial and Plain Sermons*, nor is it as explicitly theological as in his writings on the relation of faith and revelation, for example, in his "Papers on Inspiration."[79] In the University Sermons, faith is not viewed or developed mainly as a product of grace, of the Gospel, or of any source distinct from what nature supplies.

It is as if Newman had chosen in this faith-reason series not to go inside the cathedral, but rather, like Monet, to view it in its various aspects and appearances from outside, according to the "humanly speaking" view. But we also know that all of Cardinal Newman's "humanly speaking" views really stem from his faith-filled vision from within the cathedral, that is, from within the church catholic and from within the sanctified temple of his inmost being. As for Monet, it was not until a few days before he finished his magnificent cathedral series, the arduous work of two long years, that he finally entered the cathedral for the first time. Monet's views are from without; Newman's are from within and rely on the religious imagination of the predisposed moral self to make the connections and coherences, to create the integral whole. This difference between the two great artists is, perhaps, at least as much a difference as the materials, tools, and genres of their expression.

Newman's vision of how faith informs the life of the ordinary Christian believer is reflected in a passage which may well describe what Claude Monet viewed upon entering into that great object of his imagination, the cathedral of Rouen.

> [A] Catholic Cathedral is a sort of world, everyone going about his own business, but that business a religious one; groups of worshippers, and solitary ones—kneeling, standing—some at shrines, some at altars—hearing Mass and communicating—currents of worshippers intercepting and passing by each other—altar after altar lit up for worship, like stars in the firmament—or the bell giving notice of what is going on in parts you do not see—and all the while the canons in the choir going through their hours matins and lauds or Vespers, and at the end of it incense

rolling up from the high altar, and all this in one of the most wonderful buildings in the world and every day—lastly, all of this without any show or effort, but what every one is used to—every one at his own work, and leaving every one else to his.[80]

Notes

1. To Mrs. J. Mozley in *Letters and Correspondence of John Henry Newman during his Life in the English Church,* ed. Anne Mozley, 2 vols. (London: Longmans Green, 1903), 2: 366, and *The Letters and Diaries of John Henry Newman* (hereafter *LD*), ed. Charles Stephen Dessain et al., vols. 11–22 (London, 1961–72), vols. 23–31 (Oxford, 1973–77), vols. 1–7 (Oxford, 1978–95), 12: 30. See also Ian Ker, *John Henry Newman: A Biography* (Oxford: Oxford University Press, 1988), 272, as well as pages 257–269, which emphasize in particular the last six sermons. My debt, and that of other Newman scholars, to Ian Ker, for this authoritative biography as well as for his many other studies of Newman's thought, is incalculable. My thanks are owed as well to the Fathers of the Birmingham Oratory in England, especially to C. J. G. Winterton, and to the Venerable John Henry Newman Association of the United States, in particular to Vincent J. Giese.

2. For the intriguing story of the Oxford Movement for reform in the Church of England, narrated in relation to the singular personalities and uncommon influence of its leaders, see *The Oxford Conspirators: A History of the Oxford Movement, 1833–1845* (New York: Macmillan, 1969) by Marvin R. O'Connell, whose generous colleagueship in Newman Studies, including the critical reading of this introduction, I most gratefully acknowledge. In his editor's introduction to *From Oxford to the People* (Leominster, Herefordshire: Fowler Wright Books, 1996), Paul Vaiss refers to Marvin O'Connell's *Oxford Conspirators* as "the first full history of the Oxford Movement since R. W. Church's [1891] and E. A. Knox's [1933]" and reviews English and French studies of the last three decades that have had some bearing on the Oxford Movement.

3. Mozley, 2: 363.

4. Ibid., 367.

5. Ibid., 368.

6. Wilfrid Ward, *The Life of John Henry Cardinal Newman,* 2 vols., (London: Longmans, Green, and Co., 1912), 1: 59.

7. Mozley, 2: 363.

8. See Henry Tristram, "Cardinal Newman's Theses de Fide and his proposed Introduction to the French Translation of the University Sermons," *Gregorianum* 18 (1937): 219–260.

9. *LD,* 12: 55.

10. Newman, as quoted in Ker, *Biography,* 257, in a sentence omitted from the letter as published in Mozley, 2: 363.

11. John Henry Newman, *Fifteen Sermons Preached before the University of Oxford* (London: Longmans, Green, and Co., 1872), preface to the 3d ed., p. x. (Hereafter *US*).

12. *LD,* 12: 29–30.

13. Ibid., 5; see also notes 1–4.

14. *US,* Advertisement, vii.

15. Ibid.

16. *LD,* 12: 29. Emphasis Newman's.

17. Ibid., 32. Emphasis added.

18. Ibid., 8–9. Emphases Newman's.

19. *US,* preface, ix–x.

20. *LD,* 15: 381.

21. See Catalogue d'exposition, *Rouen, Les Cathédrales de Monet* (Rouen: Musée des Beaux-Arts, 1994), 10, 40–41, 50. For this section, I am also indebted to chap. 3, "Pictorial Composition and Choice of Viewpoint," and chap. 12, "The Evolution of Monet's Series," in John House, *Monet: Nature into Art* (New Haven and London: Yale University Press, 1986); chap. 6, "Monet in the 1890s: The Series Paintings," in Paul Hayes Tucker, *Claude Monet, Life and Art* (New Haven and London: Yale University Press, 1995); and the Exhibition Catalogue, *Claude Monet 1840–1926* (Chicago: Art Institute of Chicago, 1995).

22. Frédéric Henriet in Jean-Paul Hoschedé's account, as quoted in House, *Monet,* 45.

23. W. lettre 1208, to Alice Monet, 5 April 1893, as cited by Sylvie Patin in Catalogue d'exposition, *Rouen*, 42.

24. As quoted in House, *Monet*, 195. See also Tucker, *Claude Monet*, 153 and Patin in Catalogue d'exposition, *Rouen*, 42–43.

25. Tucker, *Claude Monet*, 153.

26. Patin in Catalogue d'exposition, *Rouen*, 40–41. See House, *Monet*, 193: "The word *[série]* became Monet's standard term after 1890 for his more tightly integrated groups of paintings." See also Tucker, *Claude Monet*, 139: Monet "was developing something entirely new. For no other painter up until then had ever conceived of painting a large number of pictures that concentrated on the same subject and that would be differentiated only by formal factors. . . ."

27. See Patin in Catalogue d'exposition, *Rouen*, 40–41. See also House, *Monet*, 201: "After 1891, Monet increasingly systematised the procedures he had used for the Grain Stacks, in a succession of series each intended to be seen as an integrated, organic whole." Among Monet's more well-known series painted after *Les Cathédrales* are: what he called his *Londons* (the largest series he ever produced, nearly a hundred views of Waterloo Bridge, Charing Cross Bridge, and the buildings of Parliament), the twenty-four *Mornings on the Seine* (uniquely painted in strictly chronological order—all at dawn—and intended to be so exhibited), and the *Water Lilies* (which alone remain exhibited together in the order that Monet wished, in Musée de l'Orangerie, Paris).

28. As quoted by Patin in Catalogue d'exposition, *Rouen*, 45. See also House, *Monet*, 204.

29. Tucker, *Claude Monet*, 131.

30. House, *Monet*, 195–196.

31. Ibid., 213.

32. Ibid., 196.

33. Tucker, *Claude Monet*, 165.

34. Ibid., 142.

35. Ibid., 152.

36. Marcel Proust, as quoted by John Gross in *Brief Lives*, ed. Louis Kronenberger (Boston and Toronto: Little Brown and Co., 1965) 611 (translation my own).

37. Proust in *Contre Sainte-Beuve,* as cited by Michel Hogg in Catalogue d'exposition, *Rouen,* 49 (translation my own).

38. *US,* sermon III, sec. 1.

39. Newman, *An Essay on the Development of Christian Doctrine,* 1845 (rpt. Notre Dame, Ind: University of Notre Dame Press, 1989), chap. I, sec. I, no. 7 (p. 40). (Hereafter *Dev.*) See also *US,* sermon XV, "The Theory of Developments in Religious Doctrine."

40. *US,* IV, 35.

41. *LD,* 24: 242.

42. John Henry Newman, *The Idea of a University* (1854; rpt. Notre Dame: University of Notre Dame Press, 1982), discourse VII, no. 1 (p. 114). (Hereafter *Idea*).

43. Two recently published books study the close affinities between the thought of Newman and that of Hans-Georg Gadamer. See Thomas K. Carr, *Newman and Gadamer: Towards a Hermeneutics of Religious Knowledge* (Atlanta: Scholars Press, 1996), a penetrating study but one which, to its own detriment, does not take into account an outstanding work by Joseph Dunne on Newman and Gadamer (together with R. G. Collingwood, Hannah Arendt, and Jürgen Habermas—all in relation to Aristotle): *Back to the Rough Ground: 'Phronesis and Techne' in Modern Philosophy and in Aristotle* (Notre Dame: University of Notre Dame Press, 1993).

44. *Idea,* VI, 5 (p. 101).

45. In addition to the sections on the "illative sense" in Newman's *Grammar of Assent,* see "On the Office of the Judgment or Prudentia (as the arbiter) in determining the Evidentia Credibilitatis" in *The Theological Papers of John Henry Newman on Faith and Certainty,* ed. J. Derek Holmes (Oxford: Clarendon Press, 1976), 24–25 and *The Philosophical Notebook of John Henry Newman,* ed. Edward Sillem, 2 vols. (Louvain: Nauwelaerts, 1969–70) 2: 163.

46. *Dev,* I, I, 2 (pp. 34–35).

47. *LD,* 1: 226.

48. Ian Ker writes: "What is so striking is the resemblance between his idea of the Church and his earlier idea of the university, a similarity which suggests if not influence at least a common source in a unified vision" (Ker, *Biography,* 396).

49. Originally written by Newman as a series of individual articles for the *Catholic University Gazette* (1854), then published in a single volume as *Office and Work of Universities* (1856), then renamed by Newman as *Rise and Progress of Universities* and placed by him in *Historical Sketches* III (London: Longmans, Green, and Co., 1872).

50. First published by Newman in the *Rambler* (1859), then reprinted in the Appendix to the third edition of *The Arians of the Fourth Century* (London: Longmans, Green, and Co., 1871), now separately available from Sheed and Ward (Kansas City, Mo., 1961), ed. John Coulson.

51. *Idea*, V, 1 (p. 75). In keeping with the traditional usage of the Latin term *scientia* to mean knowledge, Newman most often uses the term "the sciences" to refer to all of the academic disciplines. "These various partial views or abstractions, by means of which the mind looks out upon its object, are called sciences . . ." (ibid., III, 2, p. 34). It is usually clear from the context when he is using the term "science" in the narrower, more specialized sense we use today, as, for example, in his lecture on "Christianity and Physical Science" where he discusses "the independence of the fields of Theology and general Science severally," saying that "[i]n Physics is comprised that family of sciences which is concerned with the sensible world, . . . with matter" (ibid., Part 2, VII, 3, p. 324).

52. Ibid., V, 1 (p. 75).

53. Ibid., preface, xliv–xlv.

54. *LD*, 12: 31: "We are speaking of faith and reason not in the abstract, but in the individual, in the ordo chronologicus, not logicus."

55. Newman, *An Essay in Aid of a Grammar of Assent* (Notre Dame: University of Notre Dame Press, 1979), chap. 9, sec. 3, no. 2 (p. 291). For a superb discussion of Newman's general epistemology in relation to that of Aristotle and selected contemporary philosophers, see chap. 1 in Dunne, *Back to the Rough Ground.*

56. John Henry Newman, *Autobiographical Writings*, ed. Henry Tristram (New York: Sheed and Ward, 1957), 272–273.

57. *Idea*, preface, xliv–xlv.

58. *Dev*, I, I, 2 (pp. 34–35).

59. *Autobiographical Writings,* 204.

60. *US,* V, 21. See also preface, sec. 5.

61. John Henry Newman, *The Arians of the Fourth Century,* 3d ed. (London: Longmans, Green, and Co., 1897), 135.

62. John Henry Newman, *The Via Media of the Anglican Church,* ed. H. D. Weidner (Oxford: Clarendon, 1990), 20–21. Newman's Anglican work, the *Lectures on the Prophetical Office of the Church Viewed Relatively to Romanism and Popular Protestantism* (1837, 1838), was reprinted by him as a Catholic in 1877 with the new title, *The Via Media of the Anglican Church.* Revised by Newman to eliminate elements of anti-Romanism, this third edition includes an important preface containing his mature ecclesiology, added notes, and a second volume of Oxford Movement tracts and articles.

63. John Henry Newman, *Lectures on the Doctrine of Justification* (London, Oxford, and Cambridge: Rivingtons, 3d ed., 1874), vi.

64. John Henry Newman, *Certain Difficulties Felt by Anglicans in Catholic Teaching,* 2 vols. (London: Longmans, Green, and Co., 1898), 2: 18.

65. *Via Media,* 29; *Grammar,* 196–197 (emphasis mine).

66. *US,* XV, 20.

67. *Grammar,* 316.

68. John Henry Newman, *The Theological Papers of John Henry Newman on Faith and Certainty,* ed. J. Derek Holmes (Oxford: Clarendon Press, 1976), 71–72.

69. *US,* XIII, 21. See also *US,* I, 10 on "excessive attachment to system."

70. *Grammar,* 202–203.

71. See Gilles Grandjean, "Monet et Rouen," in Catalogue d'exposition, *Rouen,* 23ff.

72. *US,* IV, 6.

73. *LD,* 28: 71–72; 24: 77.

74. *Idea,* IV, 2 (p. 55).

75. *US,* XIII, 7, 8.

76. *US,* XIII, 38.

77. The quotations in this paragraph are taken mainly from *US,* XII and XIII.

78. See *US*, XI for these and other arguments from analogy. For further discussion of Newman's important method of analogical reasoning, see Walter Jost, *Rhetorical Thought in John Henry Newman* (Columbia: University of South Carolina Press, 1989), especially pp. 135–137, 160–161; and Terrence Merrigan, *Clear Heads and Holy Hearts* (Louvain: Peters Press, 1991), especially pp. 25–29.

79. See *The Theological Papers of John Henry Newman on Biblical Inspiration and on Infallibility,* part 1.

80. *LD*, 11: 253.

SERMONS

PREACHED BEFORE

The University of Oxford.

FIFTEEN SERMONS

The University of Oxford,

BETWEEN A.D. 1826 AND 1843

By JOHN HENRY NEWMAN

SOMETIME FELLOW OF ORIEL COLLEGE

" Mane semina semen tuum, et vespere ne cesset manus tua. Quia nescis, quid magis oriatur, hoc aut illud ; et si utrumque simul, melius erit."

VERY REV. RICHARD WILLIAM CHURCH, M.A.

DEAN OF ST. PAUL'S.

My dear Dean,

WHEN I lately asked your leave to prefix your
name to this Volume of Sermons preached before
the University of Oxford, I felt I had to explain to
myself and to my readers, why I had not offered it
to you on its first publication, rather than now, when
the long delay of nearly thirty years might seem to
have destroyed the graciousness of my act.

For you were one of those dear friends, resident in
Oxford, (some, as Charles Marriott and Charles Cornish,
now no more,) who in those trying five years, from
1841 to 1845, in the course of which this Volume was
given to the world, did so much to comfort and uphold
me by their patient, tender kindness, and their zealous
services in my behalf.

I cannot forget, how, in the February of 1841, you
suffered me day after day to open to you my anxieties
and plans, as events successively elicited them; and
much less can I lose the memory of your great act of
friendship, as well as of justice and courage, in the

February of 1845, your Proctor's year, when you, with another now departed, shielded me from the "civium ardor prava jubentium," by the interposition of a prerogative belonging to your academical position.

Much as I felt your generous conduct towards me at the time, those very circumstances which gave occasion to it deprived me then of the power of acknowledging it. That was no season to do what I am doing now, when an association with any work of mine would have been a burden to another, not a service; nor did I, in the Volumes which I published during those years, think of laying it upon any of my friends, except in the case of one who had had duties with me up at Littlemore, and overcame me by his loyal and urgent sympathy.

Accept then, my dear Church, though it be late, this expression of my gratitude, now that the lapse of years, the judgment passed on me by (what may be called) posterity, and the dignity of your present position, encourage me to think that, in thus gratifying myself, I am not inconsiderate towards you.

I am, my dear Dean,

Your very affectionate friend,

JOHN H. NEWMAN.

Advent, 1871.

ADVERTISEMENT.

OF the following Sermons, the First, Third, and Sixth were preached by the Author in Vice-Chancellor's Preaching Turns; the Second in his own; the Fourth, Fifth, Seventh, Eighth, and Ninth in his turns as Select Preacher.

The Six since 1832, which close the series, were preached in private College turns, which were made available to him, as being either at his own disposal or at that of his personal friends.

Though he has employed himself for the most part in discussing portions of one and the same subject, yet he need scarcely say, that his Volume has not the method, completeness, or scientific exactness in the use of language, which are necessary for a formal Treatise upon it; nor, indeed, was such an undertaking compatible with the nature and circumstances of the composition.

The above is the Advertisement prefixed to the Original Edition, dated February 4, 1843, except that, an additional Sermon being added to the present Edition—viz., No. 3—alterations in its wording were unavoidable.

THE ORATORY,
December, 1871.

PREFACE TO THE THIRD EDITION

THESE Discourses were originally published, except as regards some verbal corrections, just as they were preached. The author would gladly at that time have made considerable alterations in them, both in the way of addition and of omission; but, professing, as they did, to be "preached before the University," he did not feel himself at liberty to do so. Much less does he alter them now; all that he has thought it right to do has been, by notes in brackets at the foot of the page, to draw attention to certain faults which are to be found in them, either of thought or of language, and, as far as possible, to set these right.

Such faults were only to be expected in discussions of so difficult a character as some of them pursue, written at intervals, and on accidental, not to say sudden opportunities, and with no aid from Anglican, and no

knowledge of Catholic theologians. He is only surprised himself, that, under such circumstances, the
errors are not of a more serious character. This
remark especially applies to the Discourses upon the
relation of Faith to Reason, which are of the nature
of an exploring expedition into an all but unknown
country, and do not even venture on a definition of
either Faith or Reason on starting. As they proceed,
however, they become more precise, as well as more
accurate, in their doctrine, which shall here be stated
in a categorical form, and, as far as possible, in the
words used in the course of them.

1. Before setting down a definition of Faith and of
Reason, it will be right to consider what is the popular
notion of Faith and Reason, in contrast with each
other.

"I have not yet said what Reason really is, or what is its relation
to Faith, but have merely contrasted the two together, taking
Reason in the sense popularly ascribed to the word," x. 45.
Vide also xii. 7, 11, 36; xiii. 1, 4; xiv. 32.

2. According to this popular sense, Faith is the
judging on weak grounds in religious matters, and
Reason on strong grounds. Faith involves easiness, and
Reason slowness in accepting the claims of Religion;
by Faith is meant a feeling or sentiment, by Reason
an exercise of common sense; Faith is conversant

with conjectures or presumptions, Reason with proofs.

"Whatever be the real distinction and relation between Faith and Reason, the contrast which would be made between them on a popular view, is this,—that Reason requires strong evidence before it assents, and Faith is content with weaker evidence," x. 17.

"Faith and Reason are popularly contrasted with each other; Faith consisting of certain exercises of Reason which proceed mainly on presumption, and Reason of certain exercises which proceed mainly upon proof," xii. 3.

Vide also 2, 7, 10, 36; and v. 19; x. 26, 32; xi. 17.

3. But now, to speak more definitely, what ought we to understand by the faculty of Reason largely understood?

"By Reason is properly understood any process or act of the mind, by which, from knowing one thing, it advances on to know another," xii. 2.

Vide also xi. 6, 7; xiii. 7, 9; xiv. 28.

4. The process of the Reasoning Faculty is either explicit or implicit: that is, either with or without a direct recognition, on the part of the mind, of the starting-point and path of thought from and through which it comes to its conclusion.

"All men have a reason, but not all men can give a reason. We may denote these two exercises of mind as reasoning and arguing," xiii. 9. Vide the whole of the discourse.

5. The process of reasoning, whether implicit or explicit, is the act of one and the same faculty, to

which also belongs the power of analyzing that process, and of thereby passing from implicit to explicit. Reasoning, thus retrospectively employed in analyzing itself, results in a specific science or art, called logic, which is a sort of rhetoric, bringing out to advantage the implicit acts on which it has proceeded.

" Clearness in argument is not indispensable to reasoning well. The process of reasoning is complete in itself, and independent; the analysis is but an account of it," xiii. 10; vide 8.

" The warfare between Error and Truth is necessarily advantageous to the former, as being conducted by set speech or treatise; and this, not only from . . . the deficiency of truth in the power of eloquence, and even of words, but moreover, from the very neatness and definiteness of method, required in a written or spoken argument. Truth is vast and far stretching, viewed as a system . . . hence it can hardly be exhibited in a given number of sentences. . . Its advocate, unable to exhibit more than a fragment of the whole, must round off its rugged extremities, etc. . . . This, indeed, is the very art of composition," &c., v. 21.

" They who wish to shorten the dispute, look out for some strong and manifest argument, which may be stated tersely, handled conveniently, and urged rhetorically," &c., xiii. 36.

Vide xiv. 30.

6. Again: there are two methods of reasoning— *à priori,* and *à posteriori ;* from antecedent probabilities or verisimilitudes, and from evidence, of which the method of verisimilitude more naturally belongs to implicit reasoning, and the method of evidence to explicit.

" Proofs may be strong or slight, not in themselves, but according to the circumstances under which the doctrine professes to come to us, which they are brought to prove ; and they will have a great or small effect upon our minds, according as we admit those circumstances or not. Now, the admission of those circumstances involves a variety of antecedent views, presumptions, implications, associations, and the like, many of which it is very difficult to detect and analyze," &c., xiii. 33.

Vide also 9, and xii. 36.

7. Again :—though the Reasoning Faculty is in its nature one and the same in all minds, it varies, without limit, in point of strength, as existing in the concrete, that is, in individuals, and that, according to the subject-matter to which it is applied. Thus, a man may reason well on matters of trade, taken as his subject, but be simply unable to bring out into shape his reasoning upon them, or to write a book about them, because he has not the talent of analyzing—that is, of reasoning upon his own reasonings, or finding his own middle terms.

" How a man reasons is as much a mystery as how he remembers. He remembers better and worse on different subject-matters, and he reasons better and worse. The gift or talent may be distinct, but the process of reasoning is the same," xiii. 10.

Vide also xi. 6.

8. This inequality of the faculty in one and the same individual, with respect to different subject-matters, arises from two causes :—from want of experience and familiarity in the details of a given subject-matter ; and

from ignorance of the principles or axioms, often recondite, which belong to it.

" The man who neglected experiments, and trusted to his vigour
of talent, would be called a theorist; and the blind man who
seriously professed to lecture on light and colours could scarcely
hope to gain an audience. . . He might discourse with ease and
fluency, till we almost forgot his lamentable deprivation; at length
on a sudden, he would lose himself in some inexpressibly great
mistake," iv. 8.

" However full and however precise our producible grounds may
be, however systematic our method, however clear and tangible our
evidence, yet, when our argument is traced down to its simple
elements, there must ever be something which is incapable of proof,"
xi. 18.

9. Hence there are three senses of the word
"Reason," over and above the large and true sense.
Since what is not brought out into view cannot be
acknowledged as existing, it comes to pass that exercises of reasoning not explicit are commonly ignored.
Hence by Reason, relatively to Religion, is meant, first,
expertness in logical argument.

" Reason has a power of analysis and criticism in all opinions and
conduct, and nothing is true or right but what may be justified, and,
in a certain sense, proved by it; and unless the doctrines received
by Faith are approvable by Reason, they have no claim to be
regarded as true," x. 13.
Vide also 14, 16.

10. And again, since Evidences are more easily

analyzed than verisimilitudes, hence reasonings, that is, investigations, on the subject of Religion, are commonly considered to be nothing but à *posteriori* arguments; and Reason relatively to Religion becomes a faculty of framing Evidences. This, again, is a popular sense of the word, as applied to the subject of Religion, and a second sense in which I have used it.

" Reason is influenced by direct and definite proof: the mind is supposed to reason severely, when it rejects antecedent proof of a fact, rejects every thing but the actual evidence producible in its favour," x. 26.

" Reason, as the word is commonly used, rests on the evidence," x. 32.

11. The word " Reason " is still more often used in these Discourses in a third sense, viz., for a certain popular abuse of the faculty ; viz., when it occupies itself upon Religion, without a due familiar acquaintance with its subject-matter, or without a use of the first principles proper to it. This so-called Reason is in Scripture designated " the wisdom of the world ;" that is, the reasoning of secular minds about Religion, or reasonings about Religion based upon secular maxims, which are intrinsically foreign to it; parallel to the abuse of Reason in other subject-matters, as when chemical truths are made the axioms and starting-points in medical science, or the doctrine of final causes

is introduced into astronomical or geological inquiries.

Hence one of these Discourses is entitled "The Usurpations of
Reason;" and in the course of it mention is made of "captious
Reason," "forward Reason," &c. Vide note on iv. 9.

12. Faith is properly an assent, and an assent
without doubt, or a certitude.

"Faith is an acceptance of things as real," xi. 9.
"Faith simply accepts testimony," x. 8.
"Faith is not identical with its grounds and its object," xiii. 4.
"Faith starts with probabilities, yet it ends in peremptory state-
ments; it believes an informant amid doubt, yet accepts his infor-
mation without doubt," xiv. 34.
Vide also 39; x. 34; xi. 1; xv. 3.

13. Since, in accepting a conclusion, there is a
virtual recognition of its premisses, an act of Faith
may be said (improperly) to include in it the reasoning
process which is its antecedent, and to be in a certain
aspect an exercise of Reason; and thus is co-ordinate,
and in contrast, with the three (improper) senses of
the word "Reason" above enumerated, viz., explicit,
evidential, and secular Reason.

"If Reason is the faculty of gaining knowledge upon grounds
given, an act or process of Faith is an exercise of Reason, as being
an instrument of indirect knowledge concerning things external to
us," xi. 8, 9.

14. Faith, viewed in contrast with Reason in these

three senses, is implicit in its acts, adopts the method of verisimilitude, and starts from religious first principles.

Vide iv. 6 ; x. 27, 44; xi. 1, 25 ; xii. 3, 27, 37.

15. Faith is kept from abuse, e. g. from falling into superstition, by a right moral state of mind, or such dispositions and tempers as religiousness, love of holiness and truth, &c.

This is the subject of the twelfth discourse ; in which, however, stress ought to have been also laid upon the availableness, against such an abuse of Faith, of Reason, in the first and second (improper) senses of the word.

The Author has lately pursued this whole subject at considerable length in his " Essay in Aid of a Grammar of Assent."

CONTENTS.

SERMON I.

SERMON II.

a 2

SERMON VI.

ON JUSTICE, AS A PRINCIPLE OF DIVINE GOVERNANCE.

(Preached on Sunday afternoon, April 8, 1832,
By appointment of the Vice-Chancellor.)

𝔍𝔢𝔯. 𝔳𝔦𝔦𝔦. 11.

SERMON VII.

CONTEST BETWEEN FAITH AND SIGHT.

(Preached on Sunday afternoon, May 27, 1832,
In the Author's turn as Select Preacher.)

1 𝔍𝔬𝔥𝔫 𝔳. 4.

SERMON VIII.

HUMAN RESPONSIBILITY, AS INDEPENDENT OF CIRCUMSTANCES.

(Preached on Sunday afternoon, November 4, 1832,
In his turn as Select Preacher.)

𝔊𝔢𝔫. 𝔦𝔦𝔦. 13.

SERMON IX.

WILFULNESS, THE SIN OF SAUL.

(Preached on Sunday morning, December 2, 1832,
In his turn as Select Preacher.)

1 𝔖𝔞𝔪. 𝔵𝔳. 11.

Contents. xxiii

SERMON I.

THE PHILOSOPHICAL TEMPER, FIRST ENJOINED BY
THE GOSPEL.

(Preached July 2, 1826, Act Sunday.)

JOHN viii. 12.

*" Then spake Jesus again unto them, saying, I am the Light of the
world."*

FEW charges have been more frequently urged by
unbelievers against Revealed Religion, than that
it is hostile to the advance of philosophy and science.
That it has discouraged the cultivation of literature
can never with any plausibility be maintained, since
it is evident that the studies connected with the
history and interpretation of the Scriptures have, more
than any others, led to inquiries into the languages,
writings, and events of ancient times. Christianity
has always been a learned religion; it came into the
world as the offspring of an elder system, to which it
was indebted for much which it contained, and which
its professors were obliged continually to consult.
The Pagan philosopher, on enrolling himself a member of the Christian Church, was invited, nay, required, to betake himself to a line of study almost
unknown to the schools of Greece. The Jewish

[UNIV. S.]   B

books were even written in a language which he did
not understand, and opened to his view an account of
manners and customs very different from those with
which he was familiar. The writings of the ancients
were to be collected, and their opinions examined;
and thus those studies which are peculiarly called
learned would form the principal employment of one
who wished to be the champion of the Christian
faith. The philosopher might speculate, but the
theologian must submit to learn.

2. It cannot, then, be maintained that Christianity
has proved unfavourable to literary pursuits; yet,
from the very encouragement it gives to these, an
opposite objection has been drawn, as if on that very
account it impeded the advancement of philosophical
and scientific knowledge. It has been urged, with
considerable plausibility, that the attachment to the
writings of the ancients which it has produced has
been prejudicial to the discovery of new truths, by
creating a jealousy and dislike of whatever was contrary to received opinions. And thus Christianity
has been represented as a system which stands in
the way of improvement, whether in politics, education, or science; as if it were adapted to the state
of knowledge, and conducive to the happiness, of the
age in which it was introduced, but a positive evil
in more enlightened times; because, from its claim
to infallibility, it cannot itself change, and therefore
must ever be endeavouring to bend opinion to its own
antiquated views. Not to mention the multitude of
half-educated men who are avowedly hostile to Re-

vealed Religion, and who watch every new discovery or theory in science, in hope that something to its disadvantage may hence be derived, it is to be lamented that many even of the present respectable advocates of improvements in the condition of society, and patrons of general knowledge, seem to consider the interests of the human race quite irreconcilable with those of the Christian Church; and though they think it indecorous or unfeeling to attack Religion openly, yet appear confidently to expect that the progress of discovery and the general cultivation of the human mind must terminate in the fall of Christianity.

3. It must be confessed that the conduct of Christians has sometimes given countenance to these erroneous views respecting the nature and tendency of Revealed Religion. Too much deference has been paid to ancient literature. Admiration of the genius displayed in its writings, an imagination excited by the consideration of its very antiquity, not unfrequently the pride of knowledge and a desire of appearing to be possessed of a treasure which the many do not enjoy, have led men to exalt the sentiments of former ages to the disparagement of modern ideas. With a view, moreover, to increase (as they have supposed) the value and dignity of the sacred volume, others have been induced to set it forth as a depository of all truth, philosophical as well as religious; although St. Paul seems to limit its utility to profitableness for doctrine, reproof, correction, and instruction in righteousness. Others, again, have been too diligent and too hasty in answering every frivolous

and isolated objection to the words of Scripture, which
has been urged,—nay, which they fancied might possibly be urged,—from successive discoveries in science;
too diligent, because their minute solicitude has occa-
sioned them to lose sight of the Christian Evidence as a
whole, and to magnify the objection, as if (though it
were unanswerable) it could really weigh against the
mass of argument producible on the other side; and
too hasty because, had they been patient, succeeding
discoveries would perhaps of themselves have solved
for them the objection, without the interference of a
controversialist.   The ill consequences of such a procedure are obvious: the objection has been recognized
as important, while the solution offered has too often
been inadequate or unsound.   To feel jealous and appear timid, on witnessing the enlargement of scientific
knowledge, is almost to acknowledge that there may
be some contrariety between it and Revelation.

4. Our Saviour, in the text, calls Himself the Light
of the world; as David had already said, in words
which especially belong to this place [1] and this day [2],
"The Lord is my Light;" and though He so speaks

[1] [The motto of the University is "Dominus illuminatio mea."]

[2] [Act Sunday. "The candidate," says Huber on the English Universities, "emancipated from his teacher, makes himself known to the other
teachers by taking part in the disputations in the schools.   These services afterwards become formal public acts, *disputationes, responsiones,
lecturæ cursoriæ*.   A more especially solemn Act formed the actual close
of the whole course of study.   The licence was then conferred on him by
the Chancellor.   A custom arose that all the final and solemn exercises
should fall in the second term of the year (hence called the Act Term),
and be closed on the last Saturday in term by a solemn general Act, the
Vesperiæ, by keeping which the candidates of all degrees in their diffe-

of Himself as bringing religious knowledge to an ignorant and apostate race, yet we have no reason to suppose that He forbids lawful knowledge of any kind, and we cannot imagine that He would promulgate, by His inspired servants, doctrines which contradict previous truths which He has written on the face of nature.

5. The objection to Christianity, to which the foregoing remarks relate, may be variously answered.

First, by referring to the fact that the greatest Philosophers of modern times—the founders of the new school of discovery, and those who have most extended the boundaries of our knowledge—have been forced to submit their reason to the Gospel; a circumstance which, independent of the argument for the strength of the Christian Evidence which the conviction of such men affords, at least shows that Revealed Religion cannot be very unfavourable to scientific inquiries, when those who sincerely acknowledge the former still distinguish themselves above others in the latter.

6. Again, much might be said on the coincidence which exists between the general principles which the evidence for Revelation presupposes, and those on which inquiries into nature proceed. Science and

rent Faculties were considered qualified and entitled to begin the exercises connected with their new degree upon the following Monday. This fresh beginning (*inceptio*) took place with the greatest solemnity, and formed the point of richest brilliancy in the scholastic year. In Oxford it was called emphatically 'the Act,' in Cambridge 'the Commencement.'" (Abridged from F. W. Newman's translation.) The Act Sunday is or was the Sunday next before the Act, which falls in the first week of July.]

Revelation agree in supposing that nature is governed by uniform and settled laws. ⌈Scripture, properly understood, is decisive in removing all those irregular agents which are supposed to interrupt, at their own pleasure, the order of nature.⌉ Almost every religion but that of the Bible and those derived from it, has supposed the existence of an indefinite number of beings, to a certain extent independent of each other, able to interfere in the affairs of life, and whose interference (supposing it to exist) being reducible to no law, took away all hope of obtaining any real information concerning the actual system of the universe. On the other hand, the inspired writers are express in tracing all miraculous occurrences to the direct interposition, or at least the permission of the Deity ; and since they also imply that miracles are displayed, not at random, but with a purpose, their declarations in this respect entirely agree with the deductions which scientific observation has made concerning the general operation of established laws, and the absence of any arbitrary interference with them on the part of beings exterior to the present course of things. The supposition, then, of a system of established laws, on which all philosophical investigation is conducted, is also the very foundation on which the evidence for Revealed Religion rests. It is the more necessary to insist upon this, because some writers have wished to confuse the Jewish and Christian faiths with those other religions and those popular superstitions which are framed on no principle, and supported by no pretence of reasoning.

7. Without enlarging, however, on arguments of this nature, it is proposed now to direct attention to the moral character which both the Jewish and Christian Religions hold up as the excellence and perfection of human nature; for we shall find that some of those habits of mind which are throughout the Bible represented as alone pleasing in the sight of God, are the very habits which are necessary for success in scientific investigation, and without which it is quite impossible to extend the sphere of our knowledge. If this be so, then the fact is accounted for without difficulty, why the most profound philosophers have acknowledged the claims of Christianity upon them. And further, considering that the character, which Scripture draws of the virtuous man, is as a whole (what may be called) an original character,—only the scattered traces of it being found in authors unacquainted with the Bible,—an argument will almost be established in favour of Christianity, as having conferred an intellectual as well as a spiritual benefit on the world.

8. For instance, it is obvious that to be in earnest in seeking the truth is an indispensable requisite for finding it. Indeed, it would not be necessary to notice so evident a proposition, had it not been for the strange conduct of the ancient philosophers in their theories concerning nature and man. It seems as though only one or two of them were serious and sincere in their inquiries and teaching. Most of them considered speculations on philosophical subjects rather in the light of an amusement than of a grave employment,—

as an exercise for ingenuity, or an indulgence of fancy,
—to display their powers, to collect followers, or for
the sake of gain.   Indeed, it seems incredible that any
men, who were really in earnest in their search after
truth, should have begun with theorizing, or have imagined that a system which they were conscious they
had invented almost without data, should happen, when
applied to the actual state of things, to harmonize with
the numberless and diversified phenomena of the world.
Yet, though it seems to be so obvious a position when
stated, that in forming any serious theory concerning
nature, we must begin with investigation, to the exclusion of fanciful speculation or deference to human
authority, it was not generally recognized or received
as such, till a Christian philosopher forced it upon the
attention of the world.   And surely he was supported
by the uniform language of the whole Bible, which
tells us that truth is too sacred and religious a thing to
be sacrificed to the mere gratification of the fancy, or
amusement of the mind, or party spirit, or the prejudices
of education, or attachment (however amiable) to the
opinions of human teachers, or any of those other
feelings which the ancient philosophers suffered to
influence them in their professedly grave and serious
discussions.

9. Again : modesty, patience, and caution, are dispositions of mind quite as requisite in philosophical inquiries
as seriousness and earnestness, though not so obviously
requisite.   Rashness of assertion, hastiness in drawing
conclusions, unhesitating reliance on our own acuteness
and powers of reasoning, are inconsistent with the

homage which nature exacts of those who would know her hidden wonders. She refuses to reveal her mysteries to those who come otherwise than in the humble and reverential spirit of learners and disciples. So, again, that love of paradox which would impose upon her a language different from that which she really speaks, is as unphilosophical as it is unchristian. Again, indulgence of the imagination, though a more specious fault, is equally hostile to the spirit of true philosophy, and has misled the noblest among the ancient theorists, who seemed to think they could not go wrong while following the natural impulses and suggestions of their own minds, and were conscious to themselves of no low and unworthy motive influencing them in their speculations.

10. Here, too, may be mentioned the harm which has been done to the interests of science by excessive attachment to system. The love of order and regularity, and that perception of beauty which is most keen in highly-gifted minds, has too often led men astray in their scientific researches. From seeing but detached parts of the system of nature, they have been carried on, without data, to arrange, supply, and complete. They have been impatient of knowing but in part, and of waiting for future discoveries; they have inferred much from slender premises, and conjectured when they could not prove. It is by a tedious discipline that the mind is taught to overcome those baser principles which impede it in philosophical investigation, and to moderate those nobler faculties and feelings which are prejudicial when in excess. To be dispassionate and cautious, to

be fair in discussion, to give to each phenomenon which nature successively presents its due weight, candidly to admit those which militate against our own theory, to be willing to be ignorant for a time, to submit to difficulties, and patiently and meekly proceed, waiting for further light, is a temper (whether difficult or not at this day) little known to the heathen world; yet it is the only temper in which we can hope to become interpreters of nature, and it is the very temper which Christianity sets forth as the perfection of our moral character.

11. Still further, we hear much said in praise of the union of scientific men, of that spirit of brotherhood which should join together natives of different countries as labourers in a common cause. But were the philosophers of ancient times influenced by this spirit? In vain shall we look among them for the absence of rivalry; and much less can we hope to find that generosity of mind, which in its desire of promoting the cause of science, considers it a slight thing to be deprived of the credit of a discovery which is really its due. They were notoriously jealous of each other, and anxious for their personal consequence, and treasured up their supposed discoveries with miserable precaution, allowing none but a chosen few to be partakers of their knowledge. On the contrary, it was Christianity which first brought into play on the field of the world the principles of charity, generosity, disregard of self and country, in the prospect of the universal good; and which suggested the idea of a far-spreading combination, peaceful yet secure.

12. It cannot be denied, however, that the true philosophical spirit did not begin to prevail till many ages
after the preaching of Christianity, nay, till times comparatively of recent date ; and it has, in consequence,
been maintained that our own superiority over the
ancients in general knowledge, is not owing to the
presence of the Christian Religion among us, but to the
natural course of improvement in the world. And
doubtless it may be true, that though a divine philosophy had never been given us from above, we might
still have had a considerable advantage over the ancients
in the method and extent of our scientific acquirements.
Still, admitting this, it is also true that Scripture was,
in matter of fact, the first to describe and inculcate that
single-minded, modest, cautious, and generous spirit,
which was, after a long time, found so necessary for
success in the prosecution of philosophical researches.
And though the interval between the propagation of
Christianity and the rise of modern science is certainly
very long, yet it may be fairly maintained that the philosophy of the Gospel had no opportunity to extend
itself in the province of matter till modern times.   It
is not surprising if the primitive Christians, amid their
difficulties and persecutions, and being for the most part
private persons in the less educated ranks of life, should
have given birth to no new school for investigating
nature ; and the learned men who from time to time
joined them were naturally scholars in the defective
philosophies of Greece, and followed their masters in
their physical speculations ; and having more important
matters in hand, took for granted what they had no

means of ascertaining. Nor is it wonderful, considering how various is the subject-matter, and how multiform have been the developments of Christianity at successive eras, that the true principles of scientific research were not elicited in the long subsequent period. Perhaps the trials and errors through which the Church has passed in the times which have preceded us, are to be its experience in ages to come.

13. It may be asked how it comes to pass, if a true philosophical temper is so allied to that which the Scriptures inculcate as the temper of a Christian, that any men should be found distinguished for discoveries in science, who yet are ill disposed towards those doctrines which Revelation enjoins upon our belief. The reason may be this: the humility and teachableness which the Scripture precepts inculcate are connected with principles more solemn and doctrines more awful than those which are necessary for the temper of mind in which scientific investigation must be conducted; and though the Christian spirit is admirably fitted to produce the tone of thought and inquiry which leads to the discovery of truth, yet a slighter and less profound humility will do the same. The philosopher has only to confess that he is liable to be deceived by false appearances and reasonings, to be biassed by prejudice, and led astray by a warm fancy; he is humble because sensible he is ignorant, cautious because he knows himself to be fallible, docile because he really desires to learn. But Christianity, in addition to this confession, requires him to acknowledge himself to be a rebel in

the sight of God, and a breaker of that fair and
goodly order of things which the Creator once established. The philosopher confesses himself to be imperfect; the Christian feels himself to be sinful and
corrupt. The infirmity of which the philosopher must
be conscious is but a relative infirmity—imperfection
as opposed to perfection, of which there are infinite
degrees. Thus he believes himself placed in a certain
point of the scale of beings, and that there are beings
nearer to perfection than he is, others farther removed
from it. But the Christian acknowledges that he has
fallen away from that rank in creation which he originally
held; that he has passed a line, and is in consequence
not merely imperfect, but weighed down with positive,
actual evil. Now there is little to lower a man in his
own opinion, in his believing that he holds a certain
definite station in an immense series of creatures, and
is in consequence removed, by many steps, from perfection; but there is much very revolting to the minds of
many, much that is contrary to their ideas of harmony
and order, and the completeness of the system of nature,
and much at variance with those feelings of esteem with
which they are desirous of regarding themselves, in the
doctrine that man is disgraced and degraded from his
natural and original rank; that he has, by sinning,
introduced a blemish into the work of God; that he is
guilty in the court of heaven, and is continually doing
things odious in the sight of the Divine holiness. And
as the whole system of the Christian faith depends upon
this doctrine, since it was to redeem man from deserved
punishment that Christ suffered on the cross, and in

order to strengthen him in his endeavours to cleanse himself from sin, and prepare for heaven, that the Holy Spirit has come to rule the Church, it is not wonderful that men are found, admirable for their philosophical temper and their success in investigating nature, and yet unworthy disciples in the school of the Gospel.

14. Such men often regard Christianity as a slavish system, which is prejudicial to the freedom of thought, the aspirations of genius, and the speculations of enterprise; an unnatural system, which sets out with supposing that the human mind is out of order, and consequently bends all its efforts to overthrow the constitution of feeling and belief with which man is born, and to make him a being for which nature never intended him; and a pernicious system, which unfits men for this life by fixing their thoughts on another, and which, wherever consistently acted upon, infallibly leads (as it often has led) to the encouragement of the monastic spirit, and the extravagances of fanaticism.

15. Although, then, Christianity seems to have been the first to give to the world the pattern of the true spirit of philosophical investigation, yet, as the principles of science are, in process of time, more fully developed, and become more independent of the religious system, there is much danger lest the philosophical school should be found to separate from the Christian Church, and at length disown the parent to whom it has been so greatly indebted. And this evil has in a measure befallen us; that it does not increase, we must look to that early religious training, to which there can be no doubt all

persons—those in the higher as well as in the poorer classes of the community—should be submitted.

16. To conclude. The ignorance of the first preachers of Christianity has been often insisted on, particularly by the celebrated historian of the Roman Empire, as a presumption or proof of their hostility to all enlightened and liberal philosophy. If, however, as has been here contended, from the precepts they delivered the best canons may be drawn up for scientific investigation, the fact will only tend to prove that *they* could not, unassisted, have originated or selected precepts so enlarged and so profound; and thus will contribute something to the strength of those accumulated probabilities, which on other grounds are so overpowering, that they spoke not of themselves, but as they were moved by the inspiration of God Himself.

SERMON II.

THE INFLUENCE OF NATURAL AND REVEALED RELIGION RESPECTIVELY.

(Preached on Easter Tuesday, April 13, 1830.)

1 JOHN i. 1—3.

"That which was from the beginning, which we have heard, which we have seen with our eyes, which we have looked upon, and our hands have handled, of the Word of life; (For the Life was manifested, and we have seen It, and bear witness, and show unto you that Eternal Life, which was with the Father, and was manifested unto us;) That which we have seen and heard declare we unto you, that ye also may have fellowship with us."

THE main purpose of our Saviour's incarnation, as far as we are permitted to know it, was that of reconciling us to God, and purchasing for us eternal life by His sufferings and death. This purpose was accomplished when He said, " It is finished," and gave up the ghost.

2. But on His rising from the dead, He extended to us two additional acts of grace, as preparatory to the future blessing, and of which, as well as of our resurrection, that miracle itself was made the evidence. " Go ye, teach all nations, baptizing them in the name of the Father, and of the Son, and of the Holy Ghost." In this commission to His disciples was intimated, on

the one hand, His merciful design of "gathering together in one the children of God that were scattered
abroad," by the gracious operation of the Holy Spirit;
and on the other hand, His intended grant of a system
of religious truth, grounded on that mysterious economy
of Divine Providence in which His own incarnation
occupies the principal place.

3. It is proposed, in the following discourse, to treat
of a subject connected with the latter of these two
great Christian blessings—viz. to attempt to determine
the relation which this revealed system of doctrine and
precept bears to that of Natural Religion, and to compare the two together in point of practical efficacy.
The other and still greater mercies of the Christian
Covenant have been mentioned only, lest, in discussing
the subject of religious knowledge, any disregard should
be implied of those fundamental doctrines of our faith,
the Atonement, and the abiding presence of the Holy
Spirit in the Church.

4. Now, in investigating the connexion between
Natural and Revealed Religion, it is necessary to explain in what sense religious doctrines of any kind can
with propriety be called natural. For from the abuse
of the term "Natural Religion," many persons will not
allow the use of it at all.

5. When, then, religion of some sort is said to be
natural, it is not here meant that any religious system
has been actually traced out by unaided Reason. We
know of no such system, because we know of no time
or country in which human Reason *was* unaided.

[UNIV. S.]   C

Scripture informs us that revelations were granted
to the first fathers of our race, concerning the nature
of God and man's duty to Him; and scarcely a people
can be named, among whom there are not traditions,
not only of the existence of powers exterior to this
visible world, but also of their actual interference with
the course of nature, followed up by religious communications to mankind from them. The Creator has
never left Himself without such witness as might anticipate the conclusions of Reason, and support a wavering conscience and perplexed faith. No people (to
speak in general terms) has been denied a revelation
from God, though but a portion of the world has
enjoyed an authenticated revelation.

6. Admitting this fully, let us speak of *the fact;* of
the actual state of religious belief of pious men in
the heathen world, as attested by their writings still
extant; and let us call this attainable creed Natural
Religion.

7. Now, in the first place, it is obvious that Conscience is the essential principle and sanction of Religion in the mind. Conscience implies a relation
between the soul and a something exterior, and that,
moreover, superior to itself; a relation to an excellence
which it does not possess, and to a tribunal over which
it has no power. And since the more closely this inward monitor is respected and followed, the clearer, the
more exalted, and the more varied its dictates become,
and the standard of excellence is ever outstripping,
while it guides, our obedience, a moral conviction is
thus at length obtained of the unapproachable nature

as well as the supreme authority of That, whatever it is, which is the object of the mind's contemplation. Here, then, at once, we have the elements of a religious system; for what is Religion but the system of relations existing between us and a Supreme Power, claiming our habitual obedience: "the blessed and only Potentate, who only hath immortality, dwelling in light unapproachable, whom no man hath seen or can see"?

8. Further, Conscience implies a difference in the nature of actions, the power of acting in this way or that as we please, and an obligation of acting in one particular way in preference to all others; and since the more our moral nature is improved, the greater inward power of improvement it seems to possess, a view is laid open to us both of the capabilities and prospects of man, and the awful importance of that work which the law of his being lays upon him. And thus the presentiment of a future life, and of a judgment to be passed upon present conduct, with rewards and punishments annexed, forms an article, more or less distinct, in the creed of Natural Religion.

9. Moreover, since the inward law of Conscience brings with it no proof of its truth, and commands attention to it on its own authority, all obedience to it is of the nature of Faith; and habitual obedience implies the direct exercise of a clear and vigorous faith in the truth of its suggestions, triumphing over opposition both from within and without; quieting the murmurs of Reason, perplexed with the disorders of the present scheme of things, and subduing the appe-

tites, clamorous for good which promises an immediate and keen gratification.

10. While Conscience is thus ever the sanction of Natural Religion, it is, when improved, the rule of Morals also. But here is a difference : it is, as such, essentially religious ; but in Morals it is not necessarily a guide, only in proportion as it happens to be refined and strengthened in individuals. And here is a solution of objections which have been made to the existence of the moral sense, on the ground of the discordancy which exists among men as to the excellence or demerit of particular actions. These objections only go to prove the uncertain character (if so be) of the inward law of right and wrong ; but are not, even in their form, directed against the certainty of that general religious sense, which is implied in the remorse and vague apprehension of evil which the transgression of Conscience occasions.

11. Still, unformed and incomplete as is this law by nature, it is quite certain that obedience to it is attended by a continually growing expertness in the science of Morals. A mind, habitually and honestly conforming itself to its own full sense of duty, will at length enjoin or forbid with an authority second only to an inspired oracle. Moreover, in a heathen country, it will be able to discriminate with precision between the right and wrong in traditionary superstitions, and will thus elicit confirmation of its faith even out of corruptions of the truth. And further, it will of course realize in its degree those peculiar rewards of virtue which appetite cannot comprehend ; and will detect in

this world's events, which are but perplexities to mere unaided Reason, a general connexion existing between right moral conduct and happiness, in corroboration of those convictions which the experience of its own private history has created.

12. Such is the large and practical religious creed attainable (as appears from the extant works of heathen writers) by a vigorous mind which rightly works upon itself, under (what may be called) the Dispensation of Paganism. It may be even questioned whether there be any essential character of Scripture doctrine which is without its place in this moral revelation. For here is the belief in a principle exterior to the mind to which it is instinctively drawn, infinitely exalted, perfect, incomprehensible; here is the surmise of a judgment to come; the knowledge of unbounded benevolence, wisdom, and power, as traced in the visible creation, and of moral laws unlimited in their operation; further, there is even something of hope respecting the availableness of repentance, so far (that is) as suffices for religious support; lastly, there is an insight into the rule of duty, increasing with the earnestness with which obedience to that rule is cultivated.

13. This sketch of the religious knowledge not impossible to Heathen Philosophy, will be borne out by its writings, yet will be only obtained by a selection of the best portions of them. Hence we derive two conclusions: that the knowledge was *attainable*—for what one man may attain is open to another; on the other hand, that, in general, it was not *actually attained*— for else there would be no need of so confined a

selection of them. And thus we are carried on to the
inquiry already proposed—viz. *where* it was that
Natural Religion failed in practical effect, and how
Revealed Religion supplies the deficiency. Out of the
many answers which might be given to this question,
let us confine ourselves to that which is suggested by
the text.

14. Natural Religion teaches, it is true, the infinite
power and majesty, the wisdom and goodness, the presence, the moral governance, and, in one sense, the
unity of the Deity ; but it gives little or no information [1]
respecting what may be called His *Personality*. It follows that, though Heathen Philosophy knew so much
of the moral system of the world, as to see the duties
and prospects of man in the same direction in which
Revelation places them, this knowledge did not pre-
clude a belief in fatalism, which might, of course,
consist in unchangeable moral laws, as well as physical.
And though Philosophy acknowledged an intelligent,
wise, and beneficent Principle of nature, still this too
was, in fact, only equivalent to the belief in a pervading Soul of the Universe, which consulted for its
own good, and directed its own movements, by instincts similar to those by which the animal world is
guided ; but which, strictly speaking, was not an
object of worship, inasmuch as each intelligent being
was, in a certain sense, himself a portion of it. Much
less would a conviction of the Infinitude and Eternity
of the Divine Nature lead to any just idea of His

---

[1] [This seems to me too strongly said, and inconsistent with what is
said *infra*, vi. 10. Vide Essay on Assent, v. i.]

Personality, since there can be no circumscribing lineaments nor configuration of the Immeasurable, no external condition or fortune to that Being who is all in all.
Lastly, though Conscience seemed to point in a certain
direction as a witness for the real moral locality (so to
speak,) of the unseen God, yet, as it cannot prove its
own authority, it afforded no argument for a Governor
and Judge, distinct from the moral system itself, to
those who disputed its informations.

15. While, then, Natural Religion was not without
provision for all the deepest and truest religious feelings, yet presenting no tangible history of the Deity, no
points of His personal character[2] (if we may so speak
without irreverence), it wanted that most efficient
incentive to all action, a starting or rallying point,
—an object on which the affections could be placed,
and the energies concentrated. Common experience
in life shows how the most popular and interesting
cause languishes, if its head be removed; and how
political power is often vested in individuals, merely
for the sake of the definiteness of the practical impression which a personal presence produces. How,
then, should the beauty of virtue move the heart,
while it was an abstraction? "Forma quidem hones-
tatis, *si oculis cerneretur*, admirabiles amores excitaret
sapientiæ;" but, till "seen and heard and handled,"
It did but witness against those who disobeyed, while

---

[2] The author was not acquainted, at the time this was written, with
Mr. Coleridge's Works, and a remarkable passage in his **Biographia
Literaria**, in which several portions of this Sermon are anticipated. It
has been pointed out to him since by the kindness of a friend, [Mr.
Thomas D. Acland.]—Vide Biogr. Lit. vol. i. p. 199.

they acknowledged It; and who, seemingly conscious where their need lay, made every effort to embody It in the attributes of individuality, embellishing their " Logos," as they called It, with figurative actions, and worshipping It as the personal development of the Infinite Unknown.

16. But, it may be asked, was Heathen Religion of no service here? It testified, without supplying the need;—it bore testimony to it, by attempting to attribute a personal character and a history to the Divinity; but it failed, as degrading His invisible majesty by unworthy, multiplied and inconsistent images, and as shattering the moral scheme of the world into partial and discordant· systems, in which appetite and expedience received the sanction due only to virtue. And thus refined philosophy and rude natural feeling each attempted separately to enforce obedience to a religious rule, and each failed on its own side. The God of philosophy was infinitely great, but an abstraction; the God of paganism was intelligible, but degraded by human conceptions. Science and nature could produce no joint-work ; it was left for an express Revelation to propose the Object in which they should both be reconciled, and to satisfy the desires of both in a real and manifested incarnation of the Deity.

17. When St. Paul came to Athens, and found the altar dedicated to the Unknown God, he professed his purpose of declaring to the Heathen world Him " whom they ignorantly worshipped." He proceeded to condemn their polytheistic and anthropomorphic

errors, to disengage the notion of a Deity from the base earthly attributes in which Heathen religion had enveloped it, and to appeal to their own literature in behalf of the true nature of Him in whom " we live, and move, and have our being." But, after thus acknowledging the abstract correctness of the philosophical system, as far as it went, he preaches unto them Jesus and the Resurrection; that is, he embodies the moral character of the Deity in those historical notices of it which have been made the medium of the Christian manifestation of His attributes.

18. It is hardly necessary to enter into any formal proof that this is one principal object, as of all revelation, so especially of the Christian; viz. to relate some course of action, some conduct, a life (to speak in human terms) of the One Supreme God. Indeed, so evidently is this the case, that one very common, though superficial objection to the Scriptures, is founded on their continually ascribing to Almighty God human passions, words, and actions. The first chapter of the book of Job is one instance which may suggest many more; and those marks of character are especially prominent in Scripture, which imply an extreme opposition to an eternal and fated system, inherent freedom of will, power of change, long-suffering, placability, repentance, delight in the praises and thanksgivings of His creatures, failure of purpose, and the prerogative of dispensing His mercies according to His good pleasure. Above all, in the New Testament, the Divine character is exhibited to us, not merely as love, or mercy, or holiness (attributes which have a

vagueness in our conceptions of them from their im-
mensity), but these and others as seen in an act of *self-
denial*—a mysterious quality when ascribed to Him,
who is all things in Himself, but especially calculated
(from the mere meaning of the term) to impress upon
our minds the personal character of the Object of our
worship. "God so loved the world," that He *gave up*
His only Son: and the Son of God "*pleased not Himself.*" In His life we are allowed to discern the attributes of the Invisible God, drawn out into action in
accommodation to our weakness. The passages are too
many to quote, in which this object of His incarnation
is openly declared. "In Him dwelleth all the fulness
of the Godhead bodily." "He that hath seen Him, hath
seen the Father." He is a second Creator of the world,
I mean, as condescending to repeat (as it were) for our
contemplation, in human form, that distinct personal
work, which made "the morning stars sing together,
and all the sons of God shout for joy." In a word,
the impression upon the religious mind thence made is
appositely illustrated in the words of the text, "That
which was from the beginning, which we have heard,
which we have seen with our eyes, which we have
looked upon, and our hands have handled, of the Word
of Life; (For the Life was manifested, and we have
seen It, and bear witness, and show unto you that
Eternal Life, which was with the Father, and was
manifested unto us;) That which we have seen and
heard declare we unto you, that ye also may have
fellowship with us."

19. No thought is more likely to come across and

haunt the mind, and slacken its efforts under Natural
Religion, than that after all we may be following a vain
shadow, and disquieting ourselves without cause, while
we are giving up our hearts to the noblest instincts
and aspirations of our nature. The Roman Stoic, as
he committed suicide, complained he had worshipped
virtue, and found it but an empty name. It is even
now the way of the world to look upon the religious
principle as a mere peculiarity of temper, a weakness,
or an enthusiasm, or refined feeling (as the case may
be), characteristic of a timid and narrow, or of a
heated or a highly-gifted mind. Here, then, Revelation
meets us with simple and distinct *facts* and *actions*, not
with painful inductions from existing phenomena, not
with generalized laws or metaphysical conjectures, but
with *Jesus and the Resurrection;* and *"if Christ be not
risen"* (it confesses plainly), "then is our preaching
vain, and your faith is also vain." Facts such as this
are not simply evidence of the truth of the revelation,
but the media of its impressiveness. The life of Christ
brings together and concentrates truths concerning the
chief good and the laws of our being, which wander
idle and forlorn over the surface of the moral world,
and often appear to diverge from each other. It
collects the scattered rays of light, which, in the first
days of creation, were poured over the whole face of
nature, into certain intelligible centres, in the firmament of the heaven, to rule over the day and over the
night, and to divide the light from the darkness. Our
Saviour has in Scripture all those abstract titles of
moral excellence bestowed upon Him which philo-

sophers have invented. He is the Word, the Light, the Life, the Truth, Wisdom, the Divine Glory. St. John announces in the text, "The Life was manifested, and we *have seen* It."

20. And hence will follow an important difference in the moral character formed in the Christian school, from that which Natural Religion has a tendency to create. The philosopher aspires towards a divine *principle ;* the Christian, towards a Divine *Agent.* Now, dedication of our energies to the service of a person is the occasion of the highest and most noble virtues, disinterested attachment, self-devotion, loyalty ; habitual humility, moreover, from the knowledge that there must ever be one that is above us. On the other hand, in whatever degree we approximate towards a mere standard of excellence, we do not really advance towards it, but bring it to us ; the excellence we venerate becomes part of ourselves—we become a god to ourselves. This was one especial consequence of the pantheistic system of the Stoics, the later Pythagoreans, and other philosophers ; in proportion as they drank into the spirit of eternal purity, they became divine in their own estimation ; they contrasted themselves with those who were below them, knowing no being above them by whom they could measure their proficiency. Thus they began by being humble, and, as they advanced, humility and faith wore away from their character. This is strikingly illustrated in Aristotle's description of a perfectly virtuous man. An incidental and unstudied greatness of mind is said by him to mark the highest moral excellence, and truly ; but the genuine nobleness of the

virtuous mind, as shown in a superiority to common temptations, forbearance, generosity, self-respect, calm high-minded composure, is deformed by an arrogant contempt of others, a disregard of their feelings, and a harshness and repulsiveness of external manner. That is, the philosopher saw clearly the tendencies of the moral system, the constitution of the human soul, and the ways leading to the perfection of our nature; but when he attempted to delineate the ultimate complete consistent image of the virtuous man, how could he be expected to do this great thing, who had never seen Angel or Prophet, much less the Son of God manifested in the flesh ?

21. At such pains is Scripture, on the other hand, to repress the proud self-complacency just spoken of, that not only is all moral excellence expressly referred to the Supreme God, but even the principle of good, when implanted and progressively realized in our hearts, is still continually revealed to us as a Person, as if to mark strongly that it is not our own, and must lead us to no preposterous self-adoration. For instance, we read of Christ being formed in us—dwelling in the heart— of the Holy Spirit making us His temple; particularly remarkable is our Saviour's own promise : " If a man love Me, he will keep My words; and My Father will love him, and We will *come unto him, and make our abode with him.*"

22. It may be observed, that this method of persona- tion (so to call it) is carried throughout the revealed system. The doctrine of the Personality of the Holy Spirit has just been referred to. Again, the doctrine

of original sin is centred in the person of Adam, and in this way is made impressive and intelligible to the mass of mankind. The Evil Principle is revealed to us in the person of its author, Satan. Nay, not only thus, in the case of really existing beings, as the first man and the Evil Spirit, but even when a figure must be used, is the same system continued. The body of faithful men, or Church, considered as the dwelling-place of the One Holy Spirit, is invested with a metaphorical personality, and is bound to act as one, in order to those practical ends of influencing and directing human conduct in which the entire system may be considered as originating. And, again, for the same purpose of concentrating the energies of the Christian body, and binding its members into close union, it was found expedient, even in Apostolic times, to consign each particular church to the care of one pastor, or bishop, who was thus made a personal type of Christ mystical, the new and spiritual man ; a centre of action and a living witness against all heretical or disorderly proceedings.

23. Such, then, is the Revealed system compared with the Natural—teaching religious truths historically, not by investigation ; revealing the Divine Nature, not in works, but in action ; not in His moral laws, but in His spoken commands; training us to be subjects of a kingdom, not citizens of a Stoic republic; and enforcing obedience, not on Reason so much as on Faith.

24. And now that we are in possession of this great gift of God, Natural Religion has a use and impor-

tance which it before could hardly possess. For as
Revealed Religion enforces doctrine, so Natural Religion
recommends it. It is hardly necessary to observe, that
the whole revealed scheme rests on nature for the validity
of its evidence. The claim of miraculous power or
knowledge assumes the existence of a Being capable of
exerting it; and the matter of the Revelation itself is
evidenced and interpreted by those awful, far-reaching
analogies of mediation and vicarious suffering, which
we discern in the visible course of the world. There is,
perhaps, no greater satisfaction to the Christian than
that which arises from his perceiving that the Revealed
system is rooted deep in the natural course of things,
of which it is merely the result and completion; that
his Saviour has interpreted for him the faint or
broken accents of Nature; and that in them, so
interpreted, he has, as if in some old prophecy, at once
the evidence and the lasting memorial of the truths of
the Gospel.

25. It remains to suggest some of the conclusions
which follow from this view, thus taken, of the relation
of Revealed to Natural Religion.

(1.) First, much might be said on the evidence thence
deducible for the truth of the Christian system. It is
one point of evidence that the two systems coincide in
declaring the same substantial doctrines : viz., as being
two independent witnesses in one and the same question;
an argument contained by implication, though not
formally drawn out, in Bishop Butler's Analogy. It is
a further point of evidence to find that Scripture com-

pletes the very deficiency of nature; and, while its doctrines of Atonement and Mediation are paralleled by phenomena in the visible course of things, to discern in it one solitary doctrine, which from its nature has no parallel in this world, an Incarnation of the Divine Essence, an intrinsic evidence of its truth in the benefit thus conferred on religion.

26. (2.) Next, light is thus thrown upon the vast practical importance of the doctrines of the Divinity of our Lord, and of the Personality of the Holy Spirit. It is the impiety, indeed, involved in the denial of these, which is the great guilt of anti-Trinitarians; but, over and above this, such persons go far to destroy the very advantages which the Revealed system possesses over the Natural; and throw back the science of morals and of human happiness into that state of vagueness and inefficiency from which Christianity has extricated it. On the other hand, we learn besides, the shallowness of the objection to the doctrine of the Holy Trinity, grounded on its involving a plurality of Persons in the Godhead; since, if it be inconceivable, as it surely is, how Personality can in any way be an attribute of the infinite, incommunicable Essence of the Deity, or in what particular sense it is ascribed to Him, Unitarians, so called (to be consistent), should find a difficulty in the doctrine of an Unity of Person, as well as of a Trinity; and, having ceased to be Athanasians, should not stop till they become Pantheists.

27. (3.) Further, the same view suggests to us the peculiar perverseness of schism, which tends to undo the very arrangement which our Lord has made, for

arresting the attention of mankind, and leading them to seek their true moral good; and which (if followed to its legitimate results) would reduce the world to the very state in which it existed in the age of the heathen moralist, so familiar to us in this place, who, in opening his treatise, bears witness to the importance of a visible Church, by consulting the opinions of mankind as to the means of obtaining happiness; and not till disappointed in sage and statesman, the many and the educated, undertakes himself an examination of man's nature, as if the only remaining means of satisfying the inquiry.

28. (4.) And hence, at the same time, may be learned the real religious position of the heathen, who, we have reason to trust, are not in danger of perishing, except so far as all are in such danger, whether in heathen or Christian countries, who do not follow the secret voice of conscience, leading them on by faith to their true though unseen good. For the prerogative of Christians consists in the possession, not of exclusive knowledge and spiritual aid, but of gifts high and peculiar; and though the manifestation of the Divine character in the Incarnation is a singular and inestimable benefit, yet its absence is supplied in a degree, not only in the inspired record of Moses, but even, with more or less strength, as the case may be, in those various traditions concerning Divine Providences and Dispensations which are scattered through the heathen mythologies.

29. (5.) Further, a comment is hence afforded us on the meaning of a phrase perplexed by controversy—that

of   preaching Christ." By which is properly meant,
not the putting Natural Religion out of sight, nor the
separating one doctrine of the Gospel from the rest, as
having an exclusive claim to the name of Gospel; but
the displaying *all* that Nature and Scripture teach
concerning Divine Providence (for they teach the same
great truths), whether of His majesty, or His love, or
His mercy, or His holiness, or His fearful anger, through
the medium of the life and death of His Son Jesus
Christ.   A mere moral strain of teaching duty and
enforcing obedience fails in persuading us to practice, not
because it appeals to conscience, and commands and
threatens (as is sometimes supposed), but because it
does not urge and illustrate virtue in the Name and by
the example of our blessed Lord.   It is not that natural
teaching gives merely the Law, and Christian teaching
gives the tidings of pardon, and that a command chills
or formalizes the mind, and that a free forgiveness converts it (for nature speaks of God's goodness as well
as of His severity, and Christ surely of His severity as
well as of His goodness); but that in the Christian
scheme we find *all* the Divine Attributes (not mercy
only, though mercy pre-eminently) brought out and
urged upon us, which were but latent in the visible
course of things.

30. (6.) Hence it appears that the Gospels are the
great instruments (under God's blessing) of fixing
and instructing our minds in a religious course,
the Epistles being rather comments on them than intended to supersede them, as is sometimes maintained.
Surely it argues a temper of mind but partially moulded

to the worship and love of Christ, to make this distinction between His teaching and that of His Apostles,
when the very promised office of the Comforter in His
absence was, not to make a new revelation, but expressly "to bring all things to their remembrance"
which "*He* had said to them;" *not* to "speak of Himself," but "to receive of Christ's, and show it unto
them." The Holy Spirit came "to glorify Christ," to
declare openly to all the world that *He* had come on
earth, suffered, and died, who was also the Creator and
Governor of the world, the Saviour, the final Judge of
men. It is the Incarnation of the Son of God rather
than any doctrine drawn from a partial view of Scripture (however true and momentous it may be) which is
the article of a standing or a falling Church. "Every
spirit that confesseth not that Jesus Christ is come *in
the flesh*, is not of God; . . . this is that spirit of anti-
Christ;" for, not to mention other more direct considerations, it reverses, as far as in it lies, all that the
revealed character of Christ has done for our faith and
virtue. And hence the Apostles' speeches in the book
of Acts and the primitive Creeds insist almost exclusively upon the history, not the doctrines, of Christianity; it being designed that, by means of our Lord's
Economy, the great doctrines of theology should be
taught, the facts of that Economy giving its peculiarity
and force to the Revelation.

31. May it ever be our aim thus profitably to use
that last and complete manifestation of the Divine
Attributes and Will contained in the New Testament,

setting the pattern of the Son of God ever before us, and studying so to act as if He were sensibly present, by look, voice, and gesture, to approve or blame us in all our private thoughts and all our intercourse with the world !

SERMON III.[1]

EVANGELICAL SANCTITY THE COMPLETION OF NATURAL VIRTUE.

(Preached March 6, 1831.)

Eph. v. 8, 9.

" Ye were sometimes darkness, but now are ye light in the Lord: walk as children of light: for the fruit of the Spirit is in all goodness and righteousness and truth."

WHILE Christianity reveals the pardon of sin and the promise of eternal life through the mediation of Christ, it also professes to point out means for the present improvement of our moral nature itself. This improvement, we know, is referred in Scripture to the Holy Spirit, as a first cause; and, as coming from Him, both the influence itself upon the mind and the moral character formed under that influence are each in turn called " the spirit." Thus, St. Paul speaks of the law of "the spirit of life in Christ Jesus[2]," and contrasts it with that character and conduct which are sin and death. He speaks too of receiving " the spirit of faith[3]," or the temper of which faith is the essence; and in the

---

[1] [This discourse was omitted in former editions, as having been written in haste on a sudden summons to preach.]

[2] Rom. viii. 2.   [3] 2 Cor. iv. 13.

text, which is found in the Epistle for this Sunday, he refers to the outward manifestation or fruit of the same spirit, " goodness, righteousness, and truth." " Light" is another word, used as in the text—to express the same moral change which the Gospel offers us ; but this title is proper to our Lord, who is the true Light of men. Christians are said to be " called into His marvellous light," to " walk as children of light," to " abide in the light," to " put on the armour of light [4]." Another similar term is newness or renewal of mind. Indeed, it is quite obvious that the phraseology of the New Testament is grounded in such views of the immediate inward benefits to be conferred upon the Church on the coming of Christ.

2. What, then, is meant by this language ? language, which, if great words stand for great ideas, and an Apostle does not aim at eloquent speech rather than at the simple truth, must raise our expectations concerning the fulness of the present benefits resulting to us in the present state of things from Christianity. That it is not mere ordinary religious obedience, such as the Holy Spirit may foster among the heathen ; nor, on the other hand, miraculous endowment of which St. Paul speaks, when he prays that " the Father of glory" might give to the Ephesians " the spirit of wisdom and revelation," " enlightened understanding," " knowledge of the riches of the glory of the Saints' inheritance [5]," this surely is evident without formal proof, and least of all need be insisted on in this place.

3. Nor, again, does the question find its answer in the

1 Pet. ii. 9. 1 John i. 7 ; ii. 10. Rom. xiii. 12.   [5] Eph. i. 17, 18.

view of certain men of deeper piety than the mass of mankind,—of those, I mean, who, clearly perceiving that Christian morality and devotion are something extraordinarily excellent and divine, have sought to embody them in a strict outward separation from the world, a ceremonial worship, severe austerities, and a fixed adjustment of the claims of duty in all the varying *minutiæ* of daily conduct; and who, in consequence, have at length substituted dead forms for the " spirit " which they desired to honour.

4. Nor further may we seek an explanation of the difficulty from such men as consult their feelings and imaginations rather than the sure Word of God, and place that spiritual obedience, which all confess to be the very test of a Christian, in the indulgence of excited affections, in an impetuous, unrefined zeal, or in the language of an artificial devotion. For this view of spirituality, also, except in the case of minds peculiarly constituted, ends in a formal religion.

5. Moreover, the aspect of the Christian world affords us no elucidation of St. Paul's language concerning the great gift of grace. Far from concurring with Scripture and interpreting it for us, doubtless the manners and habits even of the most refined society are rather calculated to prejudice the mind against any high views of religious and moral duty. And this has been the case even from the Apostle's age, as may be inferred from his Epistle to the Corinthians, who could hardly have understood their own titles, as "sanctified in Christ," " called to be saints[6]," at the time that they

[6] 1 Cor. i. 2.

have among them, "debates, envyings, whisperings, swellings, tumults, uncleanness, lasciviousness[7]," unrepented of.

6. It is indeed by no means clear that Christianity has at any time been of any great spiritual advantage to the world at large. The general temper of mankind, taking man individually, is what it ever was, restless and discontented, or sensual, or unbelieving. In barbarous times, indeed, the influence of the Church was successful in effecting far greater social order and external decency of conduct than are known in heathen countries; and at all times it will abash and check excesses which conscience itself condemns. But it has ever been a restraint on the world rather than a guide to personal virtue and perfection on a large scale; its fruits are negative.

7. True it is, that in the more advanced periods of society a greater innocence and probity of conduct and courtesy of manners will prevail; but these, though they have sometimes been accounted illustrations of the peculiar Christian character, have in fact no necessary connexion with it. For why should they not be referred to that mere advancement of civilization and education of the intellect, which is surely competent to produce them? Morals may be cultivated as a science; it furnishes a subject-matter on which reason may exercise itself to any extent whatever, with little more than the mere external assistance of conscience and Scripture. And, when drawn out into system, such a moral teaching will attract general admiration

[7] 2 Cor. xii. 20, 21.

from its beauty and refinement; and from its evident expediency will be adopted as a directory (so to say) of conduct, whenever it does not occasion any great inconvenience, or interfere with any strong passion or urgent interest. National love of virtue is no test of a sensitive and well-instructed conscience,—of nothing beyond intellectual culture. History establishes this: the Roman moralists write as admirably, as if they were moral men.

8. And, if this be the case, as I think it is, do we not compromise the dignity of Christianity by anxiously referring unbelievers to the effects of the Gospel of Jesus in the world at large, as if a sufficient proof of its divine origin, when the same effects to all appearance are the result of principles which do not " spring from the grace of Christ and the inspiration of His Spirit"? For it is not too much to say, that, constituted as human nature is, any very wide influence and hearty reception of given principles among men argues in fact their earthly character,—" they are of the world, therefore speak they of the world, and the world heareth them[5]." The true light of the world offends more men than it attracts; and its divine origin is shown, not in its marked effects on the mass of mankind, but in its surprising power of elevating the moral character where it is received in spirit and in truth. Its scattered saints, in all ranks of life, speak of it to the thoughtful inquirer: but to the world at large, its remarkable continuance on the earth is its witness, —its pertinacity of existence, confronting, as it has in

[5] 1 John iv. 5.

turn, every variety of opinion, and triumphing over them all. To the multitude it does not manifest itself[9]; —not that it willingly is hid from them, but that the perverse freedom of their will keeps them at a distance from it.

9. Besides, it must not be forgotten, that Christianity professes to prepare us for the next life. It is nothing strange then, if principles, which avowedly direct the science of morals to present beneficial results in the community, should show to the greater advantage in their own selected field of action. Exalted virtue cannot be fully appreciated, nay, is seldom recognized on the public stage of life, because it addresses itself to an unseen tribunal. Its actual manifestations on this confused and shifting scene are but partial; just as the most perfect form loses its outline and its proportions, when cast in shadow on some irregular surface.

10. Let it be assumed, then, as not needing proof, that the freedom of thought, enlightened equitableness, and amiableness, which are the offspring of civilization, differ far more even than the piety of form or of emotion from the Christian spirit, as being "not pleasant to God, forasmuch as they spring not of faith in Jesus Christ, yea, rather, 'doubtless,' having the nature of sin."

11. How then, after all, must the gift be described, which Christianity professes to bestow? I proceed, in answer to this question, to consider what is said on the subject by Scripture itself, where alone we ought to look for the answer. Not as if any new light could be

[9] Vide John xiv. 21—23.

thrown upon the subject, or any statements made, which have not the assent of sober Christians generally, but in order to illustrate and enforce an all-important truth ; and, while at every season of the year practical views of Christianity are befitting, they are especially suggested and justified by the services of humiliation in which we are at present [1] engaged.

12. The difference, then, between the extraordinary Christian " spirit," and human faith and virtue, viewed apart from Christianity, is simply this :—that, while the two are the same in nature, the former is immeasurably higher than the other, more deeply rooted in the mind it inhabits, more consistent, more vigorous, of more intense purity, of more sovereign authority, with greater promise of victory—the choicest elements of our moral nature being collected, fostered, matured into a determinate character by the gracious influences of the Holy Ghost, differing from the virtue of heathens somewhat in the way that the principle of life in a diseased and wasted frame differs from that health, beauty, and strength of body, which is nevertheless subject to disorder and decay.

13. That the spiritual and the virtuous mind are essentially the same, is plain from the text as from other Scriptures : " The fruit of the Spirit is in all goodness and righteousness and truth." Let us rather confine our attention to the point of difference between them ; viz. that the Christian graces are far superior in rank and dignity to the moral virtues. The following may serve as illustrations of this difference :—

[1] Lent.

14. (1.) Take at once our Lord's words, when enjoining the duty of love, "If ye love them who love you, what reward have ye? do not even the publicans the same?" Or St. Peter's, on the duty of patience! "What glory is it, if, when ye be buffeted for your faults, ye shall take it patiently? but if, when ye do well and suffer for it, ye take it patiently, this is acceptable with God [2]."

15. This contrast between ordinary and transcendant virtue, the virtues of nature and the virtues of Christianity, may be formally drawn out in various branches of our duty. For instance; duties are often divided into religious, relative, personal; the characteristic excellence in each of those departments of virtue being respectively faith, benevolence and justice, and temperance. Now in Christianity these three are respectively perfected in hope, charity, and self-denial, which are the peculiar fruits of the "spirit" as distinguished from ordinary virtue. This need not be proved in detail; it is sufficient to refer to St. Paul's Epistle to the Romans, and his first to the Corinthians. These three cardinal graces of the Christian character are enforced by our Saviour, when He bids us take no thought for the morrow; do as we would be done by; and deny ourselves, take up our cross, and follow Him [3].

16. Other virtues admit of a similar growth and contrast. Christian patience is contrasted with what is ordinary patience in the passage from St. Peter just cited. St. John speaks of the "love of God casting out fear;" and whatever difficulty may lie in the interpretation of these words, they are at least clear in marking the tran-

[2] Matt. v. 46. 1 Pet. ii. 20.　　[3] Matt. vi. 34; vii. 12; x. 38.

scendant quality of the Christian grace, compared with
the ordinary virtue, as seen under former dispensations
of religion.   And in the Epistle to the Hebrews, the
inspired writer contrasts the elementary objects of faith
with those which are the enjoyment of a perfect and
true Christian; the doctrines which spring from the
Atonement being the latter, and the former such as the
Being of a God, His Providence, the Resurrection and
eternal judgment.

17. (2.) In the next place, we may learn what is the
peculiar gift of the Spirit even without seeking in Scripture for any express contrast between graces and virtues,
by considering the Christian moral code as a whole,
and the general impression which it would make on
minds which had been instructed in nothing beyond the
ordinary morality which nature teaches.   Such are the
following passages—we are bid not to resist evil, but
to turn the cheek to the smiter; to forgive from our
hearts our brother, though he sin against us until
seventy times seven; to love and bless our enemies;
to love without dissimulation; to esteem others better
than ourselves; to bear one another's burdens; to
condescend to men of low estate; to minister to our
brethren the more humbly, the higher our station is; to
be like little children in simplicity and humility.   We
are to guard against every idle word, and to aim at
great plainness of speech; to make prayer our solace,
and hymns and psalms our mirth; to be careless about
the honours and emoluments of the world; to maintain
almost a voluntary poverty (at least so far as re-
nouncing all superfluous wealth may be called such);

to observe a purity severe as an utter abhorrence of uncleanness can make it to be; willingly to part with hand or eye in the desire to be made like to the pattern of the Son of God; and to think little of friends or country, or the prospects of ordinary domestic happiness, for the kingdom of heaven's sake [4].

18. Now, in enumerating these maxims of Christian morality, I do not attempt to delineate the character itself, which they are intended to form as their result. Without pretending to interpret rules, which the religious mind understands only in proportion to its progress in sanctification, I may assume, what is enough for the present purpose, that they evidently point out to some very exalted order of moral excellence as the characteristic of a genuine Christian. Thus they are adequate to the explanation of the Apostle's strong language about the Spirit of *glory* and God [5] as the present gift gained for us by our Saviour's intercession, which in the text is evidently declared to be a moral gift, yet as evidently to be something more than what is meant by ordinary faith and obedience.

19. (3.) And next, let us see what may be gained on the subject by examining the lives of the Apostles, and of their genuine successors. Here their labours and sufferings attract our attention first. Not that pain and privation have any natural connexion with virtue; but because, when virtue is pre-supposed, these conditions exert a powerful influence in developing and ele-

---

[4] Matt. v. 28. 37. 39. 44; vi. 25; xii. 36; xviii. 3. 8. 35; xix. 12. 29; xx. 27. Rom. xii. 9. 16. 1 Cor. vi. 18—20. Gal. vi. 2. James v. 13.
[5] 1 Pet. iv. 14.

vating it. Considering St. Paul's ready and continued sacrifices of himself and all that was his in the cause of the Gospel, could the texture of his religion bear any resemblance to that weak and yielding principle which constitutes the virtue of what we now consider the more conscientious part of mankind? He and his brethren had a calm strength of mind, which marked them out, more than any other temper, to be God's elect who could not be misled, stern weapons of God, purged by affliction and toil to do His work on earth and to persevere to the end.

20. And let us view such men as these, whom we rightly call Saints, in the combination of graces which form their character, and we shall gain a fresh insight into the nature of that sublime morality which the Spirit enforces. St. Paul exhibits the union of zeal and gentleness; St. John, of overflowing love with uncompromising strictness of principle Firmness and meekness is another combination of virtues, which is exemplified in Moses, even under the first Covenant. To these we may add such as self-respect and humility, the love and fear of God, and the use of the world without the abuse of it. This necessity of being "sanctified wholly," in the Apostle's language, is often forgotten. It is indeed comparatively easy to profess one side only of moral excellence, as if faith were to be all in all, or zeal, or amiableness; whereas in truth, religious obedience is a very intricate problem, and the more so the farther we proceed in it. The moral growth within us must be symmetrical, in order to be beautiful or lasting; hence mature sanctity is seldom

recognized by others, where it really exists, never by the world at large. Ordinary spectators carry off one or other impression of a good man, according to the accidental circumstances under which they see him. Much more are the attributes and manifestations of the Divine Mind beyond our understanding, and, appearing inconsistent, are rightly called mysterious.

21. (4.) A last illustration of the special elevation of Christian holiness is derived from the anxious exhortation made to us in Scripture to be diligent in aiming at it. There is no difficulty in realizing in our own persons the ordinary virtues of society; nay, it is the boast of some ethical systems that they secure virtue, on the admission of a few simple and intelligible principles, or that they make it depend on the knowledge of certain intellectual truths. This is a shallow philosophy; but Christian perfection is as high as the commands and warnings of Scripture are solemn : " Watch and pray ;" " many are called, few chosen ;" "strait is the gate, and narrow is the way ;" " strive to enter in," "many shall seek," only; " a rich man shall hardly enter ;" " he that is able to receive it, let him receive it[6];" and others of a like character.

22. Such, then, is the present benefit which Christianity offers us ; not only a renewal of our moral nature after Adam's original likeness, but a blending of all its powers and affections into the one perfect man, " after the measure of the stature of the fulness of Christ." Not that heathens are absolutely precluded from this transforma-

[6] Matt. vii.; xix.; xxii.; xxvi. Luke xiii.

tion from sin to righteousness ; nor as if we dare limit
the actual progress made by individuals among them ;
nor, further, as if it were not every one's duty to aim
at perfection in all things under any Dispensation ; but
neither the question of duty nor that of God's dealings
with heathen countries has come under consideration
here; but what it is that Christians have pledged to
them from above on their regeneration ; what that great
gift is of Christ's passion, of which the Apostles speak
in language so solemn and so triumphant, as at first
sight to raise a difficulty about its meaning.

23. Considering, then, the intense brightness and
purity of that holiness to which we are called, and on the
other hand our ignorant and sensual condition, as we are
really found, our Church teaches us to put away from
ourselves the title of "Saint," and to attribute it to
such especially as "have laboured and not fainted;[7] "
those who, like the Apostles and primitive martyrs, have
fought a good fight, and finished their course, and kept
the faith.

24. Nor let it seem to any one, that, by so doing, the
timid Christian is debarred of his rights and discouraged;
or, on the other hand, that the indolent are counte-
nanced in low views of duty by setting before them what
they may consider a double standard of virtue.   For
indolent minds will content themselves with the performance of a meagre heartless obedience, whether or not
a higher excellence is also proposed to them.   And as
to the sincere but anxious disciple of Christ, let it
relieve his despondency to reflect that on him as much

[7] Rev. ii. 3.

as on the matured saint, have been bestowed the titles of God's everlasting favour and the privileges of election. God's will and purpose are pledged in his behalf; and the first fruits of grace are vouchsafed to him, though his character be not yet brought into the abiding image of Christ. While the distance from him of the prize must excite in him an earnest desire of victory and a fear of failure, there is no impassable barrier between him and it, to lead him to despair of it. And there is a point in a Christian's progress at which his election may be considered as secured; whether or not he can assure himself of this, at least there may be times when he will "feel within him the working of the spirit of Christ, mortifying the flesh, and drawing up his mind to high and heavenly things." Thus St. Paul on one occasion says, "Not as though I had attained;" yet, far from desponding, he adds, "I press towards the mark for the prize." Again, at the close of his life, he says, "Henceforth there is laid up for me a crown of righteousness[8]."

25. The subject which has come before us naturally leads on to one or two reflections, with which I shall conclude.

On the one hand, it suggests the question, Are there in this age saints in the world, such as the Apostles were? And this at least brings us to a practical reflection. For, if there are such any where, they ought to exist in our own Church, or rather, since the Apostles were men of no higher nature than ourselves, if there are not

[8] Phil. iii. 12—14. 2 Tim. iv. 8.

among us such as they were, no reason can possibly bo given for the deficiency, but the perverse love of sin in those who are not such. There are Christians who do not enjoy a knowledge of the pure truth; and others, who wander without the pale of the divinely privileged Church of Christ; but we are enabled justly to glory in our membership with the body which the Apostles founded, and in which the Holy Spirit has especially dwelt ever since, and we are blessed with the full light of Scripture, and possess the most formally correct creed of any of the Churches. Yet, on the other hand, when we look at the actual state of this Christian country, it does not seem as if men were anxiously escaping the woe, which, first pronounced on an apostate Apostle, assuredly hangs over them. They do not appear to recognize any distinction between natural and spiritual excellence; they do not aim at rising above the morality of unregenerate men, which, though commendably in heathen, is not available for Christian salvation. And they are apt to view Christian morality as a mere system, as one of the Evidences for Revealed Religion, and as a mark of their superior knowledge in comparison with Jews and Pagans, far more than as it enjoins on them a certain ethical character, which they are commanded to make their own.

26. When, moreover, to the imperative duty, which lies upon us, of being true Christians, and to the actual signs of carelessness and unbelief which the Christian world exhibits, we add the extreme difficulty of turning from sin to obedience, the prospect before us becomes still more threatening. It is difficult even to form a

notion of the utter dissimilarity between the holiness
to which we are called and the habits which we still
imperceptibly form for ourselves, if we leave the tendencies of our nature to take their spontaneous course.
What two things are more opposed to each other than
a mind revelling in the keen indulgence of its passions,
and the same mind, when oppressed with self-reproach
and bodily suffering, and loathing the sins in which it
before exulted ? Yet, great as this contrast is, remorse
does not more differ from profligate excess, than both
of them differ from a true religious habit of mind. As
the pleasure of sinning is contrary to remorse, so
remorse is not repentance, and repentance is not reformation, and reformation is not habitual virtue, and
virtue is not the full gift of the Spirit. How shall we
limit the process of sanctification ? But of these its
higher stages deliberate sinners are as ignorant, and as
ignorant of their ignorance, as of those "heavenly things,"
to which our Saviour refers.

27. And lastly, when the shortness of our probation
is added to the serious thoughts already dwelt upon, who
shall estimate the importance of every day and hour of
a Christian's life in its bearing on his eternal destiny ?
Not that life is not long enough to ascertain each man's
use of his own gifts,—rather, our probation could not
be materially longer, for our nature is such, that, though
life were ten times its present length, yet our eternal
prospects would, as it appears, still be decided by our
first start on its course. We cannot keep from forming
habits of one kind or another, each of our acts influences
the rest, gives character to the mind, narrows its free-

will in the direction of good or evil, till it soon con-
verges in all its powers and principles to some fixed
point in the unbounded horizon before it. This at least
is the general law of our moral nature; and such fearful
expression does it give to every event which befalls us,
and to every corresponding action of our will, and
especially with such appalling interest does it invest
the probation of our early years, that nothing but the
knowledge of the Gospel announcements, and above all
of the gracious words and deeds of our Redeemer, is
equal to the burden of it. And these are intended to
sustain the threatenings of the visible system of things,
which would overwhelm us except for the promise, as
the hearing of the promise on the other hand might puff
us up with an unseeming presumption, had we no experience of the terrors of Natural Religion.

28. The day, we know, will come, when every Christian
will be judged, not by what God has done for him, but
by what he has done for himself : when, of all the varied
blessings of Redemption, in which he was clad here,
nothing will remain to him, but what he has incorporated
in his own moral nature, and made part of himself.
And, since we cannot know what measure of holiness
will be then accepted in our own case, it is but left to us
to cast ourselves individually on God's mercy in faith,
and to look steadily, yet humbly, at the Atonement for
sin which He has appointed; so that when He comes
to judge the world, He may remember us in His kingdom.

SERMON IV.

THE USURPATIONS OF REASON[1].

(Preached December 11, 1831.)

MATT. xi. 19.

" Wisdom is justified of her children."

SUCH is our Lord's comment upon the perverse conduct of His countrymen, who refused to be satisfied
either with St. John's reserve or His own condescension.
John the Baptist retired from the world, and when men
came to seek him, spoke sternly to them. Christ, the
greater Prophet, took the more lowly place, and freely
mixed with sinners. The course of God's dealings with
them was varied to the utmost extent which the essential truth and unchangeableness of His moral government permitted ; but in neither direction of austereness
nor of grace did it persuade. Having exposed this remarkable fact in the history of mankind, the Divine
Speaker utters the solemn words of the text, the truth
which they convey being the refuge of disappointed

---

[1] [Wisdom, Reason, in this Discourse, is taken for secular Reason, or
the "wisdom of the world," that is, Reason exercising itself on secular
principles in the subject-matter of religion and morals, whereas every
department of thought has its own principles, homogeneous with itself,
and necessary for reasoning justly in it. Vide Preface.]

mercy, as well as a warning addressed to all whom they might concern. "Wisdom is justified of her children:" as if He said, "There is no act on God's part, no truth of religion, to which a captious Reason may not find objections; and in truth the evidence and matter of Revelation are not addressed to the mere unstable Reason of man, nor can hope for any certain or adequate reception with it. Divine Wisdom speaks, not to the world, but to her own children, or those who have been already under her teaching, and who, knowing her voice, understand her words, and are suitable judges of them. These justify her."

2. In the text, then, a truth is expressed in the form of a proverb, which is implied all through Scripture as a basis on which its doctrine rests—viz. that there is no necessary connexion between the intellectual and moral principles of our nature[2]; that on religious subjects we may prove any thing or overthrow any thing, and can arrive at truth but accidentally, if we merely investigate by what is commonly called Reason[3], which is in such matters but the instrument at best, in the hands of the legitimate judge, spiritual discernment. When we consider how common it is in the world at large to consider the intellect as the characteristic part of our nature, the silence of Scripture in regard to it (not to mention its positive disparagement of it) is very striking. In the

---

[2] [That is, as found in individuals, in the concrete.]

[3] [Because we may be reasoning from wrong principles, principles unsuitable to the subject-matter reasoned upon. Thus, the moral sense, or "spiritual discernment" must supply us with the assumptions to be used as premisses in religious inquiry.]

Old Testament scarcely any mention is made of the existence of the Reason as a distinct and chief attribute of mind; the sacred language affording no definite and proper terms expressive either of the general gift or of separate faculties in which it exhibits itself. And as to the New Testament, need we but betake ourselves to the description given us of Him who is the Only-begotten Son and Express Image of God, to learn how inferior a station in the idea of the perfection of man's nature is held by the mere Reason? While there is no profaneness in attaching to Christ those moral attributes of goodness, truth, and holiness, which we apply to man, there would be an obvious irreverence in measuring the powers of His mind by any standard of intellectual endowments, the very names of which sound mean and impertinent when ascribed to Him. St. Luke's declaration of His growth " in *wisdom* and stature," with no other specified advancement, is abundantly illustrated in St. John's Gospel, in which we find the Almighty Teacher rejecting with apparent disdain all intellectual display, and confining Himself to the enunciation of deep truths, intelligible to the children of wisdom, but conveyed in language altogether destitute both of argumentative skill, and what is commonly considered eloquence.

3. To account for this silence of Scripture concerning intellectual excellence, by affirming that the Jews were not distinguished in that respect, is hardly to the point, for surely a lesson is conveyed to us in the very circumstance of such a people being chosen as the medium of a moral gift. If it be further objected, that to speak

concerning intellectual endowments fell beyond the range of inspiration, which was limited by its professed object, this is no objection, but the very position here maintained. No one can deny to the intellect its own excellence, nor deprive it of its due honours; the question is merely this, whether it be not limited in its turn, as regards its range [4], so as not without intrusion to exercise itself as an independent authority in the field of morals and religion.

4. Such surely is the case; and the silence of Scripture concerning intellectual gifts need not further be insisted on, either in relation to the fact itself, or the implication contained in it. Were a being unacquainted with mankind to receive information concerning human nature from the Bible, would he ever conjecture its actual state, as developed in society, in all the various productions and exhibitions of what is called talent? And, next viewing the world as it is, and the Bible in connexion with it, what would he see in the actual history of Revelation, but the triumph of the moral powers of man over the intellectual, of holiness over ability, far more than of mind over brute force? Great as was the power of the lion and the bear, the leopard, and that fourth nameless beast, dreadful and terrible and strong exceedingly, God had weapons of their own kind to bruise and tame them. The miracles of the Church displayed more physical power than the hosts of Pharaoh and Sennacherib. Power, not mind, was op-

---

[4] [That is, the secular Reason, or Reason, as informed by a secular spirit, or starting from secular principles, as, for instance, utilitarian, or political, epicurean, or forensic.]

posed to power; yet to the refined Pagan intellect, the rivalry of intellect was not granted. The foolish things of the world confounded the wise, far more completely than the weak the mighty. Human philosophy was beaten from its usurped province, but not by any counter-philosophy; and unlearned Faith, establishing itself by its own inherent strength, ruled the Reason as far as its own interests were concerned [b], and from that time has employed it in the Church, first as a captive, then as a servant; not as an equal, and in nowise (far from it) as a patron.

5. I propose now to make some remarks upon the place which Reason holds in relation to Religion, the light in which we should view it, and certain encroachments of which it is sometimes guilty; and I think that, without a distinct definition of the word, which would carry us too far from our subject, I can make it plain what I take it to mean. Sometimes, indeed, it stands for all in which man differs from the brutes, and so includes in its signification the faculty of distinguishing between right and wrong, and the directing principle in conduct. In this sense I certainly do not here use it, but in that narrower signification, which it usually bears, as representing or synonymous with the intellectual powers, and as opposed as such to the moral qualities, and to Faith.

6. This opposition between Faith and Reason takes

---

[b] [That is, unlearned Faith was strong enough, in matters relating to its own province, to compel the reasoning faculty, as was just, to use as its premises in that province the truths of Natural Religion.]

place in two ways, when either of the two encroaches upon the province of the other[6]. It would be an absurdity to attempt to find out mathematical truths by the purity and acuteness of the moral sense. It is a form of this mistake which has led men to apply such Scripture communications as are intended for religious purposes to the determination of physical questions. This error is perfectly understood in these days by all thinking men. This was the usurpation of the schools of theology in former ages, to issue their decrees to the subjects of the Senses and the Intellect. No wonder Reason and Faith were at variance. The other cause of disagreement takes place when Reason is the aggressor, and encroaches on the province of Religion, attempting to judge of those truths which are subjected to another part of our nature, the moral sense[7]. For instance, suppose an acute man, who had never conformed his life to the precepts of Scripture, attempted to decide on the degree and kind of intercourse which a Christian ought to have with the world, or on the measure of guilt involved in the use of light and profane words, or which of the Christian doctrines were generally necessary to salvation, or to judge of the wisdom or use of consecrating places of worship, or to determine what kind and extent of reverence should be paid to the Lord's Day, or what portion of our possessions set apart for religious purposes; questions these which are addressed to the cultivated moral perception, or, what is sometimes im-

[6] [Vide "Discourses on University Education," Nos. ii. and iii., 2nd edition.]

[7] [By "aggressive Reason" is meant the mind reasoning unduly, that is, on assumptions foreign and injurious to religion and morals.]

properly termed, "*feeling ;*"—improperly, because feeling comes and goes, and, having no root in our nature, speaks with no divine authority; but the moral perception, though varying in the mass of men, is fixed in each individual, and is an original element within us. Hume, in his Essay on Miracles, has well propounded a doctrine, which at the same time he misapplies. He speaks of " those dangerous friends or disguised enemies to the Christian Religion, who have undertaken to defend it by the principles of human Reason." " Our most holy Religion," he proceeds, " is founded on *Faith,* not on Reason." This is said in irony ; but it is true as far as every important question in Revelation is concerned, and to forget this is the error which is at present under consideration.

7. That it is a common error is evident from the anxiety generally felt to detach the names of men of ability from the infidel party. Why should we be desirous to disguise the fact, if it be such, that men distinguished, some for depth and originality of mind, others for acuteness, others for prudence and good sense in practical matters, yet have been indifferent to Revealed Religion,—why, unless we have some misconceived notion concerning the connexion between the intellect and the moral principle ? Yet, is it not a fact, for the proof or disproof of which we need not go to history or philosophy, when the humblest village may show us that those persons who turn out badly, as it is called,—who break the laws first of society, then of their country,—are commonly the very men who have received more than the ordinary share of intel-

lectual gifts? Without turning aside to explain or
account for this, thus much it seems to show us, that
the powers of the intellect (in that degree, at least, in
which, in matter of fact, they are found amongst us) do
not necessarily lead us in the direction of our moral
instincts, or confirm them; but if the agreement between
the two be but matter of accident, what testimony do
we gain from the mere Reason to the truths of
Religion?

8. Why should we be surprised that one faculty of
our compound nature should not be able to do that
which is the work of another? It is as little strange
that the mind, which has only exercised itself on
matters of literature or science, and never submitted
itself to the influence of divine perceptions, should be
unequal to the contemplation of a moral revelation, as
that it should not perform the office of the senses.
There is a strong analogy between the two cases. Our
Reason assists the senses in various ways, directing the
application of them, and arranging the evidence they
supply; it makes use of the facts subjected to them,
and to an unlimited extent deduces conclusions from
them, foretells facts which are to be ascertained, and
confirms doubtful ones; but the man who neglected
experiments and trusted to his vigour of talent, would
be called a theorist; and the blind man who seriously
professed to lecture on light and colours could scarcely
hope to gain an audience [8]. Or suppose his lecture

[8] [That is, not only are the *principles* proper to a given subject-matter
necessary for a successful inquiry into that subject-matter, but there
must be also a *personal familiarity* with it. Vide the Preface.]

proceeded, what might be expected from him ? Starting from the terms of science which would be the foundation and materials of his system, instead of apprehended facts, his acuteness and prompt imagination might carry him freely forward into the open field of the science, he might discourse with ease and fluency, till we almost forgot his lamentable deprivation ; at length on a sudden, he would lose himself in some inexpressibly great mistake, betrayed in the midst of his career by some treacherous word, which he incautiously explained too fully or dwelt too much upon ; and we should find that he had been using words without corresponding ideas :— on witnessing his failure, we should view it indulgently, qualifying our criticism by the remark, that the exhibition was singularly good for a blind man.

9. Such would be the fate of the officious Reason [9], busying itself without warrant in the province of sense.   In its due subordinate place there, it acts but as an instrument; it does but assist and expedite, saving the senses the time and trouble of working.   Give a man a hundred eyes and hands for natural science, and you materially loosen his dependence on the ministry of Reason.

10. This illustration, be it observed, is no adequate parallel of the truth which led to it; for the subject of light and colours is at least within the grasp of scientific definitions, and therefore cognizable by the intellect

[9] [And so "captious Reason," supr. 1; "mere Reason," 2; "human Reason," 6; "forward Reason," infr. 12; "usurping Reason," 23; "rebellious Reason," v. 18; "versatile Reason," v. 27, that is, the reason of secular minds, venturing upon religious questions.]

far better than morals. Yet apply it, such as it is, to
the matter in hand, not, of course, with the extravagant
object of denying the use of the Reason in religious
inquiries, but in order to ascertain what is its real place
in the conduct of them. And in explanation of it I
would make two additional observations :—first, we
must put aside the indirect support afforded to Revelation by the countenance of the intellectually gifted
portion of mankind; I mean, in the way of *influence.*
Reputation for talent, learning, scientific knowledge,
has natural and just claims on our respect, and recommends a cause to our notice. So does power; and
in this way power, as well as intellectual endowments,
is necessary to the maintenance of religion, in order to
secure from mankind a hearing for an unpleasant
subject; but power, when it has done so much, attempts
no more; or if it does, it loses its position, and is
involved in the fallacy of persecution. Here the
parallel holds good—it is as absurd to argue men, as to
torture them, into believing.

11. But in matter of fact (it will be said) Reason *can*
go farther; for we can reason about Religion, and we
frame its Evidences. Here, then, secondly, I observe,
we must deduct from the real use of the Reason in
religious inquiries, whatever is the mere setting right
of its own mistakes. The blind man who reasoned
himself into errors in Optics might possibly reason
himself out of them; yet this would be no proof that
extreme acuteness was necessary or useful in the
science itself. It was but necessary for a blind man;
that is, supposing he was bent on attempting to do

what from the first he ought not to have attempted;
and, after all, with the uncertainty whether he would
gain or lose in his search after scientific truth by such
an attempt. Now, so numerous and so serious have
been the errors of theorists on religious subjects (that
is, of those who have speculated without caring to act
on their sense of right; or have rested their teaching on
mere arguments, instead of aiming at a direct contemplation of its subject-matter), that the correction of those
errors has required the most vigorous and subtle exercise
of the Reason, and has almost engrossed its efforts.
Unhappily the blind teacher in morals can ensure himself a blind audience, to whom he may safely address
his paradoxes, which are sometimes admitted even by
religious men, on the ground of those happy conjectures which his acute Reason now and then makes,
and which they can verify. ⌈What an indescribable confusion hence arises between truth and falsehood, in
systems, parties and persons!⌋ What a superhuman
talent is demanded to unravel the chequered and
tangled web; and what gratitude is due to the gifted
individual who by his learning or philosophy in part
achieves the task! yet not gratitude in such a case to
the Reason as a principle of research, which is merely
undoing its own mischief, and poorly and tardily re-
dressing its intrusion into a province not its own; but
to the man, the moral being, who has subjected it in
his own person to the higher principles of his nature.

12. To take an instance. What an extreme exercise
of intellect is shown in the theological teaching of the
Church! Yet how was it necessary? chiefly, from the

previous errors of heretical reasonings, on subjects addressed to the moral perception. For while Faith was engaged in that exact and well-instructed devotion to Christ which no words can suitably describe, the forward Reason stepped in upon the yet unenclosed ground of doctrine, and attempted to describe there, from its own resources [1], an image of the Invisible. Henceforth the Church was obliged, in self-defence, to employ the gifts of the intellect in the cause of God, to trace out (as near as might be) the faithful shadow of those truths, which unlearned piety admits and acts upon, without the medium of clear intellectual representation.

13. This obviously holds good as regards the Evidences [2] also, great part of which are rather answers to objections than direct arguments for Revelation; and even the direct arguments are far more effective in the confutation of captious opponents, than in the conviction of inquirers. Doubtless the degree in which we depend on argument in religious subjects varies with each individual, so that no strict line can be drawn: still, let it be inquired whether these Evidences are not rather to be viewed as splendid philosophical investigations than practical arguments; at best bulwarks intended for

---

[1] ["Canons, founded on physics, were made" by the early heretics, "the basis of discussions about possibilities and impossibilities in a spiritual substance. A contemporary writer, after saying that they supported their 'God-denying apostasy' by syllogistic forms of argument, proceeds, 'Abandoning the inspired writings they devote themselves to geometry.' And Epiphanius: 'Aiming to exhibit the divine nature by means of Aristotelic syllogisms and geometrical data they are led on to declare, &c.'" History of Arians, p. 35, Edit. 3.]

[2] [By the Evidences of Christianity are meant exercises of Reason in proof of its divinity, *explicit* and *à posteriori*. Vide Preface.]

overawing the enemy by their strength and number, rather than for actual use in war. In matter of fact, *how* many men do we suppose, in a century, out of the whole body of Christians, have been primarily brought to belief, or retained in it, by an intimate and lively perception of the force of what are technically called the Evidences? And why are there so few? Because to the mind already familiar with the truths of Natural Religion, enough of evidence is at once afforded by the mere fact of the present existence of Christianity; which, viewed in its connexion with its principles and upholders and effects[3], bears on the face of it the signs of a divine ordinance in the very same way in which the visible world attests to us its own divine origin;—a more accurate investigation, in which superior talents are brought into play, merely bringing to light an innumerable alternation of arguments, for and against it, which forms indeed an ever-increasing series in its behalf, but still does not get beyond the first suggestion of plain sense and religiously-trained reason; and in fact, perhaps, never comes to a determination. Nay, so alert is the instinctive power of an educated conscience, that by some secret faculty, and without any intelligible reasoning process[4], it seems to detect moral truth wherever it lies hid, and feels a conviction of its own accuracy which bystanders cannot account for; and this especially in the case of Revealed Religion, which is one comprehensive moral fact,—according to the say-

---

[3] [That is, viewed in the light of *verisimilitudes* or "the Notes of the Church."]

[4] [That is, by an *implicit* act of reasoning.]

ing which is parallel to the text, "I know My sheep,
and am known of Mine[5]."

14. From considerations such as the foregoing, it
appears that exercises of Reason are either external, or
at least only ministrative, to religious inquiry and knowledge : accidental to them, not of their essence ; useful
in their place, but not necessary. But in order to obtain further illustrations, and a view of the importance
of the doctrine which I would advocate, let us proceed
to apply it to the circumstances of the present times.
Here, first, in finding fault with the times, it is right to
disclaim all intention of complaining of them. To
murmur and rail at the state of things under which we
find ourselves, and to prefer a former state, is not merely
indecorous, it is absolutely unmeaning. We are ourselves necessary parts of the existing system, out of
which we have individually grown into being, into our
actual position in society. Depending, therefore, on the
times as a condition of existence, in wishing for other
times we are, in fact, wishing we had never been born.
Moreover, it is ungrateful to a state of society, from
which we daily enjoy so many benefits, to rail against it.
Yet there is nothing unbecoming, unmeaning, or
ungrateful in pointing out its faults and wishing them
away.

15. In this day, then, we see a very extensive
development of an usurpation which has been been pre-
paring, with more or less of open avowal, for some
centuries,—the usurpation of Reason in morals and

[5] John x. 14.

religion [6]. In the first years of its growth it professed
to respect the bounds of justice and sobriety : it was
little in its own eyes; but getting strength, it was
lifted up; and casting down all that is called God, or
worshipped, it took its seat in the temple of God, as His
representative. Such, at least, is the consummation at
which the Oppressor is aiming;—which he will reach,
unless He who rids His Church of tyrants in their hour
of pride, look down from the pillar of the cloud, and
trouble his host.

16. Now, in speaking of an usurpation of the Reason
at the present day, stretching over the province of
Religion, and in fact over the Christian Church, no admission is made concerning the degree of cultivation
which the Reason has at present reached in the territory
which it has unjustly entered. A tyrant need not be
strong; he keeps his ground by prescription and through
fear. It is not the profound thinkers who intrude with
their discussions and criticisms within the sacred limits
of moral truth. A really philosophical mind, if unhappily it has ruined its own religious perceptions, will
be silent; it will understand that Religion does not lie
in its way : it may disbelieve its truths, it may account
belief in them a weakness, or, on the other hand, a
happy dream, a delightful error, which it cannot itself
enjoy;—any how, it will not usurp. But men who know
but a little, are for that very reason most under the

---

[6] [That is, the usurpation of *secular* Reason, or the claim of men of
the world to apply their ordinary sentiments and conventional modes of
judging to the subject of religion; parallel to the conduct of the man in
the fable, who felt there was "nothing like leather."]

power of the imagination, which fills up for them at
pleasure those departments of knowledge to which they
are strangers; and, as the ignorance of abject minds
shrinks from the spectres which it frames there, the
ignorance of the self-confident is petulant and pre-
suming.

17. The usurpations of the Reason may be dated from
the Reformation. Then, together with the tyranny, the
legitimate authority of the ecclesiastical power was more
or less overthrown; and in some places its ultimate
basis also, the moral sense. One school of men resisted
the Church; another went farther, and rejected the
supreme authority of the law of Conscience. Accordingly, Revealed Religion was in a great measure stripped
of its proof; for the existence of the Church had been
its external evidence, and its internal had been supplied
by the moral sense. Reason now undertook to repair
the demolition it had made, and to render the proof of
Christianity independent both of the Church and of the
law of nature. From that time (if we take a general
view of its operations) it has been engaged first in
making difficulties by the mouth of unbelievers, and then
claiming power in the Church as a reward for having,
by the mouth of apologists, partially removed them.

18. The following instances are in point, in citing
which let no disrespect be imagined towards such really
eminent men as were at various times concerned in
them. Wrong reason could not be met, when miracle
and inspiration were suspended, except by rightly-
directed Reason.

19. (1.) As to the proof of the authority of Scripture.

This had hitherto rested on the testimony borne to it by the existing Church. Reason volunteered proof, not different, however, in kind, but more subtle and complicated in its form,—took the evidence of past ages, instead of the present, and committed its keeping (as was necessary) to the oligarchy of learning: at the same time, it boasted of the service thus rendered to the cause of Revelation, that service really consisting in the external homage thus paid to it by learning and talent, not in any great direct practical benefit, where men honestly wish to find and to do God's will, to act for the best, and to prefer what is safe and pious, to what shows well in argument.

20. (2.) Again, the Evidences themselves have been elaborately expanded; thus satisfying, indeed, the liberal curiosity of the mind, and giving scope for a devotional temper to admire the manifold wisdom of God, but doing comparatively little towards keeping men from infidelity, or turning them to a religious life. The same remark applies to such works on Natural Theology as treat of the marks of design in the creation, which are beautiful and interesting to the believer in a God; but, when men have not already recognized God's voice within them, ineffective, and this moreover possibly from some unsoundness in the intellectual basis of the argument[7].

---

[7] [This remark does not touch the argument from *order* as seen in the universe. "As a cause implies a will, so does order imply a purpose. Did we see flint celts, in their various receptacles all over Europe, scored always with certain special and characteristic marks, even though those marks had no assignable meaning or final cause whatever, we should take that very repetition, which indeed is the principle of order, to be a

21. (3.) A still bolder encroachment was contemplated by the Reason, when it attempted to deprive the Moral Law of its intrinsic authority, and to rest it upon a theory of present expediency. Thus, it constituted itself the court of ultimate appeal in religious disputes, under pretence of affording a clearer and more scientifically-arranged code than is to be collected from the obscure precedents and mutilated enactments of the Conscience.

22. (4.) A further error, connected with the assumption just noticed, has been that of making intellectually-gifted men arbiters of religious questions, in the place of the children of wisdom. As far as the argument for Revelation is concerned, it is only necessary to show that Christianity has had disciples among men of the highest ability; whereas a solicitude already alluded to has been shown to establish the orthodoxy of some great names in philosophy and science, as if truly it were a great gain to religion, and not to themselves, if they *were* believers. Much more unworthy has been the practice of boasting of the admissions of infidels concerning the beauty or utility of the Christian system, as if it were a great thing for a divine gift to obtain praise for human excellence from proud or immoral men. Far different is the spirit of our own Church, which, re-

proof of intelligence. The agency, then, which has kept up and keeps up the general laws of nature, energizing at once in Sirius and on the earth, and on the earth in its primitive period as well as in the nineteenth century, must be Mind, and nothing else ; and Mind at least as wide and as enduring in its living action as the immeasurable ages and spaces of the universe on which that agency has left its traces." Essay on Assent, iv. i. 4.]

joicing, as she does, to find her children walking in truth, never forgets the dignity and preciousness of the gifts she offers ; as appears, for instance, in the warnings prefacing the Communion Service, and in the Commination,—above all, in the Athanasian Creed, in which she but follows the example of the early Church, which first withdrew her mysteries from the many, then, when controversy exposed them, guarded them with an anathema,—in each case, lest curious Reason might rashly gaze and perish.

23. (5.) Again,—another dangerous artifice of the usurping Reason has been, the establishment of Societies, in which literature or science has been the essential bond of union, to the exclusion of religious profession. These bodies, many of them founded with no bad intention, have gradually led to an undue exaltation of the Reason, and have formed an unconstitutional power, advising and controlling the legitimate authorities of the soul. In troubled times, such as the present, associations, the most inoffensive in themselves, and the most praise-worthy in their object, hardly escape this blame. Of this nature have been the literary meetings and Societies of the last two centuries, not to mention recently-established bodies of a less innocent character.

24. (6.) And lastly, let it be a question, whether the theories on Government, which exclude Religion from the essential elements of the state, are not also off-shoots of the same usurpation.

25. And now, what remains but to express a con-fidence, which cannot deceive itself, that, whatever be

the destined course of the usurpations of the Reason in the scheme of Divine Providence, its fall must at last come, as that of other proud aspirants before it ? "Fret not thyself," says David, "because of evil doers, neither be thou envious against the workers of iniquity ; for they shall soon be cut down like the grass, and wither as the green herb ;" perishing as that high-minded power, which the Prophet speaks of, who sat in the seat of God, as if wiser than Daniel, and acquainted with all secrets, till at length he was cast out from the holy place as profane, in God's good time[8]. Our plain business, in the meantime, is to ascertain and hold fast our appointed station in the troubled scene, and then to rid ourselves of all dread of the future ; to be careful, while we freely cultivate the Reason in all its noble functions, to keep it in its subordinate[9] place in our nature : while we employ it industriously in the service of Religion, not to imagine that, in this service, we are doing any great thing, or directly advancing its influence over the heart; and, while we promote the education of others in all useful knowledge, to beware of admitting any principle of union, or standard of reward, which may practically disparage the supreme authority of Christian fellowship. Our great danger is, lest we should not understand our own principles, and should weakly surrender customs and institutions, which go far to constitute the Church what she is, the pillar and ground of moral truth,—

[8] Ezek. xxviii. 3. 16.

[9] [Subordinate, because the knowledge of God is the highest function of our nature, and, as regards that knowledge, Reason only holds the place of an instrument.]

lest, from a wish to make religion acceptable to the world in general, more free from objections than any moral system can be made, more immediately and visibly beneficial to the temporal interests of the community than God's comprehensive appointments condescend to be, we betray it to its enemies; lest we rashly take the Scriptures from the Church's custody, and commit them to the world, that is, to what is called public opinion; which men boast, indeed, will ever be right on the whole, but which, in fact, being the opinion of men who, as a body, have not cultivated the internal moral sense, and have externally no immutable rules to bind them, is, in religious questions, only by accident right, or only on very broad questions, and to-morrow will betray interests which to-day it affects to uphold.

26. However, what are the essentials of our system, both in doctrine and discipline; what we may safely give up, and what we must firmly uphold; such practical points are to be determined by a more mature wisdom than can be expected in a discussion like the present, or indeed can be conveyed in any formal treatise. It is a plainer and a sufficiently important object, to contribute to the agitation of the general subject, and to ask questions which others are to answer.

SERMON V.

PERSONAL INFLUENCE, THE MEANS OF PROPAGATING
THE TRUTH.

(Preached January 22, 1832.)

HEB. xi. 34.

" Out of weakness were made strong."

THE history of the Old Testament Saints, conveyed in
these few words, is paralleled or surpassed in its
peculiar character by the lives of those who first proclaimed the Christian Dispensation. " Behold, I send
you forth as lambs among wolves," was the warning
given them of their position in the world, on becoming
Evangelists in its behalf. Their miraculous powers
gained their cause a hearing, but did not protect themselves. St. Paul records the fulfilment of our Lord's
prophecy, as it contrasts the Apostles and mankind at
large, when he declares, " Being reviled, we bless;
being persecuted, we suffer it; being defamed, we
entreat; we are made as the filth of the world, and are
the offscouring of all things unto this day [1]." Nay,
these words apply not only to the unbelieving world;
the Apostle had reason to be suspicious of his Christian

[1] 1 Cor. iv. 12, 13.

brethren, and even to expostulate on that score, with
his own converts, his "beloved sons." He counted it
a great gain, such as afterwards might be dwelt upon
with satisfaction, that the Galatians did not despise nor
reject him on account of the infirmity which was in his
flesh; and, in the passage already referred to, he
mourns over the fickleness and coldness of the Corinthians, who thought themselves wise, strong, and
honourable, and esteemed the Apostles as fools, weak,
and despised.

2. Whence, then, was it, that in spite of all these
impediments to their success, still they succeeded?
How did they gain that lodgment in the world, which
they hold down to this day, enabling them to per-
petuate principles distasteful to the majority even of
those who profess to receive them? What is that
hidden attribute of the Truth, and how does it act,
prevailing, as it does, single-handed, over the many
and multiform errors, by which it is simultaneously and
incessantly attacked?

3. Here, of course, we might at once refer its success
to the will and blessing of Him who revealed it, and
who distinctly promised that He would be present with
it, and with its preachers, "alway, even unto the end."
And, of course, by realizing this in our minds, we learn
dependence upon His grace in our own endeavours to
recommend the Truth, and encouragement to persevere.
But it is also useful to inquire into the human means
by which His Providence acts in the world, in order to
take a practical view of events as they successively come
before us in the course of human affairs, and to under-

stand our duty in particulars; and, with reference to these means, it is now proposed to consider the question.

4. Here, first of all,—

It is plain that we cannot rightly ascribe the influence of moral truth in the world to the gift of miracles, which was entrusted to the persons who promulgated it in that last and perfect form, in which we have been vouchsafed it; that gift having been withdrawn with the first preaching of it. Nor, again, can it be satisfactorily maintained that the visible Church, which the miracles formed, has taken their place in the course of Divine Providence, as the basis, strictly speaking, on which the Truth rests; though doubtless it is the appointed instrument, in even a fuller sense than the miracles before it, by which that Truth is conveyed to the world: for though it is certain that a community of men, who, as individuals, were but imperfectly virtuous, would, in the course of years, gain the ascendancy over vice and error, however well prepared for the contest, yet no one pretends that the visible Church is thus blessed; the Epistle to the Corinthians sufficiently showing, that, in all ages, true Christians, though contained in it, and forming its life and strength, are scattered and hidden in the multitude, and, but partially recognizing each other, have no means of combining and co-operating. On the other hand, if we view the Church simply as a political institution, and refer the triumph of the Truth, which is committed to it, merely to its power thence resulting,—then, the question recurs, first, how is it that this mixed and heterogeneous body, called the Church, has, through so many centuries, on the whole, been true to the principles on which it was first established; and then, how, thus preserving its principles, it has, over and above this, gained on its side, in so many countries and times, the countenance and support of the civil authorities. Here, it would be sufficient to consider the three first centuries of its existence, and to inquire by what means, in spite of its unearthly principles, it grew and strengthened in the world; and how, again, corrupt body as it was then as now, still it preserved, all the while, with such remarkable fidelity, those same unearthly principles which had been once delivered to it.

5. Others there are who attempt to account for this prevalence of the Truth, in spite of its enemies, by imagining, that, though at first opposed, yet it is, after a time, on mature reflection, accepted by the world in general from a real understanding and conviction of its excellence; that it is in its nature level to the comprehension of men, considered merely as rational beings, without reference to their moral character, whether good or bad; and that, in matter of fact, it is recognized and upheld by the mass of men, taken as individuals, not merely approved by them, taken as a mass, in which some have influence over others,— not merely submitted to with a blind, but true instinct, such as is said to oppress inferior animals in the presence of man, but literally advocated from an enlightened capacity for criticizing it; and, in con-

sequence of this notion, some men go so far as to advise that the cause of Truth should be frankly committed to the multitude as the legitimate judges and guardians of it.

6. Something may occur to expose the fallacy of this notion, in the course of the following remarks on what I conceive to be the real method by which the influence of spiritual principles is maintained in this carnal world. But here, it is expedient at once to appeal to Scripture against a theory, which, whether plausible or not, is scarcely Christian. The following texts will suggest a multitude of others, as well as of Scripture representations, hostile to the idea that moral truth is easily or generally discerned. " The natural man receiveth not the things of the Spirit of God [2]." " The light shineth in darkness, and the darkness comprehended it not [3]." " Whosoever hath, to him shall be given [4]." " Wisdom is justified by her children [5]."

7. On the other hand, that its real influence consists directly in some inherent moral power, in virtue in some shape or other, not in any evidence or criterion level to the undisciplined reason of the multitude, high or low, learned or ignorant, is implied in texts, such as those referred to just now :—" I send you forth as sheep in the midst of wolves ; *be ye, therefore,* wise as serpents, and harmless as doves."

8. This being the state of the question, it is proposed to consider, whether the influence of Truth in the world at large does not arise from *the personal influence,*

[2] 1 Cor. ii. 14.   [3] John i. 5.   [4] Matt. xiii. 12.   [5] Matt. xi. 19.

direct and indirect, of those who are commissioned to teach it.

9. In order to explain the sense in which this is asserted, it will be best to begin by tracing the mode in which the moral character of such an organ of the Truth is formed; and, in a large subject, 1 must beg permission to be somewhat longer (should it be necessary) than the custom of this place allows.

10. We will suppose this Teacher of the Truth so circumstanced as One alone among the sons of Adam has ever been, such a one as has never transgressed his sense of duty, but from his earliest childhood upwards has been only engaged in increasing and perfecting the light originally given him. In him the knowledge and power of acting rightly have kept pace with the enlargement of his duties, and his inward convictions of Truth with the successive temptations opening upon him from without to wander from it. Other men are surprised and overset by the sudden weight of circumstances against which they have not provided; or, losing step, they strain and discompose their faculties in the effort, even though successful, to recover themselves; or they attempt to discriminate for themselves between little and great breaches of the law of conscience, and allow themselves in what they consider the former; thus falling down precipices (as I may say) when they meant to descend an easy step, recoverable the next moment. Hence it is that, in a short time, those who started on one line make such different progress, and diverge in so many directions. Their conscience still speaks, but having been trifled with, it does not tell

truly; it equivocates, or is irregular. Whereas in him who is faithful to his own divinely implanted nature, the faint light of Truth dawns continually brighter; the shadows which at first troubled it, the unreal shapes created by its own twilight-state, vanish; what was as uncertain as mere feeling, and could not be distinguished from a fancy except by the commanding urgency of its voice, becomes fixed and definite, and strengthening into principle, it at the same time developes into habit. As fresh and fresh duties arise, or fresh and fresh faculties are brought into action, they are at once absorbed into the existing inward system, and take their appropriate place in it. Doubtless beings, disobedient as most of us, from our youth up, cannot comprehend even the early attainments of one who thus grows in wisdom as truly as he grows in stature; who has no antagonist principles unsettling each other— no errors to unlearn; though something is suggested to our imagination by that passage in the history of our Blessed Lord, when at twelve years old He went up with His parents to the Temple. And still less able are we to understand the state of such a mind, when it had passed through the temptations peculiar to youth and manhood, and had driven Satan from him in very despair.

11. Concerning the body of opinions formed under these circumstances,—not accidental and superficial, the mere reflection of what goes on in the world, but the natural and almost spontaneous result of the formed and finished character within,—two remarks may be offered. (1.) That every part of what may be called

this moral creed will be equally true and necessary; and (if, as we may reasonably suppose, the science of morals extends without limit into the details of thought and conduct) numberless particulars, which we are accustomed to account indifferent, may be in fact indifferent in no truer sense, than in physics there is really any such agent as chance ; our ignorance being the sole cause of the seeming variableness on the one hand in the action of nature, on the other in the standard of faith and morals. This is practically important to remember, even while it is granted that no exemplar of holiness has been exhibited to us, at once faultless yet minute ; and again, that in all existing patterns, besides actual defects, there are also the idiosyncrasies and varieties of disposition, taste, and talents, nay of bodily organization, to modify the dictates of that inward light which is itself divine and unerring. It is important, I say, as restraining us from judging hastily of opinions and practices of good men into which we ourselves cannot enter ; but which, for what we know, may be as necessary parts of the Truth, though too subtle for our dull perceptions, as those great and distinguishing features of it, which we, in common with the majority of sincere men, admit. And particularly will it preserve us from rash censures of the Primitive Church, which, in spite of the corruptions which disfigured it from the first, still in its collective holiness may be considered to make as near an approach to the pattern of Christ as fallen man ever will attain ; being, in fact, a Revelation in some sort of that Blessed Spirit in a bodily shape, who was promised to us as a second

Teacher of Truth after Christ's departure, and became such upon a subject-matter far more diversified than that on which our Lord had revealed Himself before Him. For instance, for what we know, the Episcopal principle, or the practice of Infant Baptism, which is traceable to Apostolic times, though not clearly proved by the Scripture records, may be as necessary in the scheme of Christian truth as the doctrines of the Divine Unity, and of man's responsibility, which in the artificial system are naturally placed as the basis of Religion, as being first in order of succession and time. And this, be it observed, will account for the omission in Scripture of express sanctions of these and similar principles and observances; provided, that is, the object of the Written Word be, not to unfold a system for our intellectual contemplation, but to secure the formation of a certain character.

12. (2.) And in the second place, it is plain, that the gifted individual whom we have imagined, will of all men be least able (as such) to defend his own views, inasmuch as he takes no external survey of himself. Things which are the most familiar to us, and easy in practice, require the most study, and give the most trouble in explaining; as, for instance, the number, combination, and succession of muscular movements by which we balance ourselves in walking, or utter our separate words; and this quite independently of the existence or non-existence of language suitable for describing them. The longer any one has persevered in the practice of virtue, the less likely is he to recollect how he began it; what were his difficulties on starting,

and how surmounted; by what process one truth led to another ; the less likely to elicit justly the real reasons latent in his mind for particular observances or opinions. He holds the whole assemblage of moral notions almost as so many collateral and self-evident facts. Hence it is that some of the most deeply-exercised and variously gifted Christians, when they proceed to write or speak upon Religion, either fail altogether, or cannot be understood except on an attentive study ; and after all, perhaps, are illogical and unsystematic, assuming what their readers require proved, and seeming to mistake connexion or antecedence for causation, probability for evidence. And over such as these it is, that the minute intellect of inferior men has its moment of triumph, men who excel in a mere short-sighted perspicacity ; not understanding that, even in the case of intellectual excellence, it is considered the highest of gifts to possess an intuitive knowledge of the beautiful in art, or the effective in action, without reasoning or investigating ; that this, in fact, is *genius ;* and that they who have a corresponding insight into moral truth (as far as they have it) have reached that especial perfection in the spiritual part of their nature, which is so rarely found and so greatly prized among the intellectual endowments of the soul.

13. Nay, may we not further venture to assert, not only that moral Truth will be least skilfully defended by those, as such, who are the genuine depositories of it, but that it cannot be adequately explained and defended in words at all ? Its views and human language are incommensurable. For, after all, what *is* language but

an artificial system adapted for particular purposes, which have been determined by our wants ? And here, even at first sight, can we imagine that it has been framed with a view to ideas so refined, so foreign to the whole course of the world, as those which (as Scripture expresses it) " no man can learn," but the select remnant who are " redeemed from the earth," and in whose mouth " is found no guile [6] "? Nor is it this heavenly language alone which is without its intellectual counterpart. Moral character in itself, whether good or bad, as exhibited in thought and conduct, surely cannot be duly represented in words. We may, indeed, by an effort, reduce it in a certain degree to this arbitrary medium; but in its combined dimensions it is as impossible to write and read a man (so to express it), as to give literal depth to a painted tablet.

14. With these remarks on the nature of moral Truth, as viewed externally, let us conduct our secluded Teacher, who is the embodied specimen of it, after his thirty years' preparation for his office, into the noise and tumult of the world; and in order to set him fairly on the course, let us suppose him recommended by some external gift, whether ordinary or extraordinary, the power of miracles, the countenance of rulers, or a reputation for learning, such as may secure a hearing for him from the multitude of men. This must be supposed, in consequence of the very constitution of the present world. Amid its incessant din, nothing will attract attention but what cries aloud and spares not. It is an old proverb, that

[6] Rev. xiv. 3. 5.

men profess a sincere respect for Virtue, and then let
her starve; for they have at the bottom of their hearts
an evil feeling, in spite of better thoughts, that to be
bound to certain laws and principles is a superstition
and a slavery, and that freedom consists in the actual
exercise of the will in evil as well as in good; and they
witness (what cannot be denied) that a man who throws
off the yoke of strict conscientiousness, greatly increases his producible talent for the time, and his immediate power of attaining his ends. At best they will
but admire the religious man, and treat him with
deference; but in his absence they are compelled (as
they say) to confess that a being so amiable and gentle
is not suited to play his part in the scene of life; that
he is too good for this world; that he is framed for a
more primitive and purer age, and born out of due
time. Μακαρίσαντες ὑμῶν τὸ ἀπειρόκακον, says the
scoffing politician in the History, οὐ ζηλοῦμεν τὸ ἄφρον;
—would not the great majority of men, high and low,
thus speak of St. John the Apostle, were he now
living?

15. Therefore, we must invest our Teacher with a
certain gift of power, that he may be feared. But
even then, how hopeless does this task seem to be at
first sight! how improbable that he should be able to
proceed one step farther than his external recommendation carries him forward! so that it is a marvel how
the Truth had ever been spread and maintained among
men. For, recollect, it is not a mere set of opinions
that he has to promulgate, which may lodge on the
surface of the mind; but he is to be an instrument in

changing (as Scripture speaks) the heart, and modelling all men after one exemplar; making them like himself, or rather like One above himself, who is the beginning of a new creation. Having (as has been said) no sufficient eloquence—nay, not language at his command—what instruments can he be said to possess? Thus he is, from the nature of the case, thrown upon his personal resources, be they greater or less; for it is plain that he cannot commit his charge to others as his representatives, and be translated (as it were), and circulated through the world, till he has made others like himself.

16. Turn to the history of Truth, and these anticipations are fulfilled. Some hearers of it had their conscience stirred for a while, and many were affected by the awful simplicity of the Great Teacher; but the proud and sensual were irritated into opposition; the philosophic considered His doctrines strange and chimerical; the multitude followed for a time in senseless wonder, and then suddenly abandoned an apparently falling cause. For in truth what was the task of an Apostle, but to raise the dead? and what trifling would it appear, even to the most benevolent and candid men of the world, when such a one persisted to chafe and stimulate the limbs of the inanimate corpse, as if his own life could be communicated to it, and motion would continue one moment after the external effort was withdrawn; in the poet's words,

$$\theta\rho\acute{a}\sigma os\ \dot{a}\kappa o\acute{v}\sigma\iota o\nu$$
$$\dot{a}\nu\delta\rho\acute{a}\sigma\iota\ \theta\nu\acute{\eta}\sigma\kappa o\upsilon\sigma\iota\ \kappa o\mu\acute{\iota}\zeta\omega\nu.$$

Truly such a one must expect, at best, to be accounted but a babbler, or one deranged by his "much learning"—a visionary and an enthusiast,—

κάρτ' ἀπομούσως ἦσθα γεγραμμένος,

fit for the wilderness or the temple; a jest for the Areopagus, and but a gladiatorial show at Ephesus, ἐπιθανάτιος, an actor in an exhibition which would finish in his own death.

17. Yet (blessed be God!) the power of Truth actually did, by some means or other, overcome these vast obstacles to its propagation; and what those means were, we shall best understand by contemplating it, as it now shows itself when established and generally professed; an ordinary sanction having taken the place of miracles, and infidelity being the assailant instead of the assailed party.

18. It will not require many words to make it evident how impetuous and (for the time) how triumphant an attack the rebellious Reason will conduct against the long-established, over-secure, and but silently-working system of which Truth is the vital principle.

19. (1.) First, every part of the Truth is novel to its opponent; and seen detached from the whole, becomes an objection. It is only necessary for Reason [7] to ask many questions; and, while the other party is investigating the real answer to each in detail, to claim the victory, which spectators will not be slow to award,

[7] [Here, as in the foregoing Discourse, by Reason is meant the reasoning of secular minds, (1) *explicit,* (2) *à posteriori,* and (3) based on *secular assumptions.* Vide Preface.]

fancying (as is the manner of men) that clear and ready speech is the test of Truth. And it can choose its questions, selecting what appears most objectionable in the tenets and practices of the received system; and it will (in all probability), even unintentionally, fall upon the most difficult parts; what is on the surface being at once most conspicuous, and also farthest removed from the centre on which it depends. On the other hand, its objections will be complete in themselves from their very minuteness. Thus, for instance, men attack ceremonies and discipline of the Church, appealing to common sense, as they call it; which really means, appealing to some proposition which, though true in its own province, is nothing to the purpose in theology; or appealing to the logical accuracy of the argument, when every thing turns on the real meaning of the terms employed, which can only be understood by the religious mind.

20. (2.) Next, men who investigate in this merely intellectual way, without sufficient basis and guidance in their personal virtue, are bound by no fears or delicacy. Not only from dulness, but by preference, they select ground for the contest, which a reverent Faith wishes to keep sacred; and, while the latter is looking to its stepping, lest it commit sacrilege, they have the unembarrassed use of their eyes for the combat, and overcome, by skill and agility, one stronger than themselves.

21. (3.) Further, the warfare between Error and Truth is necessarily advantageous to the former, from its very nature, as being conducted by set speech or treatise; and this, not only for a reason already as-

signed, the deficiency of Truth in the power of eloquence, and even of words, but moreover from the very neatness and definiteness of method required in a written or spoken argument. Truth is vast and far-stretching, viewed as a system; and, viewed in its separate doctrines, it depends on the combination of a number of various, delicate, and scattered evidences; hence it can scarcely be exhibited in a given number of sentences. If this be attempted, its advocate, unable to exhibit more than a fragment of the whole, must round off its rugged extremities, and unite its straggling lines, by much the same process by which an historical narrative is converted into a tale. This, indeed, is the very *art* of composition, which, accordingly, is only with extreme trouble preserved clear of exaggeration and artifice ; and who does not see that all this is favourable to the cause of error,—to that party which has not faith enough to be patient of doubt, and has just talent enough to consider perspicuity the chief excellence of a writer ? To illustrate this, we may contrast the works of Bishop Butler with those of that popular infidel writer at the end of the last century, who professed to be the harbinger of an " Age of Reason."

22. (4.) Moreover, this great, though dangerous faculty which evil employs as its instrument in its warfare against the Truth, may simulate all kinds of virtue, and thus become the rival of the true saints of God, whom it is opposing. It may draw fine pictures of virtue, or trace out the course of sacred feelings or of heavenly meditations. Nothing is so easy as to be reli-

gious on paper; and thus the arms of Truth are turned, as far as may be found necessary, against itself.

23. (5.) It must be further observed, that the exhibitions of Reason, being complete in themselves, and having nothing of a personal nature, are capable almost of an omnipresence by an indefinite multiplication and circulation, through the medium of composition: here, even the orator has greatly the advantage over the religious man; words may be heard by thousands at once,—a good deed will be witnessed and estimated at most by but a few.

24. (6.) To put an end to these remarks on the advantages accruing to Error in its struggle with Truth;—the exhibitions of the Reason, being in their operation separable from the person furnishing them, possess little or no responsibility. To be anonymous is almost their characteristic, and with it all the evils attendant on the unchecked opportunity for injustice and falsehood.

25. Such, then, are the difficulties which beset the propagation of the Truth: its want of instruments, as an assailant of the world's opinions; the keenness and vigour of the weapons producible against it, when itself in turn is to be attacked. How, then, after all, has it maintained its ground among men, and subjected to its dominion unwilling minds, some even bound to the external profession of obedience, others at least in a sullen neutrality, and the inaction of despair?

26. I answer, that it has been upheld in the world not as a system, not by books, not by argument, nor by temporal power, but by the personal influence of such

men as have already been described, who are at once
the teachers and the patterns of it; and, with some
suggestions in behalf of this statement, I shall conclude.

27. (1.) Here, first, is to be taken into account the
natural beauty and majesty of virtue, which is more or
less felt by all but the most abandoned. I do not
say virtue in the abstract,—virtue in a book. Men
persuade themselves, with little difficulty, to scoff at
principles, to ridicule books, to make sport of the
names of good men; but they cannot bear their
presence : it is holiness embodied in personal form,
which they cannot steadily confront and bear down : so
that the silent conduct of a conscientious man secures
for him from beholders a feeling different in kind from
any which is created by the mere versatile and garru-
lous Reason.

28. (2.) Next, consider the extreme rarity, in any great
perfection and purity, of simple-minded, honest devotion to God; and another instrument of influence is
discovered for the cause of Truth. Men naturally prize
what is novel and scarce; and, considering the low views
of the multitude on points of social and religious duty,
their ignorance of those precepts of generosity, self-
denial, and high-minded patience, which religion enforces, nay, their scepticism (whether known to themselves or not) of the existence in the world of severe
holiness and truth, no wonder they are amazed when
accident gives them a sight of these excellences in
another, as though they beheld a miracle; and they
watch it with a mixture of curiosity and awe.

29. (3.) Besides, the conduct of a religious man is quite

above them. They cannot imitate him, if they try. It may be easy for the educated among them to make speeches, or to write books; but high moral excellence is the attribute of a school to which they are almost strangers, having scarcely learned, and that painfully, the first elements of the heavenly science. One little deed, done against natural inclination for God's sake, though in itself of a conceding or passive character, to brook an insult, to face a danger, or to resign an advantage, has in it a power outbalancing all the dust and chaff of mere profession; the profession whether of enlightened benevolence and candour, or, on the other hand, of high religious faith and of fervent zeal.

30. (4.) And men feel, moreover, that the object of their contemplation is beyond their reach—not open to the common temptations which influence men, and grounded on a foundation which they cannot explain. And nothing is more effectual, first in irritating, then in humbling the pride of men, than the sight of a superior altogether independent of themselves.

31. (5.) The consistency of virtue is another gift, which gradually checks the rudeness of the world, and tames it into obedience to itself. The changes of human affairs, which first excited and interested, at length disgust the mind, which then begins to look out for something on which it can rely, for peace and rest; and what can then be found immutable and sure, but God's word and promises, illustrated and conveyed to the inquirer in the person of His faithful servants? Every day shows us how much depends on firmness for ob-

taining influence in practical matters; and what are all
kinds of firmness, as exhibited in the world, but like-
nesses and offshoots of that true stability of heart
which is stayed in the grace and in the contemplation
of Almighty God?

32. (6.) Such especially will be the thoughts of those
countless multitudes, who, in the course of their trial,
are from time to time weighed down by affliction, or
distressed by bodily pain. This will be in their case,
the strong hour of Truth, which, though unheard and
unseen by men as a body, approaches each one of that
body in his own turn, though at a different time. Then
it is that the powers of the world, its counsels, and its
efforts (vigorous as they seemed to be in the race), lose
ground, and slow-paced Truth overtakes it; and thus
it comes to pass, that, while viewed in its outward
course it seems ever hastening onwards to open infidelity
and sin, there are ten thousand secret obstacles,
graciously sent from God, cumbering its chariot-wheels,
so that they drive heavily, and saving it from utter
ruin.

33. Even with these few considerations before us, we
shall find it difficult to estimate the moral power which
a single individual, trained to practise what he teaches,
may acquire in his own circle, in the course of years.
While the Scriptures are thrown upon the world, as if
the common property of any who choose to appropriate
them, he is, in fact, the legitimate interpreter of them,
and none other; the Inspired Word being but a dead
letter (ordinarily considered), except as transmitted
from one mind to another. While he is unknown to the

world, yet, within the range of those who see him, he will become the object of feelings different in kind from those which mere intellectual excellence excites. The men commonly held in popular estimation are greatest at a distance; they become small as they are approached; but the attraction, exerted by unconscious holiness, is of an urgent and irresistible nature; it persuades the weak, the timid, the wavering, and the inquiring; it draws forth the affection and loyalty of all who are in a measure like-minded; and over the thoughtless or perverse multitude it exercises a sovereign compulsory sway, bidding them fear and keep silence, on the ground of its own right divine to rule them,—its hereditary claim on their obedience, though they understand not the principles or counsels of that spirit, which is "born, not of blood, nor of the will of the flesh, nor of the will of man, but of God."

34. And if such be the personal influence excited by the Teacher of Truth over the mixed crowd of men whom he encounters, what (think we) will be his power over that select number, just referred to, who have already, in a measure, disciplined their hearts after the law of holiness, and feel themselves, as it were, individually addressed by the invitation of his example? These are they whom our Lord especially calls His "elect," and came to "gather together in one," for they are worthy. And these, too, are they who are ordained in God's Providence to be the salt of the earth,—to continue, in their turn, the succession of His witnesses, that heirs may never be wanting to the royal line, though death sweeps away each successive

generation of them to their rest and their reward. These, perhaps, by chance fell in with their destined father in the Truth, not at once discerning his real greatness. At first, perhaps, they thought his teaching fanciful, and parts of his conduct extravagant or weak. Years might pass away before such prejudices were entirely removed from their minds; but by degrees they would discern more and more the traces of un-earthly majesty about him; they would witness, from time to time, his trial under the various events of life, and would still find, whether they looked above or below, that he rose higher, and was based deeper, than they could ascertain by measurement. Then, at length, with astonishment and fear, they would become aware that Christ's presence was before them; and, in the words of Scripture, would glorify God in His servant [8]; and all this while they themselves would be changing into that glorious Image which they gazed upon, and be in training to succeed him in its propagation.

35. Will it be said, This is a fancy, which no experience confirms? First, no irreligious man can know any thing concerning the hidden saints. Next, no one, religious or not, can detect them without attentive study of them. But, after all, say they are few, such high Christians; and what follows? They are enough to carry on God's noiseless work. The Apostles were such men; others might be named, in their several generations, as successors to their holiness. These communicate their light to a number of lesser luminaries, by whom, in its turn, it is distributed through the

[8] Gal. i. 24.

world; the first sources of illumination being all the
while unseen, even by the majority of sincere Christians,—unseen as is that Supreme Author of Light
and Truth, from whom all good primarily proceeds.
A few highly-endowed men will rescue the world for
centuries to come. Before now even one man* has
impressed an image on the Church, which, through
God's mercy, shall not be effaced while time lasts.
Such men, like the Prophet, are placed upon their
watch-tower, and light their beacons on the heights.
Each receives and transmits the sacred flame, trimming
it in rivalry of his predecessor, and fully purposed to
send it on as bright as it has reached him; and thus
the self-same fire, once kindled on Moriah, though
seeming at intervals to fail, has at length reached us
in safety, and will in like manner, as we trust, be
carried forward even to the end.

36. To conclude. Such views of the nature and
history of Divine Truth are calculated to make us
contented and resigned in our generation, whatever
be the peculiar character or the power of the errors of
our own times. For Christ never will reign visibly
upon earth; but in each age, as it comes, we shall read
of tumult and heresy, and hear the complaint of good
men marvelling at what they conceive to be the especial
wickedness of their own times.

37. Moreover, such considerations lead us to be
satisfied with the humblest and most obscure lot; by
showing us, not only that we may be the instruments

* Athanasius.

of much good in it, but that (strictly speaking) we could scarcely in any situation be direct instruments of good to any besides those who personally know us, who ever must form a small circle; and as to the indirect good we may do in a more exalted station (which is by no means to be lightly esteemed), still we are not absolutely precluded from it in a lower place in the Church. Nay, it has happened before now, that comparatively retired posts have been filled by those who have exerted the most extensive influences over the destinies of Religion in the times following them; as in the arts and pursuits of this world, the great benefactors of mankind are frequently unknown.

38. Let all those, then, who acknowledge the voice of God speaking within them, and urging them heavenward, wait patiently for the End, exercising themselves, and diligently working, with a view to that day when the books shall be opened, and all the disorder of human affairs reviewed and set right; when " the last shall be first, and the first last;" when "all things that offend, and they which do iniquity," shall be gathered out and removed; when " the righteous shall shine forth as the sun," and Faith shall see her God; when " they that be wise shall shine as the brightness of the firmament, and they that turn many to righteousness as the stars, for ever and ever."

SERMON VI.

(Preached April 8, 1832.)

JER. viii. 11.

*" They have healed the hurt of the daughter of My people slightly, saying,
Peace, peace, when there is no peace."*

THERE will ever be persons who take a favourable
view of human nature, as it actually is found in
the world, and of the spiritual condition and the prospects of mankind. And certainly the face of things
is so fair, and contains so much that is interesting and
lofty, that the spectator may be pardoned if, on the
first sight, he is disposed to believe them to be as
cheerful and as happy as they appear,—the evils of life
as light and transitory, and its issue as satisfactory.
Such easy confidence is natural in youth; nay, it is
even commendable at a time of life in which suspicion
and incredulity are unbecoming; that is, it *would* be
commendable, did not Scripture acquaint us from the
very first (by way of warning, previous to our actual
experience) with the deceitfulness of the world's promises and teaching; telling us of the opposition between

H 2

Sight and Faith, of that strait gate and that narrow
way, the thought of which is to calm us in youth, that
it may enliven and invigorate us in old age.

2. Yet, on the other hand, it cannot be denied that
even the information of Scripture results in a cheerful
view of human affairs, and condemns gloom and sad-
ness as a sin, as well as a mistake; and thus, in fact,
altogether sanctions the conclusions gathered from the
first sight of the course of the world. But here is an
instance, such as not unfrequently is found, of an
opinion being abstractedly true, and yet the person
who holds it wrong in his mode of holding it; so that
while the terms in which he conveys it approach indefinitely near to those in which the true view is contained, nevertheless men who maintain the very reverse
may be nearer the truth than he is. It often happens
that, in pursuing the successive stages of an investigation, the mind continually reverses its judgment to
and fro, according as the weight of argument passes
over and back again from the one alternative of the
question to the other ; and in such a case the ultimate
utility of the inquiry does not consist in the conclusion
finally adopted, which may be no other than that with
which the inquiry was commenced ; but in the position
in which we have learned to view it, and the circumstances with which we have associated it. It is plain,
too, that the man who has gone through many of these
progressive alternations of opinion, but has for some
cause or other stopped short of the true view legitimately terminating the inquiry, would be farther from
it in the mere enunciation of his sentiments, but in the

state of his mind far nearer to it, than he who has not examined the subject at all, and is right by accident. Thus it happens, men are cheerful and secure from ignorance of the evils of life; and they are secure, again, from seeing the remedy of the evils; and, on the other hand, they are desponding from seeing the evils without the remedy: so that we must never say that an individual is right, merely on the ground of his holding an opinion which happens to be true, unless he holds it in a particular manner; that is, under those conditions, and with that particular association of thought and feeling, which in fact is the interpretation of it.

3. That superficial judgment, which happens to be right without deserving to be so, is condemned in the text. The error of the prophets and priests there spoken of consisted, not in promising a *cure* for the wounded soul, but in healing the hurt of the daughter of God's people *slightly*, saying, Peace, peace, before they had ascertained either the evil or the remedy. The Gospel is in its very name a message of peace, but it must never be separated from the bad tidings of our fallen nature, which it reverses; and he who speaks of the state of the world in a sanguine way, may indeed be an advanced Christian, but he may also be much less even than a proselyte of the gate; and if his security and peace of mind be merely the calm of ignorance, surely the men whom he looks down upon as narrow-minded and superstitious, whose religion consists in fear not in love, shall go into the kingdom of heaven before him. We are reminded of this im-

portant truth by the order of our ecclesiastical year. Easter Day, our chief Festival, is preceded by the forty days of Lent, to show us that they, and they only, who sow in tears, shall reap in joy.

4. Remarks such as these are scarcely necessary, as far as we of this place are concerned, who, through God's blessing, are teachers of His truth, and "by reason of use have our senses exercised to discern both good and evil." Yet it is impossible not to observe, and it is useful to bear in mind, that mankind at large is not wiser or better than heretofore; rather, that it is an especial fault of the present day, to mistake the false security of the man of the world for the composure, cheerfulness, and benevolence of the true Christian; while all the varying shades of character between these two, though indefinitely more deserving of our respect than the former of them—I mean the superstitious, the bigot, the intolerant, and the fanatic—are thrust out of the way as inhuman and offensive, merely because their knowledge of themselves is more exact than their apprehension of the Gospel, and their zeal for God's honour more energetic than their love of mankind.

5. This in fact is the fault incident to times of political peace and safety, when the world keeps well together, no motions stirring beneath it to disturb the continuity of its surface, which for the time presents to us a consistent and finished picture. When the laws of a country are upheld and obeyed, and property secure, the world appears to realize that vision of constancy and permanence which it presented to our

youthful imagination. Human nature appears more amiable than it really is, because it is not tried with disappointments; more just, because it is then its interest to respect the rights of others; more benevolent, because it can be so without self-denial. The warnings contained in the historical Scriptures, concerning the original baseness and corruption of the heart, are, in the course of time, neglected; or, rather, these very representations are adduced as a proof how much better the world now is than it was once; how much more enlightened, refined, intellectual, manly; and this, not without some secret feeling of disrespect towards the writers of the plain facts recorded in the Bible, as if, even were the case so bad as they make it appear, it had been more judicious and humane to have said nothing about it.

6. But, fairly as this superficial view of human nature answers in peaceful times; speciously as it may argue, innocently as it may experimentalize, in the rare and short-lived intervals of a nation's tranquillity; yet, let persecution or tribulation arise, and forthwith its imbecility is discovered. It is but a theory; it cannot cope with difficulties; it imparts no strength or loftiness of mind; it gains no influence over others. It is at once shattered and crushed in the stern conflict of good and evil; disowned, or rather overlooked, by the combatants on either side, and vanishing, no one knows how or whither.

7. The opinions alluded to in the foregoing remarks, when assuming a definite doctrinal basis, will be found to centre in Socinianism or Theophilanthropism, the

name varying according as it admits or rejects the authority of Scripture. And the spirit of this system will be found to infect great numbers of men, who are unconscious of the origin and tendency of their opinions. The essential dogmas of Socinianism are such as these; that the rule of Divine government is one of benevolence, and nothing but benevolence; that evil is but remedial and temporary; that sin is of a venial nature; that repentance is a sufficient atonement for it; that the moral sense is substantially but an instinct of benevolence; and that doctrinal opinions do not influence our character or prospects, nor deserve our serious attention. On the other hand, sentiments of this character are evidently the animating principle of the false cheerfulness, and the ill-founded hope, and the blind charitableness, which I have already assigned to the man of the world.

8. In order to illustrate the untenableness of such propositions as have just been adduced, and hence to show, by way of instance, the shallowness and feebleness of the minds which maintain them, their real feebleness in all practical matters, plausibly or loudly as they may speak during the hour of tranquillity in which they display themselves, it may be useful to make some remarks on what appears to be the real judgment of God upon human sin, as far as it is discernible by the light of nature; not as if any thing new could be said on the subject, but in order to remind ourselves of truths which are peculiarly important in these times.

9. The consideration most commonly adduced by the

advocates of the absolute, unmixed benevolence of the
Divine Government, and of the venial nature of sin according to the provisions of that Government, is an *à
priori* argument, founded on an appeal to a supposed instinct of our nature. It has before now been put familiarly
thus :—" Is there any man living who would not, if he
could, accomplish the final restitution and eternal happiness of every individual ? and are we more benevolent than God ?" Or, again, the same general argument
is sometimes stated more cautiously as follows ; that
" No man can be in a perfectly right state of mind, who,
if he consider general happiness at all, is not ready
to acknowledge that a good man must regard it as
being in its own nature the most desirable of *all* objects ;
and that any habitual disposition clearly discerned to
be, in its whole result, at variance with general happiness, is unworthy of being cultivated, or fit to be rooted
out ; that accordingly, we are compelled to attribute
God's *whole* government to benevolence ; that it is as
much impossible for us to love and revere a Being, to
whom we ascribe a mixed or imperfect benevolence, as
to believe the most positive contradictions in terms ;
that is, as religion *consists* in love and reverence, *it*
cannot subsist without a belief in benevolence as the
sole principle of Divine Government."

10. Now first, it is surely not true that benevolence
is the only, or the chief, principle of our moral nature.
To say nothing of the notion of duty to an Unseen
Governor, implied in the very authoritativeness with
which conscience dictates to us (a notion which suggests
to the mind that there *is*, in truth, some object more

" desirable in its own nature " than " the general happiness " of mankind—viz. the approbation of our Maker), not to insist on this, it may be confidently asserted, that the instincts of justice and of purity are natural to us in the same sense in which benevolence is natural. If it be natural to pity and wish well to men in general, without reference to their character, or our personal knowledge of them, or any other attendant circumstance, it is also natural to feel indignation when vice triumphs, and to be dissatisfied and uneasy till the inequality is removed.

11. In order to meet this objection, it is maintained by the writers under consideration, that the good of mankind is the ultimate end, to which even the principle of justice, planted in us, tends ; that the rule of reward and punishment is a chief means of making men happy; and therefore that the feelings of indignation, resentment, and the like, must be considered as given us, not for their own sake (granting them given us), but in order to ensure the general good of mankind ; in other words, that they are no evidence of the existence of justice as an original and absolute principle of the moral law, but only of that infinite unmixed benevolence of God, to which the feelings in question are in our case really subservient. But this is nothing but an assertion, and will not stand examination; for true as it is, that the instinct of justice, implanted in us, tends to *general* good,—good on the whole,—it evidently does not tend to *universal* good, the good of each individual; and nothing short of this can be the scope of absolute and simple benevolence. Our indignation at vice tends to

the actual misery of the vicious (whether they be many or few)—nay, to their *final* misery, except indeed there be provisions in the world's system, hitherto concealed, securing the ultimate destruction of vice ; for *while* it remained, it and all connected with it would ever be the natural objects of our abhorrence, and this natural abhorrence evidently interferes with the hypothesis, that universal good is the one end to which the present system of Divine Governance tends.

12. On the other hand, so far from its being " impossible (as the theory under consideration affirms) to love and revere a Being to whom we ascribe a mixed benevolence," while undoubtedly benevolence excites our love and reverence, so does a perfect justice also ; we are under a natural attraction to admire and adore the great sight, just as we are led on (to compare small things with great) to dwell rapturously upon some exquisite work of man's designing, the beautiful and harmonious result of the highest and most accomplished genius. If we do not habitually thus search out and lovingly hang over the traces of God's justice, which are around us, it is because we are ourselves sinners ; because, having a bad conscience, we have a personal interest in denying them, and a terror in having them forced upon us. In proportion as we grow in habits of obedience, far from our vision of the eternal justice of God vanishing from our minds, and being disowned by our feelings, as if it were but the useful misconception of a less advanced virtue, doubtless it increases, as fear is cast out. The saints in heaven ascribe glory to God, " for *true and righteous* are His judgments."

"Great and marvellous are Thy works, Lord God Almighty; just and true are Thy ways, Thou King of saints[1]." If, then, the infinite benevolence of God wins our love, certainly His justice commands it; and were we able, as the Saints made perfect are able, to combine the notion of both in their separate perfections, as displayed in the same acts, doubtless our awe and admiration of the glorious vision would be immeasurably increased.

13. Moreover, that justice is a primary notion in our minds, and does not admit of resolution into other elements, may be argued from its connexion with that general love of order, congruity, and symmetry, to which I have been referring,—that very desire of arranging and adjusting, which is made use of for the purpose of denying its elementary nature, and which must, in its essence, be considered, if any thing is considered, an original principle of human nature.

14. Nay, it may be doubted whether the notion of justice be not more essential to the mental constitution of free agents, than benevolence can be. For our very consciousness of being free, and so responsible, includes in it the idea of an unchangeable rule of justice, on which the judgment is hereafter to be conducted; or rather excludes, as far as it goes, the notion of a simply benevolent Governor; a simply benevolent end being relinquished (as we may speak) by the Creator, so soon as He committed the destinies of man to his own hands, and made him a first cause, a principle of origination, in the moral world.

[1] Rev. xv. 3.

15. But even if the general happiness of mankind could be assigned in hypothesis, as the one end to which all our moral instincts tended, and though nothing could be adduced in behalf of the intrinsic authority of the notion of justice, it would not be allowable thence to infer the unmixed benevolence of the Divine Mind, seeing we have actual evidences of His justice in the course of the world, such as cannot be explained away by a mere argument from the analogy of our own nature. Should any one attempt here to repeat the process of simplification, and refer in turn Divine Justice, as seen in the world, to Divine Benevolence, as if reward and punishment were but means to the one end of general good, let such a venturous speculator bethink himself what he is essaying, when he undertakes to simplify such attributes of the Divine Mind, as the course of things happens to manifest to him. Not to insist on the presumption (as I may well call it) of the attempt, let him ask himself, merely as a philosopher, whether there is no difference between referring phenomena to an hypothetical law or system for convenience sake (as, for instance, he is accustomed to refer the movements of the physical world to gravitation), and on the other hand undertaking to assign and fix, as a matter of fact, the real, primary and universal principles which guide the acts of a Mind, unknown and infinite, and that, from a knowledge of merely one or two characteristics of His mode of acting. After all, what is meant by affirming that God has, strictly speaking, any end or design at all in what He does, external to Himself? We see the world, physical and

moral, as a fact; and we see the Attributes of God, as they are called, displayed in it; but before we attempt to decide whether or not the happiness of His creatures is the solitary all-absorbing end of His government, let us try to determine by the way of Reason what was His particular view in creating us at all. What indeed Revelation has told us, that we are able to speak con‐ fidently about, and it is our blessedness to be able; but Revelation does not come into this question. By the use of unaided Reason, we are utterly incapable of conceiving, why a Being supremely blessed in Himself from eternity should ever commence the work of creation; what the design of creation is, as such; whether, if there be any end in it, it is not one different in kind, utterly removed from any which ear hath heard or mind conceived; and whether His creation of man in the first instance, and therefore man's happiness in‐ clusively, may not be altogether subservient to further ends in the scope of His purposes. Doubtless it is our wisdom, both as to the world and as to Scripture, to take things as we find them; not to be wise above what is written, whether in nature or in grace; not to attempt a theory where we must reason without data; much less, even could we frame one, to mistake it for a fact instead of what it is, an arbitrary arrangement of our knowledge, whatever that may be, and nothing more.

16. Considerations such as these are sufficient for the purpose for which I have employed them; sufficient to act as a retort, by means of their own weapons, upon

those who would undermine our faith, little as they may mean to do so, nay, rather who would lead us, not merely to a rejection or perversion of Christianity, but even to a denial of the visible course of things as it actually exists; that is, to that unreal and unpractical view of human nature which was described in the outset. And now, before concluding, let us observe what the world teaches us, in matter of fact, concerning the light in which sin is regarded by our great Governor and Judge.

17. Here it is usual to insist on the visible consequences of single sins, as furnishing some foreboding of the full and final judgment of God upon all we do; and the survey of such instances is very striking. A solitary act of intemperance, sensuality, or anger, a single rash word, a single dishonest deed, is often the cause of incalculable misery in the sequel to the person who has been betrayed into it. Our fortunes are frequently shaped by the thoughtless and seemingly inconsiderable sins of our early life. The quarrel of an hour, the sudden yielding to temptation, will throw a man into a disadvantageous line of life, bring him into trouble, ruin his prospects; or again, into circumstances unfavourable to his religious interests, which unsettle his mind, and ultimately lead him to abandon his faith. All through life we may suffer the penalty of past disobedience; disobedience, too, which we now can hardly enter into and realize, which is most foreign to our present principles and feelings, which we can hardly recognize as belonging to us, just as if no identity existed between our present and our former selves.

18. Should it be said that this does not in all or in most cases happen, I answer, that, were there but a few such cases, they would be sufficient to destroy the hypothesis, already remarked upon, of the unmixed benevolence of the Divine Government. For they are in many instances too definite and significant to be explained as remedial measures, or as any thing short of judgments on sin; and in fact, they have been acknowledged as such by the common sense of mankind in every age; and on the other hand, it constantly happens that they neither effect, nor evince a tendency towards effecting, the moral benefit of the individuals thus punished. But further, granting that they are but isolated instances of God's judgment concerning the guilt of disobedience; yet, if we believe that His Providence proceeds on any fixed plan, and that all deeds are impartially recompensed according to their nature, it seems to follow, that, since some sins evidently do receive an after punishment, therefore all have the prospect of the like; and consequently that those who escape here, will suffer hereafter; that this is the rule, and if there be any additional law counteracting it, this has to be proved. What measure of punishment is reserved for us, we cannot tell; but the actual consequences which we witness of apparently slight offences, make the prospect before us alarming. If any law is traceable in this awful subject, it would appear to be this, that the greater the delay, the greater the punishment, if it comes at length; as if a suspension of immediate vengeance were an indulgence only to be compensated by an accumulated suffering afterwards.

19. Then, as to the efficacy of repentance, which is so much insisted on,—when repentance is spoken of as being a sufficient substitute in itself, by a self-evident fitness, though not for the consequences of sin in this life, yet at least for the future punishment, let the following remark be considered, which is a solemn one. I ask, does death, which is supposed to terminate the punishment of the penitent, terminate the consequences of his sins upon others? Are not these consequences continued long after his death, even to the end of time? And do they not thus seem to be a sort of intimation or symbol to survivors, that, in spite of his penitence, God's wrath is hot against him? A man publishes an irreligious or immoral book; afterwards he repents, and dies. What does Reason, arguing from the visible course of things, suggest concerning the efficacy of that repentance? The sin of the penitent lives; it continues to disseminate evil; it corrupts multitudes. *They* die, many of them, *without* repenting; many more receive permanent, though not fatal injury to their souls, from the perusal. Surely no evidence is here, in the course of Divine Government, of the efficacy of repentance. Shall *he* be now dwelling in Abraham's bosom, who hears on the other side of the gulf the voices of those who curse his memory as being the victims of his sin?

20. Against these fearful traces or omens of God's visitation upon sin, we are, of course, at liberty to set all the gracious intimations, given us in nature, of His placability. Certain as it is, that all our efforts and all our regrets are often unable to rid us of the consequences of previous disobedience, yet doubtless they

often alleviate these, and often remove them. And this goes to show that His Governance is not one of absolute unmixed justice, which, of course, (were it so) would reduce every one of us to a state of despair. Nothing, however, is told us in nature of the limits of the two rules, of love and of justice, or how they are to be reconciled; nothing to show that the rule of mercy, as acting on moral agents, is more than the supplement, not the substitute of the fundamental law of justice and holiness. And, let it be added, taking us even as we are, much as each of us has to be forgiven, yet a religious man would hardly wish the rule of justice obliterated. It is a something which he can depend on and recur to; it gives a character and a certainty to the course of Divine Governance; and, tempered by the hope of mercy, it suggests animating and consolatory thoughts to him; so that, far from acquiescing in the theory of God's unmixed benevolence, he will rather protest against it as the invention of those who, in their eagerness to conciliate the enemies of the Truth, care little about distressing and sacrificing its friends.

21. Different, indeed, is his view of God and of man, of the claims of God, of man's resources, of the guilt of disobedience, and of the prospect of forgiveness, from those flimsy self-invented notions, which satisfy the reason of the mere man of letters, or the prosperous and self-indulgent philosopher! It is easy to speak eloquently of the order and beauty of the physical world, of the wise contrivances of visible nature, and of the benevolence of the objects proposed in them; but none of those topics throw light upon the subject

which it most concerns us to understand, the character of the Moral Governance under which we live; yet, is not this the way of the wise in this world, viz. instead of studying that Governance as a primary subject of inquiry, to assume they know it, or to conceive of it after some work of "Natural Theology [2]," or, at best, to take their notions of it from what appears on the mere surface of human society?—as if men did not put on their gayest and most showy apparel when they went abroad! To see truly the cost and misery of sinning, we must quit the public haunts of business and pleasure, and be able, like the Angels, to see the tears shed in secret,—to witness the anguish of pride and impatience, where there is no sorrow,—the stings of remorse, where yet there is no repentance,—the wearing, never-ceasing struggle between conscience and sin,—the misery of indecision,—the harassing, haunting fears of death, and a judgment to come,—and the superstitions which these engender. Who can name the overwhelming total of the world's guilt and suffering,—suffering crying for vengeance on the authors of it, and guilt foreboding it!

22. Yet one need not shrink from appealing even to the outward face of the world, as proving to us the extreme awfulness of our condition, as sinners against the law of our being; for a strange fact it is, that boldly as the world talks of its own greatness and its enjoyments, and easily as it deceives the mere theophilanthropist, yet, when it proceeds to the thought of its

[2] [This was an allusion to Paley. Vide "Lectures on University Subjects," No. vi., p. 252.]

Maker, it has ever professed a gloomy religion, in spite
of itself. This has been the case in all times and places.
Barbarous and civilized nations here agree. The world
cannot bear up against the Truth, with all its boastings.
It makes an open mock at sin, yet secretly attempts to
secure an interest against its possible consequences in
the world to come. Where has not the custom prevailed of propitiating, if possible, the unseen powers of
heaven?—but why, unless man were universally conscious of his danger, and feared the punishment of sin,
while he "hated to be reformed"? Where have not
sacrifices been in use, as means of appeasing the Divine
displeasure?—and men have anxiously sought out what
it was they loved best, and would miss most painfully,
as if to strip themselves of it might move the compassion of God. Some have gone so far as to offer
their sons and their daughters as a ransom for their own
sin,—an abominable crime doubtless, and a sacrifice to
devils, yet clearly witnessing man's instinctive judgment upon his own guilt, and his foreboding of punishment. How much more simple a course had it been,
merely to have been sorry for disobedience, and to
profess repentance, were it a natural doctrine (as some
pretend), that repentance is an atonement for offences
committed!

23. Nor is this all. Not only in their possessions and
their offspring, but in their own persons, have men
mortified themselves, with the hope of expiating deeds
of evil. Burnt-offerings, calves of a year old, thousands
of rams, and ten thousands of rivers of oil, their first-
born for their transgression, the fruit of their body for

the sin of their soul, even these are insufficient to lull the sharp throbbings of a heavy-laden conscience. Think of the bodily tortures to which multitudes have gloomily subjected themselves, and that for years, under almost every religious system, with a view of ridding themselves of their sins, and judge what man conceives of the guilt of disobedience. You will say that such fierceness in self-tormenting is a mental disease, and grows on a man. But this answer, granting there is truth in it, does not account for the reverence in which such persons have usually been held. Have we no instinct of self-preservation? Would these same persons gain the admiration of others, unless their cruelty to their own flesh arose from a religious motive? Would they not be derided as madmen, unless they sheltered themselves under the sanction of an awful, admitted truth, the corruption and the guilt of human nature?

24. But it will be said, that Christians, at least, must admit that these frightful exhibitions of self-torture are superstition. Here I may refer to the remarks with which I began. Doubtless these desperate and dark struggles are to be called superstition, when viewed by the side of true religion; and it is easy enough to speak of them as superstition, when we have been informed of the gracious and joyful result in which the scheme of Divine Governance issues. But it is man's truest and best religion, *before* the Gospel shines on him. If our race *be* in a fallen and depraved state, what ought our religion to be but anxiety and remorse, till God comforts us? Surely, to be in gloom,—to view ourselves with horror,—to look about to the right

hand and to the left for means of safety,—to catch at
every thing, yet trust in nothing,—to do all we can,
and try to do more than all,—and, after all, to wait in
miserable suspense, naked and shivering, among the
trees of the garden, for the hour of His coming, and
meanwhile to fancy sounds of woe in every wind
stirring the leaves about us,—in a word, to be superstitious,—is nature's best offering, her most acceptable
service, her most mature and enlarged wisdom, in the
presence of a holy and offended God. They who are
not superstitious without the Gospel, will not be religious with it : and I would that even in us, who have
the Gospel, there were more of superstition than there
is ; for much is it to be feared that our security about
ourselves arises from defect in self-knowledge rather
than in fulness of faith, and that we appropriate to ourselves promises which we cannot read.

25. To conclude. Thoughts concerning the Justice
of God, such as those which have engaged our attention,
though they do not, of course, explain to us the mystery
of the great Christian Atonement for sin, show the use
of the doctrine to us sinners. Why Christ's death was
requisite for our salvation, and how it has obtained it,
will ever be a mystery in this life. But, on the other hand,
the contemplation of our guilt is so growing and so
overwhelming a misery, as our eyes open on our real
state, that some strong act (so to call it) was necessary,
on God's part, to counterbalance the tokens of His
wrath which are around us, to calm and reassure us,
and to be the ground and the medium of our faith. It

seems, indeed, as if, in a practical point of view, no mere promise was sufficient to undo the impression left on the imagination by the facts of Natural Religion; but in the death of His Son we have His *deed*—His irreversible deed—making His forgiveness of sin, and His reconciliation with our race, no contingency, but an event of past history. He has vouchsafed to evidence His faithfulness and sincerity towards us (if we may dare so to speak) as we must show ours towards Him, not in word, but by action; which becomes therefore the pledge of His mercy, and the plea on which we draw near to His presence ;—or, in the words of Scripture, whereas " all have sinned, and come short of the glory of God," Christ Jesus is " set forth as a propitiation for the remission of sins that are past," to declare and assure us, that, without departing from the just rule, by which all men must, in the main, be tried, still He will pardon and justify " him that believeth in Jesus."

SERMON VII.

CONTEST BETWEEN FAITH AND SIGHT.

(Preached May 27, 1832.)

1 JOHN v. 4.

" This is the victory that overcometh the world, even our faith."

THE danger to which Christians are exposed from the influence of the visible course of things, or the world (as it is called in Scripture), is a principal subject of St. John's General Epistle. He seems to speak of the world as some False Prophet, promising what it cannot fulfil, and gaining credit by its confident tone. Viewing it as resisting Christianity, he calls it the "spirit of anti-Christ," the parent of a numerous progeny of evil, false spirits like itself, the teachers of all lying doctrines, by which the multitude of men are led captive. The antagonist of this great tempter is the Spirit of Truth, which is " greater than he that is in the world;" its victorious antagonist, because gifted with those piercing eyes of Faith which are able to scan the world's shallowness, and to see through the mists of error into the glorious kingdom of God beyond them. " This is the victory that overcometh the world," says the text, " even our Faith." And if we inquire what

are the sights which our faith sees, the Apostle answers
by telling us of "the Spirit that beareth witness, because the Spirit is Truth." The world witnesses to an
untruth, which will one day be exposed; and Christ,
our Lord and Master, is the "Amen, the faithful and
true witness," who came into the world "by water and
blood," to "bear witness unto the Truth;" that, as the
many voices of error bear down and overpower the
inquirer by their tumult and importunity, so, on the
other hand, Truth might have its living and visible
representative, no longer cast, like the bread, at random on the waters, or painfully gained from the schools
and traditions of men, but committed to One " come
in the flesh," to One who has an earthly name and
habitation, who, in one sense, is one of the powers of
this world, who has His train and retinue, His court
and kingdom, His ministering servants, bound together
by the tie of brotherly love among themselves, and of
zeal against the Prophets of error. "Who is he that
overcometh the world, but he that believeth that Jesus
is the Son of God?" St. John then compares together
the force of the world's testimony, and of that which
the Gospel provides. "If we receive the witness of
men, the witness of God is greater; for this is the witness of God which He has testified of His Son;" as if
"the spirit, the water, and the blood," spoke for God
more loudly than the world speaks for the Evil one.
In the very opening of the Epistle, he had set before
us in another form the same gracious truth, viz., that
the Gospel, by affording us, in the Person and history
of Christ, a witness of the invisible world, addresses

itself to our senses and imagination, after the very manner in which the false doctrines of the world assail us. "That which was from the beginning, . . which we have looked upon, . . that which we have seen and heard, declare we unto you."

2. Now, here we have incidentally suggested to us an important truth, which, obvious as it is, may give rise to some profitable reflections; viz., that the world overcomes us, not merely by appealing to our reason, or by exciting our passions, but by imposing on our imagination. So much do the systems of men swerve from the Truth as set forth in Scripture, that their very presence becomes a standing fact against Scripture, even when our reason condemns them, by their persevering assertions, and they gradually overcome those who set out by contradicting them. In all cases, what is often and unhesitatingly asserted, at length finds credit with the mass of mankind; and so it happens, in this instance, that, admitting as we do from the first, that the world is one of our three chief enemies, maintaining, rather than merely granting, that the outward face of things speaks a different language from the word of God; yet, when we come to act in the world, we find this very thing a trial, not merely of our obedience, but even of our faith; that is, the mere fact that the world turns out to be what we began by actually confessing concerning it.

3. Let us now direct our attention to this subject, in order to see what it means, and how it is exemplified in the ordinary course of the world.

And let us commence with the age when men are first exposed, in any great degree, to the temptation of trusting the world's assertions—when they enter into life, as it is called. Hitherto they have learned revealed truths only as a creed or system; they are instructed and acquiesce in the great Christian doctrines; and, having virtuous feelings, and desiring to do their duty, they think themselves really and practically religious. They read in Scripture of "the course of the world," but they have little notion what it really is; they believe it to be sinful, but how it acts in seducing from the Truth, and making evil seem good, and good evil, is beyond them. Scripture, indeed, says much about the world; but they cannot learn practically what it is from Scripture; for, not to mention other reasons, Scripture being written by inspiration, represents things such as they really are in God's sight, such as they will seem to us in proportion as we learn to judge of them rightly, not as they appear to those "whose senses are" not yet "exercised to discern both good and evil."

4. Under these circumstances, youths are brought to their trial. The simple and comparatively retired life which they have hitherto enjoyed is changed for the varied and attractive scenes of mixed society. Its numberless circles and pursuits open upon them, the diversities and contrarieties of opinion and conduct, and of the subjects on which thought and exertion are expended. This is what is called seeing the world. Here, then, all at once they lose their reckoning, and let slip the lessons which they thought they had so

accurately learned. They are unable to apply in practice what they have received by word of mouth; and,
perplexed at witnessing the multiplicity of characters
and fortunes which human nature assumes, and the
range and intricacy of the social scheme, they are
gradually impressed with the belief that the religious
system which they have hitherto received is an inadequate solution of the world's mysteries, and a rule
of conduct too simple for its complicated transactions.
All men, perhaps, are in their measure subjected to
this temptation. Even their ordinary and most innocent intercourse with others, their temporal callings,
their allowable recreations, captivate their imaginations, and, on entering into this new scene, they look
forward with interest towards the future, and form
schemes of action, and indulge dreams of happiness,
such as this life has never fulfilled. Now, is it not
plain, that, after thus realizing to themselves the promises of the world, when they look back to the Bible
and their former lessons, these will seem not only un-
interesting and dull, but a theory too?—dull, colour-
less, indeed, as a sober landscape, after we have been
gazing on some bright vision in the clouds—but,
withal, unpractical, unnatural, unsuitable to the exi-
gencies of life and the constitution of man?

5. For consider how little is said in Scripture about
subjects which necessarily occupy a great part of the
attention of all men, and which, being there unnoticed,
become thereby the subject-matter of their trial. Their
private conduct day by day; their civil, social, and
domestic duties; their relation towards those events

which mark out human life into its periods, and, in the case of most men, are the source of its best pleasures, and the material of its deepest affections, are, as if purposely, passed over, that they themselves may complete the picture of true faith and sanctity which Revelation has begun.

6. And thus (as has already been said) what is primarily a trial of our obedience, becomes a trial of our faith also. The Bible seems to contain a world in itself, and not the same world as that which we inhabit; and those who profess to conform to its rules gain from us respect indeed, and praise, and yet strike us withal in some sort as narrow-minded and fanciful; tenderly to be treated, indeed, as you would touch cautiously any costly work of art, yet, on the whole, as little adapted to do good service in the world as it is, as a weapon of gold or soft clothing on a field of battle.

7. And much more, of course, does this delusion hang about the mind, and more closely does it wrap it round, if, by yielding to the temptations of the flesh, a man predisposes himself to the influence of it. The palmary device of Satan is to address himself to the pride of our nature, and, by the promise of independence, to seduce us into sin. Those who have been brought up in ignorance of the polluting fashions of the world, too often feel a rising in their minds against the discipline and constraint kindly imposed upon them; and, not understanding that their ignorance is their glory, and that they cannot really enjoy both good and evil, they murmur that they are not allowed to essay what they do not wish to practise, or to choose for themselves in

matters where the very knowledge seems to them to give a superiority to the children of corruption. Thus the temptation of becoming as gods works as in the beginning, pride opening a door to lust; and then, intoxicated by their experience of evil, they think they possess real wisdom, and take a larger and more impartial view of the nature and destinies of man than religion teaches; and, while the customs of society restrain their avowals within the bounds of propriety, yet in their hearts they learn to believe that sin is a matter of course, not a serious evil, a failing in which all have share, indulgently to be spoken of, or rather, in the case of each individual, to be taken for granted, and passed over in silence; and believing this, they are not unwilling to discover or to fancy weaknesses in those who have the credit of being superior to the ordinary run of men, to insinuate the possibility of human passions influencing them, this or that of a more refined nature, when the grosser cannot be imputed, and, extenuating at the same time the guilt of the vicious, to reduce in this manner all men pretty much to a level. A more apposite instance of this state of soul cannot be required than is given us in the celebrated work of an historian of the last century, who, for his great abilities, and, on the other hand, his cold heart, impure mind, and scoffing spirit, may justly be accounted as, in this country at least, one of the masters of a new school of error, which seems not yet to have accomplished its destinies, and is framed more exactly after the received type of the author of evil, than the other chief anti-Christs who have, in these last times, occupied the scene of the world.

8. The temptation I have been speaking of, of trust-ing the world, because it speaks boldly, and thinking that evil must be acquiesced in, because it exists, will be still stronger and more successful in the case of one who is in any situation of active exertion, and has no very definite principles to secure him in the narrow way. He was taught to believe that there was but one true faith, and, on entering into life, he meets with number-less doctrines among men, each professing to be the true one. He had learned that there was but one Church, and he falls in with countless religious sects, nay, with a prevalent opinion that all these are equally good, and that there is no divinely-appointed Church at all. He has been accustomed to class men into good and bad, but he finds their actual characters no how reducible to system; good and bad mixed in every variety of proportion, virtues and vices in endless com-binations; and, what is stranger still, a deficient creed seemingly joined to a virtuous life, and inconsistent conduct disgracing a sound profession. Further still, he finds that men in general will not act on high motives, in spite of all that divines and moralists pro-fess; and his experience of this urges him, till he be-gins to think it unwise and extravagant to insist upon the mass of mankind doing so, or to preach high morals and high doctrines; and at length he looks on the re-ligious system of his youth as beautiful indeed in itself, and practical perhaps in private life, and useful for the lower classes, but as utterly unfit for those who live in the world; and while unwilling to confess this, lest he should set a bad example, he tacitly concedes it, never

is the champion of his professed principles when assailed, nor acts upon them in an honest way in the affairs of life.

9. Or, should he be led by a speculative turn of mind, or a natural philanthropy, to investigate the nature of man, or exert himself in plans for the amelioration of society, then his opinions become ultimately impressed with the character of a more definite unbelief. Sometimes he is conscious to himself that he is opposing Christianity; not indeed opposing it wantonly, but, as he conceives, unavoidably, as finding it in his way. This is a state of mind into which benevolent men are in danger of falling, in the present age. While they pursue objects tending, as they conceive, towards the good of mankind, it is by degrees forced upon their minds that Revealed Religion thwarts their proceedings, and, averse alike to relinquish their plans, and to offend the feelings of others, they determine on letting matters take their course, and, believing fully that Christianity must fall before the increasing illumination of the age, yet they wish to secure it against direct attacks, and to provide that it no otherwise falls than as it unavoidably must, at one time or other; as every inflexible instrument, and every antiquated institution, crumbles under the hands of the Great Innovator, who creates new influences for new emergencies, and recognizes no right divine in a tumultuous and shifting world.

10. Sometimes, on the other hand, because he takes the spirit of the world as his teacher, such a one drifts away unawares from the Truth as it is in Jesus; and,

merely from ignorance of Scripture, maintains theories which Scripture anathematizes. Thus he dreams on for a time, as loth to desert his first faith; then by accident meeting with some of the revealed doctrines which he learned when a child—the Incarnation, or the eternal punishment of the wicked—he stumbles. Then he will attempt to remove these, as if accidentally attached to the Scripture creed,—little thinking that they are its very peculiarities and essentials, nor reflecting that the very fact of his stumbling at them should be taken as a test that his views coincide but in appearance with the revealed system altogether; and so he will remain at the door of the Church, witnessing against himself by his lingering there, yet missing the reward bestowed even on the proselyte of the gate in heathen times, in that he might have " known the way of righteousness," yet has " turned from the holy commandment delivered unto him."

11. And some there are who, keeping their faith in the main, give up the notion of its importance. Finding that men will not agree together on points of doctrine and discipline, and imagining that union must be effected on any terms, they consent to abandon articles of faith as the basis of Christian fellowship, and try to effect what they call a union of hearts, as a bond of fellowship among those who differ in their notions of the One God, One Lord, One Spirit, One baptism, and One body; forgetful of the express condemnation pronounced by our Saviour upon those who "believe not" the preaching of His servants[1]; and that

[1] Mark xvi. 16.

he who denicth the Son, the same hath not the Father[2].

12. And others, not being able to acquiesce in the unimportance of doctrinal truth, yet perplexed at the difficulties in the course of human affairs, which follow on the opposite view, accustom themselves gratuitously to distinguish between their public and private duties, and to judge of them by separate rules. These are often such as begin by assuming some extravagant or irrelevant test for ascertaining the existence of religious principle in others, and so are led to think it is nowhere to be found, not in the true Church more than in the sects which surround it; and thus, regarding all men (to speak generally) as equally far from the Truth, and strangers to that divine regeneration which Christ bestows on His elect few, and, on the other hand, seeing that men, as cast together in society, must co-operate on some or other principles, they drop the strict principles of Scripture in their civil relations, give no preference to those who honour the Church over those who profess opinions disrespectful towards it; perhaps take up the notion that the State, as such, has nothing to do with the subject of religion; praise and blame according to a different standard from that which Christianity reveals; and all this while cherish, perhaps, in their secret thoughts a definite creed, rigid in its decisions, stimulating in its influence, in spite of the mildness, and submissiveness, and liberality of sentiment, which their public mode of speaking and acting seems to evidence.

[2] 1 John ii. 22.

13. Nor are even the better sort of men altogether secure from the impression of the world's teaching, which is so influential with the multitude. He truly is a rare and marvellous work of heavenly grace, who when he comes into the din and tumult of the world, can view things just as he calmly contemplated them in the distance, before the time of action came. So many are the secondary reasons which can be assigned for and against every measure and every principle, so urgent are the solicitations of interest or passion when the mind is once relaxed or excited, so difficult then to compare and ascertain the relative importance of conflicting considerations, that the most sincere and zealous of ordinary Christians will, to their surprise, confess to themselves that they have lost their way in the wilderness, which they could accurately measure out before descending into it, and have missed the track which lay like a clear thread across the hills, when seen in the horizon. And it is from their experience of this their own unskilfulness and weakness, that serious men have been in the practice of making vows concerning purposes on which they were fully set, that no sudden gust of passion, or lure of worldly interest, should gain the mastery over a heart which they desire to present without spot or blemish, as a chaste virgin, to Christ.

14. Let the above be taken as a few illustrations out of many, of the influence exerted, and the doctrine enforced, in the school of the world ; that school which we all set out by acknowledging to be at enmity with the school of Christ, but from which we are content to

take our lessons of practical wisdom as life goes on. Such is the triumph of Sight over Faith. The world really brings no new argument to its aid,—nothing beyond its own assertion. In the very outset Christians allow that its teaching is contrary to Revelation, and not to be taken as authority; nevertheless, afterwards, this mere unargumentative teaching, which, when viewed in theory, formed no objection to the truth of the Inspired Word, yet, when actually heard in the intercourse of life, converts them, more or less, to the service of the " prince of the power of the air, the spirit which now worketh in the children of disobedience." It assails their *imagination.* The world sweeps by in long procession ;—its principalities and powers, its Babel of languages, the astrologers of Chaldæa, the horse and its rider and the chariots of Egypt, Baal and Ashtoreth and their false worship ; and those who witness, feel its fascination ; they flock after it ; with a strange fancy, they ape its gestures, and dote upon its mummeries ; and then, should they perchance fall in with the simple solemn services of Christ's Church, and hear her witnesses going the round of Gospel truths as when they left them : " I am the Way, the Truth, and the Life ;" " Be sober, be vigilant ;" " Strait is the gate, narrow the way ;" " If any man will come after Me, let him deny himself ;" " He is despised and rejected of men, a Man of sorrows and acquainted with grief :"—how utterly unreal do these appear, and the preachers of them, how irrational, how puerile !—how extravagant in their opinions, how weak in their reasoning !—and if they profess to pity and

bear with them, how nearly does their compassion
border on contempt !

15. The contempt of men !—why should we be
unwilling to endure it ? We are not better than our
fathers. In every age it has been the lot of Christians
far more highly endowed than we are with the riches
of Divine wisdom. It was the lot of Apostles and Prophets, and of the Saviour of mankind Himself. When
He was brought before Pilate, the Roman Governor
felt the same surprise and disdain at His avowal of His
unearthly office, which the world now expresses. "To
this end was I born, ... that I should bear witness
unto the *Truth*. Pilate saith, What is Truth ?" Again,
when Festus would explain to King Agrippa the cause
of the dispute between St. Paul and the Jews, he says,
"The accusers .... brought no accusations of such
things as I supposed, but certain questions against him
of their own superstition, and of one Jesus, which was
dead, whom Paul affirmed to be alive."

16. Such, however, are the words of men, who, not
knowing the strength of Christianity, had not the guilt
of deliberate apostasy. But what serious thoughts does
it present to the mind, to behold parallels to heathen
blindness and arrogance in a Christian country, where
men might know better, if they would inquire !—and
what a warning to us all is the sight of those who,
though nominally within the Church, are avowedly
indifferent to it ! For all of us surely are on our trial,
and, as we go forth into the world, so we are winnowed,
and the chaff gradually separated from the true seed.
This is St. John's account of it. "They went out from

us, but they were not of us ; for if they had been of us, they would no doubt have continued with us : but they went out, that they might be made manifest that they were not of us." And our Lord stands by watching the process, telling us of " the hour of temptation which shall come upon all the earth," exhorting us to " try them which say they are apostles, and are not," and to " hold fast that which we have, that no man take our crown."

17. Meanwhile, it is an encouragement to us to think how much may be done in way of protest and teaching, by the mere example of those who endeavour to serve God faithfully. In this way we may use against the world its own weapons ; and, as its success lies in the mere boldness of assertion with which it maintains that evil is good, so by the counter-assertions of a strict life and a resolute profession of the truth, we may retort upon the imaginations of men, that religious obedience is not impracticable, and that Scripture has its persuasives. A martyr or a confessor is a fact, and has its witness in itself; and, while it disarranges the theories of human wisdom, it also breaks in upon that security and seclusion into which men of the world would fain retire from the thought of religion. One prophet against four hundred disturbed the serenity of Ahab, King of Israel. When the witnesses in St. John's vision were slain, though they were but two, then " they that dwelt on the earth rejoiced over them, and made merry, and sent gifts one to another, because these two prophets tormented them that dwelt on the earth." Nay, such confessors have a witness even in

the breasts of those who oppose them, an instinct originally from God, which may indeed be perverted into a hatred, but scarcely into an utter disregard of the Truth, when exhibited before them. The instance cannot be found in the history of mankind, in which an anti-Christian power could long abstain from perse-cuting. The disdainful Festus at length impatiently interrupted his prisoner's speech ; and in our better re-gulated times, whatever be the scorn or malevolence which is directed against the faithful Christian, these very feelings show that he is really a restraint on vice and unbelief, and a warning and guide to the feeble-minded, and to those who still linger in the world with hearts more religious than their professed opinions ; and thus even literally, as the text expresses it, he overcomes the world, conquering while he suffers, and willingly accepting overbearing usage and insult from others, so that he may in some degree benefit them, though the more abundantly he loves them, the less he be loved.

SERMON VIII.

HUMAN RESPONSIBILITY, AS INDEPENDENT OF
CIRCUMSTANCES.

(Preached November 4, 1832.)

GEN. iii. 13.

" The serpent beguiled me, and I did eat."

THE original temptation set before our first parents,
was that of proving their freedom, by using it
without regard to the will of Him who gave it. The
original excuse offered by them after sinning was, that
they were not really free, that they had acted under a
constraining influence, the subtilty of the tempter. They
committed sin that they might be independent of their
Maker; they defended it on the ground that they were
dependent upon Him. And this has been the course
of lawless pride and lust ever since; to lead us, first, to
exult in our uncontrollable liberty of will and conduct;
then, when we have ruined ourselves, to plead that we
are the slaves of necessity.

2. Accordingly, it has been always the office of Religion to protest against the sophistry of Satan, and to preserve the memory of those truths which the unbelieving
heart corrupts, both the freedom and the responsibility

of man ;—the sovereignty of the Creator, the supremacy of the law of conscience as His representative within us, and the irrelevancy of external circumstances in the judgment which is ultimately to be made upon our conduct and character.

3. That we are accountable for what we do and what we are,—that, in spite of all aids or hindrances from without, each soul is the cause of its own happiness or misery,—is a truth certified to us both by Nature and Revelation. Nature conveys it to us in the feeling of guilt and remorse, which implies *self*-condemnation. In the Scriptures, on the other hand, it is the great prevailing principle throughout, in every age of the world, and through every Dispensation. The change of times, the varieties of religious knowledge, the gifts of grace, interfere not with the integrity of this momentous truth. Praise to the obedient, punishment on the transgressor, is the revealed rule of God's government from the beginning to the consummation of all things. The fall of Adam did not abolish, nor do the provisions of Gospel-mercy supersede it.

4. At the creation it was declared, " In the day that thou eatest . . . thou shalt surely die." On the calling of the Israelites, the Lord God was proclaimed in sight of their lawgiver as " merciful and gracious, long-suffering, and abundant in goodness and truth ; keeping mercy for thousands, forgiving iniquity. and transgression and sin, and that will by no means clear the guilty." And when Moses interceded for the people, with an earnestness which tended to the infringement of the Divine Rule, he was reminded that

he could not himself be really responsible for others. "Whosoever hath sinned against Me, him will I blot out of My book." The prophetical Dispensation enforced the same truth still more clearly. "With the pure Thou wilt show Thyself pure, and with the froward Thou wilt show Thyself froward." "The soul that sinneth, it shall die; make you a new heart and a new spirit, for why will ye die?" And after Christ had come, the most explicit of the inspired expounders of the New Covenant is as explicit in his recognition of the original rule. "Every man shall bear his own burden . . . Be not deceived: God is not mocked; for whatsoever a man soweth, that shall he also reap." Even in his Epistle to the Romans, where he is directly engaged in declaring another, and at first sight opposite doctrine, he finds opportunity for confessing the principle of accountableness. Though exalting the sovereign power and inscrutable purposes of God, and apparently referring man's agency altogether to Him as the vessel of His good pleasure, still he forgets not, in the very opening of his exposition, to declare the real independence and responsibility of the human will. "He will render to every man according to his deeds; . . . tribulation and anguish upon every soul of man that doeth evil . . . but glory, honour, and peace, to every man that worketh good; . . . for there is no respect of persons with God;"—declarations, which I will not say are utterly irreconcilable in their very structure with (what is called) the Calvinistic creed, but which it is certain would never have been written by an assertor of it in a formal exposition of his views for the benefit of his fellow-believers. Lastly, we have the testimony of the book which completes and seals up for ever the divine communications. "My reward is with Me; to give every man according as his work shall be. Blessed are they that do His commandments, that they may have right to the tree of life [1]."

5. Moreover, we have the limits of external aids and hindrances distinctly stated to us, so as to guarantee to us, in spite of existing influences of whatever kind, even of our original corrupt nature, the essential freedom and accountableness of our will. As regards external circumstances: "God is faithful, who will not suffer you to be tempted above that ye are able; but will with the temptation also make a way to escape, that ye may be able to bear it." As regards the corrupt nature in which we are born: "Let no man say when he is tempted, I am tempted of God; but every man is tempted, when he is drawn away of his own lust, and enticed; then, when lust hath conceived, it bringeth forth sin: and sin, when it is finished, bringeth forth death." And as regards divine assistances: "It is impossible for those who were once enlightened . . . . if they fall away, to renew them again unto repentance [2]."

6. Far be it from any one to rehearse triumphantly, and in the way of controversy, these declarations of our privilege as moral agents; rather, so fearful and burdensome is this almost divine attribute of our

[1] Gen. ii. 17. Exod. xxxiv. 7; xxxii. 33. Ps. xviii. 26. Ez. xviii. 4. 31. Gal. vi. 5—7. Rom. ii. 6—11. Rev. xxii. 12, 13.
[2] 1 Cor. x. 13. James i. 13—15. Heb. vi. 4—6.

nature, that, when we consider it attentively, it requires a strong faith in the wisdom and love of our
Maker, not to start sinfully from His gift; and at the
mere prospect, not the memory of our weakness, to
attempt to transfer it from ourselves to the agents,
animate and inanimate, by which we are surrounded,
and to lose our immortality under the shadows of the
visible world. And much more, when the sense of
guilt comes upon us, do we feel the temptation of ridding ourselves of our conviction of our own responsibility; and, instead of betaking ourselves to Him who
can reverse what we cannot disclaim, to shelter ourselves under the original unbelief of our first parents,
as if the serpent gave it to us and we did eat.

7. It is my wish now to give some illustrations of
the operation of this sophistry in the affairs of life;
not that it is a subject which admits of novelty in the
discussion, but with the hope of directing attention to
a mode of deceiving our consciences, common in all
ages since the original transgression, and not least
successful in our own.

8. To find fault with the circumstances in which we
find ourselves, is our ready and familiar excuse when
our conduct is arraigned in any particular. Yet even
the heathen moralist saw that all those actions are
voluntary, in which we ourselves are in any way ultimately the principle of action; and that praise and
blame are awarded, not according to the mode in
which we should have behaved, had circumstances
been different, but according as we actually conduct

ourselves, things being as they are. Commenting on goods thrown overboard in a storm, he remarks " that such acts must be considered voluntary, as being the objects of our choice *at the time* when they are done, for our conduct is determined according to the emergency[3]." In truth, nothing is more easy to the imagination than duty in the abstract, that is, duty in name and not in reality. It is when it assumes a definite and actual shape, when it comes upon us under circumstances (and it is obvious it can come in no other way), then it is difficult and troublesome. Circumstances are the very trial of obedience. Yet, plain as this is, it is very common to fancy our particular condition peculiarly hard, and that we should be better and happier men in any other.

9. Thus, for instance, opportunity, which is the means of temptation in the case of various sins, is converted into an excuse for them. Perhaps it is very plain that, except for some unusual combination of circumstances, we could never have been tempted at all; yet, when we fall on such an occasion, we are ready to excuse our weakness, as if our trial were extraordinary.

10. Again, the want of education is an excuse common with the lower classes for a careless and irreligious life.

11. Again, it is scarcely possible to resist the imagination, that we should have been altogether other men than we are, had we lived in an age of miracles, or in the visible presence of our Lord; that is, we cannot

[3] Arist. Eth. Nicom. iii. 17.

persuade ourselves that, whatever be the force of things
external to us in modifying our condition, it is we, and
not our circumstances, that are, after all, the main
causes of what we do and what we are.

12. Or, again, to take a particular instance, which
will perhaps come home to some who hear me, when a
young man is in prospect of ordination, he has a
conceit that his mind will be more fully his own, when
he is actually engaged in the sacred duties of his new
calling, than at present; and, in the event he is perhaps amazed and frightened, to find how little influence
the change of circumstances has had in sobering and
regulating his thoughts, whatever greater decency his
outward conduct may exhibit.

13. Further, it is the common excuse of wilful sinners, that there are peculiarities in their present engagements, connexions, plans, or professions, incom-
patible with immediate repentance; according to the
memorable words of Felix, " When I have a convenient
season, I will send for thee."

14. The operation of the same deceit discovers itself in our mode of judging the conduct of others;
whether, in the boldness with which we blame in them
what, under other circumstances, we allow in ourselves;
or, again, in the false charity which we exercise towards
them.   For instance, the vices of the young are often
regarded by beholders with an irrational indulgence,
on the ground (as it is said) that youth ever will be
wanton and impetuous; which is only saying, if put
into plain language, that there are temptations which
are not intended as trials of our obedience.   Or when,

as lately, the lower orders rise up against the powers
that be, in direct opposition to the word of Scripture,
they are excused on the ground of their rulers being
bigoted and themselves enlightened; or because they
feel themselves capable of exercising more power; or
because they have the example of other nations to in-
cite them to do so; or simply (the more common excuse) because they have the means of doing so: as if
loyalty could be called a virtue when men cannot be
disloyal, or obedience had any praise when it became a
constraint. In like manner, there is a false charity,
which, on principle, takes the cause of heresy under its
protection; and, instead of condemning it, as such,
busies itself in fancying the possible circumstances
which may, in this or that particular instance, excuse
it; as if outward fortunes could change the nature of
truth or of moral excellence, or as if, admitting the
existence of unavoidable misbelief to be conceivable,
yet it were not the duty of the Christian to take things
as they are given us in Scripture, as they are in themselves, and as they are on the whole, instead of fastening upon exceptions to the rule, or attempting to
ascertain that combination and balance of circumstances, in favour of individuals, which is only known
to the Omniscient Judge.

15. The following apology for the early profligacy
of the notorious French infidel of the last century is
found in even the respectable literature of the present day, and is an illustration of the kind of fatalism
now under consideration. "It is certain," the apologist
says, "that a brilliant, highly-gifted, and more than

commonly vivacious young man, like Voltaire, who moved in the high tide of Parisian society, must *necessarily* be imbued with the levity and laxity that on every side surrounded him, and which has rendered the period in question proverbial for profligacy and debauchery. . . . . This is not observed in defence of his moral defects, or of any one else, but in answer to those who expect the virtues of a sage from the education of an Alcibiades. His youthful career seems to have been precisely that of other young men of his age and station, neither better nor worse. It is scarcely necessary to prove the tinge which such a state of society must bestow upon every character, however intellectually gifted, which ˙is formed in the midst of it." No one can say that the doctrine contained in this extract is extravagant, as opinions go, and unfair as a specimen of what is commonly received in the world, however boldly it is expressed. Yet it will be observed, that vice is here pronounced to be the necessary effect of a certain state of society, and, as being such, not extenuated merely, as regards the individual (as it may well be), but exculpated; so that, while the actions resulting from it are allowed to be intrinsically bad, yet the agent himself is acquitted of the responsibility of committing them.

16. The sophistry in question sometimes has assumed a bolder form, and has displayed itself in the shape of system. Let us, then, now direct our attention to it in some of those fortified positions, which at various times it has taken up against the plain declarations of Scripture and Conscience.

17. (1.) Fatalism is the refuge of a conscience-stricken mind, maddened at the sight of evils which it has brought upon itself, and cannot remove. To believe and tremble is the most miserable of dooms for an immortal spirit; and bad men, whose reason has been awakened by education, resolved not to be "tormented before their time," seek in its intoxication a present oblivion of their woe. It is wretched enough to suffer, but self-reproach is the worm which destroys the inward power of resistance. Submission alone makes pain tolerable in any case; and they who refuse the Divine yoke are driven to seek a sedative in the notion of an eternal necessity. They deny that they ever could have been other than they are. "What heaven has made me, I must be," is the sentiment which hardens them into hopeless pride and rebellion.

18. And it must be confessed, so great is the force of passion and of habit, when once allowed to take possession of the heart, that these men seem to have in their actual state, nay in their past experience, long before the time of their present obduracy, an infallible witness in behalf of their doctrine. In subduing our evil nature, the first steps alone are in our own power; a few combats seem to decide the solemn question, to decide whether the sovereignty is with the spirit or the flesh; *nisi paret, imperat*, is become a proverb. When once the enemy of our souls "comes in like a flood," what hope is there that he ever will be expelled? And what servitude can be compared to the bondage which follows, when we wish to do right, yet are utterly powerless to do it? whether we be slaves to some im-

perious passion, hushed indeed in its victim's ordinary
mood, and allowing the recurrence of better thoughts
and purposes, but rising suddenly and sternly, in his
evil hour, to its easy and insulting triumph ; or, on the
other hand, to some cold sin which overhangs and
deadens the mind, sloth, for instance, or cowardice, binding it down with ten thousand subtle fastenings to the
earth, nor suffering it such motion as might suffice it
for a renewal of the contest.   Such, in its worst forms,
is the condition of the obdurate sinner ; who, feeling
his weakness, but forgetting that he ever had strength,
and the promise of aid from above, at length learns to
acquiesce in his misery as if the lot of his nature, and
resolves neither to regret nor to hope.   Next he amuses
his reason with the melancholy employment of reducing
his impressions into system ; and proves, as he thinks,
from the confessed influence of external events, and the
analogy of the physical world, that all moral phenomena proceed according to a fixed law, and that we
are not more to blame when we sin than when we die.

19. (2.) The Calvinistic doctrine, if not the result, is
at least the forerunner of a similar neglect of the doctrine of human responsibility.   Whatever be the falla-
cies of its argumentative basis, viewed as a character
of mind, it miscalculates the power of the affections, as
fatalism does that of the passions.   Its practical error
is that of supposing that certain motives and views,
presented to the heart and conscience, produce certain
effects as their necessary consequence, no room being
left for the resistance of the will, or for self-discipline,
as the medium by which faith and holiness are con-

nected together. It is the opinion of a large class of
religious people, that faith being granted, works follow
as a matter of course, without our own trouble; and
they are confirmed in their opinion by a misconception
of our Church's 12th Article, as if to assert that works
"spring out necessarily of a true and lively faith"
could only mean that they follow by a kind of physical
law. When this notion is once entertained, it follows
that nothing remains to be done but to bring these
sovereign principles before the mind, as a medicine
which must work a cure, or as sights which suddenly
enlighten and win the imagination. To care for little
duties, to set men right in the details of life, to instruct
and refine their conscience, to tutor them in self-denial,
—the Scripture methods of working onwards towards
higher knowledge and obedience,—become superfluous,
nay, despicable, while these master visions are withheld. A system such as this will of course bring with
it full evidence of its truth to such debilitated minds as
have already so given way to the imagination, that
they find themselves unable to resist its impressions as
they recur. Nor is there among the theories of the
world any more congenial to the sated and remorseful
sensualist, who, having lost the command of his will,
feels that if he is to be converted, it must be by some
sudden and violent excitement. On the other hand, it
will always have its advocates among the young and
earnest-minded, who, not having that insight into their
hearts which experience gives, think that to know is to
obey, and that their habitual love of the Truth may be
measured by their momentary admiration of it. And

it is welcomed by the indolent, who care not for the Scripture warnings of the narrowness of the way of life, provided they can but assure themselves that it is easy to those who are in it; and who readily ascribe the fewness of those who find it, not to the difficulty of connecting faith and works, but to a Divine frugality in the dispensation of the gifts of grace.

20. Such are some of the elements of that state of mind which, when scientifically developed, assumes the shape of Calvinism; the characteristic error, both of the system and of the state of mind, consisting in the assumption that there are things external to the mind, whether doctrines or influences, such, that when once presented to it, they suspend its independence and involve certain results, as if by way of physical consequence; whereas, on studying the New Testament, we shall find, that amid all that is said concerning the inscrutable decrees of God, and His mysterious interposition in the workings of the human mind, still every where the practical truths with which Revelation started are assumed and recognized; that we shall be judged by our good or evil doings, and that a principle within us is ultimately the cause of the one and the other. So that it is preposterous in us to attempt to direct our course by the distant landmarks of the Divine counsels, which are but dimly revealed to us, overlooking the clear track close before our eyes provided for our need. This perverse substitution in matters of conduct of a subtle argumentative rule for one that is plain and practical, is set before us, by way of warning, in the parable of the talents. "Lord, I knew Thee that

Thou art a hard man ... and I was afraid, and went and hid Thy talent in the earth."

21. (3.) Another illustration may be given of the systematic disparagement of human responsibility, and the consequent substitution of outward events for the inward rule of conscience in judging of conduct.

The influence of the world, viewed as the enemy of our souls, consists in its hold upon our imagination. It seems to us incredible that any thing that is said every where and always can be false. And our faith is shown in preferring the testimony of our hearts and of Scripture to the world's declarations, and our obedience in acting against them. It is the very function of the Christian to be moving against the world, and to be protesting against the majority of voices. And though a doctrine such as this may be perverted into a contempt of authority, a neglect of the Church, and an arrogant reliance on self, yet there is a sense in which it is true, as every part of Scripture teaches. "Thou shalt not follow a multitude to do evil," is its uniform injunction. Yet so irksome is this duty, that it is not wonderful that the wayward mind seeks a release from it; and, looking off from what is within to what is without, it gradually becomes perplexed and unsettled. And, should it so happen that the face of society assumes a consistent appearance, and urges the claims of the world upon the Conscience as if on the ground of principle and system, then still greater is the difficulty in which it has entangled itself. Then it is that acts which, exhibited in individual instances, would have been condemned as crimes, acquire a dignity from the number of the delinquents, or their assumption of authority, and venture to claim our acquiescence as a matter of right. What would be insubordination, or robbery, or murder, when done by one man, is hallowed by the combination of the great or the many.

22. Thus, for instance, what is more common at the present day than for philosophers to represent society as moving by a certain law through different stages, and its various elements as coming into operation at different periods; and then, not content with stating the fact (which is undeniable), to go on to speak as if what has been, and is, ought to be ; and as if because at certain eras this or that class of society gains the ascendancy, therefore it lawfully gains it ? whereas in truth the usurpation of an invader, and the development (as it is called) of the popular power, are alike facts, and alike sins, in the sight of Him who forbids us to oppose constituted authority. And yet the credulous mind hangs upon the words of the world, and falls a victim to its sophistry ; as if, forsooth, Satan could not work his work upon a law, and oppose God's will upon system. But the Christian, rejecting this pretentious guide of conduct, acts on Faith, and far from being perplexed to find the world consistent in its disobedience, recollects the declarations of Scripture which foretell it.

23. Yet so contrary to common sense is it thus to assert that our conduct ought to be determined merely by what is done by a mixed multitude, that it was to be expected that the ingenious and eager minds who practically acknowledge the principle, should wish to place it on some more argumentative basis. Accord-

ingly, attempts have been made by foreign writers to show that society moves on a law which is independent of the conduct of its individual members, who cannot materially retard its progress, nor are answerable for it, —a law which in consequence is referable only to the will of the Creator. " Historical causes and their effects being viewed, at one glance, through a long course of years, seem," it has been said, " from their steady progression, to be above any human control; an impulse is given, which beats down resistance, and sweeps away all means of opposition; century succeeds to century, and the philosopher sees the same influence still potent, still undeviating and regular; to him, considering these ages at once, following with rapid thought the slow pace of time, a century appears to dwindle to a point; and the individual obstructions and accelerations, which within that period have occurred to impede or advance the march of events, are eliminated and forgotten."

24. This is the theory; and hence it is argued that it is our wisdom to submit to a power which is greater than ourselves, and which can neither be circumvented nor persuaded; as if the Christian dare take any guide of conscience except the rule of duty, or might prefer expediency (if it be such) to principle. Nothing, for instance, is more common than to hear men speak of the growing intelligence of the present age, and to insist upon the Church's supplying its wants; the previous question being entirely left out of view, whether those wants are healthy and legitimate, or unreasonable, —whether real or imaginary,—whether they ought to be gratified or repressed: and it is urged upon us, that

unless we take the lead in the advance of mind ourselves, we must be content to fall behind. But, surely our first duty is, not to resolve on satisfying a demand at any price, but to determine whether it be innocent. If so, well; but if not, let what will happen. Even though the march of society be conducted on a superhuman law, yet, while it moves against Scripture Truth, it is not God's ordinance,—it is but the creature of Satan; and, though it shiver all earthly obstacles to its progress, the gods of Sepharvaim and Arphad, fall it must, and perish it must, before the glorious fifth kingdom of the Most High, when He visits the earth, who is called Faithful and True, whose eyes are as a flame of fire, and on His head many crowns, who smites the nations with a rod of iron, and treadeth the winepress of the fierceness and wrath of Almighty God.

My object in the foregoing remarks has been to illustrate, in various ways, the operation of an all-important truth; that circumstances are but the subject-matter, and not the rule of our conduct, nor in any true sense the cause of it. Let me conclude with one more exemplification of it, which I address to the junior part of my audience.

25. (4.) In this place, where the stated devotional services of the Church are required of all of us, it is very common with our younger members to slight them, while they attend on them, on the ground of their being forced upon them. A like excuse is sometimes urged in behalf of an unworthy participation of the Lord's Supper, as if that communion could not reasonably be

considered real, or dangerous to the impenitent, which was performed under constraint[4].

26. Now, let such an apologist be taken on his own ground. Let it be granted to him, for argument's sake, though in no other way, that this general exaction of religious duties is unwise; let him be allowed the full force of his objections to a system, which he has not yet experience to understand. Yet do these outward circumstances change the nature of the case in any practical respect, or relieve him of his responsibility ? Rather, is it not his plain duty to take things as he finds them, since he has not the power of changing them; and, leaving to his superiors what pertains to them, the task of deciding on the system to be pursued, to inquire how he ought to act under it, and to reflect what his guilt will be in the day of account, if week after week he has come into the presence of God with a deliberate profanation in his right hand, or at least with irreverence of manner, and an idle mind ?

27. And, again, as regards the Holy Communion, how do the outward circumstances which bring us thither affect the real purpose of God respecting it ? Can we in earthly matters remove what we dislike, by wishing it away ?—and shall we hope, by mere unbelief, to remove the Presence of God from His ordinance ? As well may we think of removing thereby the visible emblems of bread and wine, or of withdrawing ourselves

---

[4] [Here I ought to remark, that, from the time I became public Tutor, I was always opposed to the compulsory communion of Undergraduates, and testified my opposition to it whenever I had the opportunity.]

altogether from the Omnipresent Eye of God itself. Though Christ is savingly revealed in the Sacrament only to those who receive Him in faith, yet we have the express word of Scripture for saying, that the thoughtless communicant, far from remaining as if he did not receive it, is guilty of the actual Body and Blood of Christ,—guilty of the crime of crucifying Him anew, as not discerning that which lies hid in the rite. This does not apply, of course, to any one who communicates with a doubt merely about his own state —far from it!—nor to those who resolve heartily, yet in the event fail to perform, as is the case with the young; nor to those even who may happen to sin both before and after the reception of the Sacrament. Where there is earnestness, there is no condemnation; but it applies fearfully to such as view the Blessed Ordinance as a thing of course, from a notion that they are passive subjects of a regulation which others enforce; and, perhaps, the number of these is not small. Let such persons seriously consider that, were their argument correct, they need not be considered in a state of trial at all, and might escape the future judgment altogether. They would have only to protest (as we may speak) against their creation, and they would no longer have any duties to bind them. But what says the word of God? "That which cometh into your mind, shall not be at all, that ye say, We will be as the heathen, as the families of the countries, to serve wood and stone." And then follows the threat, addressed to those who rebel:—"As I live, saith the Lord God, surely with a mighty hand, and with a stretched out arm, and with fury poured out, will I rule over you . . . . . And I will cause you to pass under the rod, and I will bring you into the bond of the covenant."

28. And these words apply to the whole subject which has engaged us. We may amuse ourselves, for a time, with such excuses for sin as a perverted ingenuity furnishes; but there is One who is justified in His sayings, and clear when He judgeth. Our worldly philosophy and our well-devised pleadings will profit nothing at a day when the heaven shall depart as a scroll is rolled together, and all who are not clad in the wedding-garment of faith and love will be speechless. Surely it is high time for us to wake out of sleep, to chase from us the shadows of the night, and to realize our individuality, and the coming of our Judge. "The night is far spent, the day is at hand," —"let us be sober, and watch unto prayer."

SERMON IX.

WILFULNESS, THE SIN OF SAUL.

(Preached December 2, 1832.)

1 SAM. xv. 11.

" It repenteth Me that I have set up Saul to be king ; for he is turned back from following Me, and hath not performed My command-ments."

THE three chief religious patterns and divine instru-ments under the first Covenant, have each his complement in the Sacred History, that we may have a warning as well as an instruction. The distinguishing virtue, moral and political, of Abraham, Moses, and David, was their faith; by which I mean an implicit reliance in God's command and promise, and a zeal for His honour; a surrender and devotion of themselves, and all they had, to Him. At His word they each relinquished the dearest wish of their hearts, Isaac, Canaan, and the Temple; the Temple was not to be built, the land of promise not to be entered, the child of promise not to be retained. All three were tried by the anxieties and discomforts of exile and wander-ing; all three, and especially Moses and David, were very zealous for the Lord God of Hosts.

2. The faith of Abraham is illustrated in the luke-

warmness of Lot, who, though a true servant of God, and a righteous man, chose for his dwelling-place the fertile country of a guilty people. To Moses, who was faithful in all God's house, is confronted the untrue prophet Balaam, who, gifted from the same Divine Master, and abounding in all knowledge and spiritual discernment, mistook words for works, and fell through love of lucre. The noble self-consuming zeal of David, who was at once ruler of the chosen people, and type of the Messiah, is contrasted with a still more conspicuous and hateful specimen of unbelief, as disclosed to us in the history of Saul. To this history it is proposed now to draw your attention, not indeed with the purpose of surveying it as a whole, but with hope of gaining thence some such indirect illustration, in the way of contrast, of the nature of religious Faith, as it is adapted to supply.

3. It cannot be denied that the designs of Providence towards Saul and David are, at first sight, of a perplexing nature, as implying distinctions in the moral character of the two men, which their history does not clearly warrant. Accordingly, it is usual, with a view of meeting the difficulty, to treat them as mere instruments in the Divine Governance of the Israelites, and to determine their respective virtues and defects, not by a moral, but by a political standard. For instance, the honourable title by which David is distinguished, as "a man after God's own heart," is interpreted with reference merely to his activity and success in enforcing the principles of the Mosaic system, no

account being taken of the motives which influenced him, or of his general character, or of his conduct in other respects. Now, it is by no means intended here to dispute the truth of such representations, or to deny that the Church, in its political relations, must even treat men with a certain reference to their professions and outward acts, such as it withdraws in its private dealings with them ; yet, to consider the difference between Saul and David to be of a moral nature, is more consistent with the practical objects with which we believe Scripture to have been written, and more reverent, moreover, to the memory of one whose lineage the Saviour almost gloried in claiming, and whose devotional writings have edified the Church even to this day. Let us then drop, for the present, the political view of the history which it is here proposed to consider, and attempt to discover the moral lesson intended to be conveyed to us in the character of Saul, the contrast of the zealous David.

4. The unbelief of Balaam discovers itself in a love of secular distinction, and was attended by self-deception. Saul seems to have had no base ends in view; he was not self-deceived; his temptation and his fall consisted in a certain perverseness of mind, founded on some obscure feelings of self-importance, very commonly observable in human nature, and sometimes called pride,—a perverseness which shows itself in a reluctance absolutely to relinquish its own independence of action, in cases where dependence is a duty, and which interferes a little, and alters a little, as if with a view of satisfying its own fancied dignity, though it

is afraid altogether to oppose itself to the voice of
God. Should this seem, at first sight, to be a trifling
fault, it is the more worth while to trace its operation
in the history of Saul. If a tree is known by its fruit,
it is a great sin.

5. Saul's character is marked by much that is considered to be the highest moral excellence,—generosity,
magnanimity, calmness, energy, and decision. He is
introduced to us as "a choice young man, and a
goodly," and as possessed of a striking personal presence, and as a member of a wealthy and powerful
family [1].

6. The first announcement of his elevation came
upon him suddenly, but apparently without unsettling
him. He kept it secret, leaving it to Samuel, who had
made it to him, to publish it. "Saul said unto his
uncle, He (that is, Samuel) told us plainly that the
asses were found. But of the matter of the kingdom,
whereof Samuel spake, he told him not." Nay, it
would even seem as if he were averse to the dignity
intended for him; for when the Divine lot fell upon
him, he had hid himself, and was not discovered by the
people without Divine assistance.

7. The appointment was at first unpopular. "The
children of Belial said, How shall this man save us?"
Here again his high-mindedness is discovered, and his
remarkable force and energy of character. He showed
no signs of resentment at the insult. "They despised

---

[1] Some sentences which follow have already been inserted in **Parochial Sermons**, Vol. iii. Serm. 3.

him, and brought him no presents. But he held his peace." Soon the Ammonites invaded the country beyond Jordan, with the avowed intention of reducing its inhabitants to slavery. They, almost in despair, sent to Saul for relief; and the panic spread in the interior, as well as among those whose country was immediately threatened. The conduct of their new king brings to mind the celebrated Roman story. "Behold, Saul came after the herd out of the field and Saul said, What aileth the people, that they weep? And they told him the tidings of the men of Jabesh. And the Spirit of God came upon Saul, and his anger was kindled greatly." His order for an immediate gathering throughout Israel was obeyed with the alacrity with which, in times of alarm, the many yield themselves up to the will of the strong-minded. A decisive victory over the enemy followed. Then the popular cry became, "Who is he that said, Shall Saul reign over us? Bring the men, that we may put them to death. And Saul said, There shall not a man be put to death this day: for to-day the Lord hath wrought salvation in Israel."

8. We seem here to find noble traits of character; at the same time it must not be forgotten that sometimes such exhibitions are also the concomitants of a certain strangeness and eccentricity of mind, which are very perplexing to those who study it, and very unamiable. Reserve, sullenness, headstrong self-confidence, pride, caprice, sourness of temper, scorn of others, a scoffing at natural feeling and religious principle; all those characters of mind which, though dis-

tinct from mental aberration, are temptations to it, frequently take the form, and have in some degree the nature, of magnanimity. It is probable, from the sequel of Saul's history, that the apparent nobleness of his first actions was connected with some such miserable principles and feelings, which then existed only in their seeds, but which afterwards sprang up and ripened to his destruction; and this in consequence of that one fatal defect of mind which has been already noticed, as corrupting the integrity of his faith.

9. The world prevailed over the faith of Balaam; a more subtle, though not a rare temptation, overcame the faith of Saul; wilfulness, the unaccountable desire of acting short of simple obedience to God's will, a repugnance of unreserved self-surrender and submission to Him. This, it will at once be seen, was one characteristic of the Jewish nation; so that the king was but a type of the people; nor, indeed, was it likely to be otherwise, born as he was in the original sin of that very perverseness which led them to choose a king, instead of God. It is scarcely necessary to refer to the details of their history for instances of a like wilfulness,—such as their leaving the manna till the morning, their going out to gather it on the seventh day, Nadab and Abihu's offering strange fire, their obstinate transgression of the Second Commandment, their presumptuous determination to fight with the Canaanites, though Moses foretold their defeat, and, when possessed of the promised land, their putting under tribute the idolaters whom they were bid exterminate. The

[UNIV. S.]   M

same was the sin of Jeroboam, who is almost by title
the Apostate; when God had promised him the kingdom of Israel, he refused to wait God's time, but impatiently forced a crisis, which ought to have been left
to Him who promised it.

10. On the other hand, Abraham and David,
with arms in their hands, waited upon Him for the
fulfilment of the temporal promise in His good time.
It is on this that the distinction turns, so much insisted
on in the Books of Kings, of serving God with a "perfect," or not with a perfect, heart. "Ahaz went to
Damascus to meet Tiglath-pileser, King of Assyria, and
saw an altar that was at Damascus; and King Ahaz
sent to Urijah the priest the fashion of the altar, . . .
and Urijah . . . built an altar according to all that
king Ahaz had sent from Damascus." Here was a
wanton innovation on received usages, which had been
appointed by Almighty God. The same evil temper is
protested against in Hezekiah's proclamation to the
remnant of the Israelites: "Be ye not like your fathers,
and like your brethren, which trespassed against the
Lord God of their fathers, who therefore gave them up
to desolation, as ye see. Now be ye not stiff-necked,
as your fathers were, but yield yourselves unto the
Lord, and enter into His sanctuary." It is indirectly
condemned, also, in the precept given to the Israelites,
before their final deliverance from Pharaoh. When
they were on the Red Sea shore, Moses said, "Fear ye
not, stand still, and see the salvation of the Lord . . . .
The Lord shall fight for you, and ye shall hold your
peace." Again, in the Book of Psalms, "Be still, and

know that I am God. I will be exalted among the
heathen, I will be exalted in the earth;" the very trial
of the people consisting in their doing nothing out of
their place, but implicitly following when the Almighty
took the lead.

11. The trial and the sin of the Israelites were continued to the end of their history. They fell from their
election on Christ's coming, in consequence of this very
wilfulness; refusing to receive the terms of the New
Covenant, *as* they were vouchsafed to them, and attempting to incorporate them into their own ceremonial
system. "They being ignorant of God's righteousness
and going about to establish their own righteousness,
have not submitted themselves unto the righteousness of
God."

12. Such was one distinguishing sin of the Israelites
as a nation; and, as it proved the cause of their rejection, so had it also, ages before, corrupted the faith, and
forfeited the privileges, of their first king. The signs
of wilfulness run through his history from first to last:
but his formal trial took place at two distinct times,
and in both cases terminated in his deliberate fall. Of
these, the latter is more directly to our purpose. When
sent to inflict a Divine judgment upon the Amalekites,
he spared those whom he was bid slay; their king Agag,
the best of the sheep and cattle, and all that was good.
We are not concerned with the general state of mind
and opinion which led him to this particular display of
wilfulness. Much might be said of that profaneness,
which, as in the case of Esau, was a distinguishing trait
in his character. Indeed, we might even conjecture

that from the first he was an unbeliever in heart; that
is, that he did not recognize the exclusive divinity of
the Mosaic theology, compared with those of the sur-
rounding nations, and that he had by this time learned
to regard the pomp and splendour of the neighbouring
monarchies with an interest which made him ashamed
of the seeming illiberality and the singularity of the
institutions of Israel. A perverse will easily collects
together a system of notions to justify itself in its obli-
quity. The real state of the case was this, that he
preferred his own way to that which God had determined. When directed by the Divine Hand towards
the mark for which he was chosen, he started aside like
a broken bow. He obeyed, but with a reserve, yet
distinctly professing to Samuel that he had performed the commandment of the Lord, because the
sheep and cattle were reserved for a pious purpose,
a sacrifice to the Lord. The Prophet, in his reply,
explained the real moral character of this limited and
discretionary obedience, in words which are a warning
to all who are within the hearing of Revealed Religion to the end of time: "Hath the Lord as great
delight in burnt offerings and sacrifices, as in obeying
the voice of the Lord? Behold, to obey is better than
sacrifice; and to hearken, than the fat of rams. For
rebellion is as the sin of witchcraft, and stubbornness is
as iniquity and idolatry."

13. The moral of Saul's history is forced upon us by
the events which followed this deliberate offence. By
wilful resistance to God's will, he opened the door to
those evil passions which till then, at the utmost, only

served to make his character unamiable, without stamping it with guilt. The reserve and mysteriousness, which, when subordinate to such magnanimity as he possessed, were even calculated to increase his influence as a ruler, ended in an overthrow of his mind, when they were allowed full scope by the removal of true religious principle, and the withdrawal of the Spirit of God. Derangement was the consequence of disobedience. The wilfulness which first resisted God, next preyed upon himself, as a natural principle of disorder; his moods and changes, his compunctions and relapses, what were they but the convulsions of the spirit, when the governing power was lost? At length the proud heart, which thought it much to obey its Maker, was humbled to seek comfort in a witch's cavern; essaying, by means which he had formerly denounced, to obtain advice from that Prophet when dead, whom in his lifetime he had dishonoured.

14. In contemplating this miserable termination of a history which promised well in the beginning, it should be observed, how clearly the failure of the divine purpose which takes place in it is attributable to man. Almighty God chose an instrument adapted, as far as external qualifications were concerned, to fulfil His purpose; adapted in all those respects which He reserved in His own hands, when He created a free agent; in character and gifts, in all respects except in that in which all men are, on the whole, on a level,—in will. No one could be selected in talents or conduct more suitable for maintaining political power at home than the reserved, mysterious monarch whom God gave to His people;

none more suitable for striking terror into the sur-
rounding nations than a commander gifted with his
coolness and promptitude in action.   But he fell from
his election, because of unbelief,—because he would
take another part, and not the very part which was
actually assigned him in the decrees of the Most
High.

15. And again, considering his character according
to the standard of moral excellence, here also it was one
not without great promise. It is from such stern
materials that the highest and noblest specimens of our
kind are formed. The pliant and amiable by nature,
generally speaking, are not the subjects of great purposes. They are hardly capable of extraordinary discipline; they yield or they sink beneath the pressure of
those sanctifying processes which do but mature the
champions of holy Church.   "Unstable as water, thou
shalt not excel," is a representation true in its degree
in the case of many, who nevertheless serve God
acceptably in their generation, and whose real place in
the ranks of the unseen world we have no means of
ascertaining.   But those minds, which naturally most
resemble the aboriginal chaos, contain within them the
elements of a marvellous creation of light and beauty,
if they but open their hearts to the effectual power of
the Holy Spirit. Pride and sullenness, obstinacy and
impetuosity, then become transformed into the zeal,
firmness, and high-mindedness of religious Faith. It
depended on Saul himself whether or not he became
the rival of that exalted saint, who, being once a fierce
avenger of his brethren, at length became " the meekest

of men," yet not losing thereby, but gaining, moral strength and resoluteness.

16. Or again, a comparison of him in this respect with the Apostle who originally bore his name, is not perhaps so fanciful as it may appear at first sight. St. Paul was distinguished by a furiousness and vindictiveness equally incongruous as Saul's pride, with the obedience of Faith. In the first persecution against the Christians, he is described by the sacred writer as ravening like a beast of prey. And he was exposed to the temptation of a wilfulness similar to that of Saul— the wilfulness of running counter to God's purposes, and interfering in the course of Dispensations which he should have humbly received. He indeed was called miraculously, but scarcely more so than Saul, who, when he least expected it, was called by Samuel, and was, at his express prediction, suddenly filled by the Spirit of God, and made to prophesy. But, while Saul profited not by the privilege thus vouchsafed to him, St. Paul was "not disobedient to the heavenly vision," and matured in his after-life in those exalted qualities of mind which Saul forfeited. Every attentive reader of his Epistles must be struck with the frequency and force of the Apostle's declarations concerning un- reserved submission to the Divine will, or rather of his exulting confidence in it. But the wretched king of Israel, what is his ultimate state, but the most forlorn of which human nature is capable? "How are the mighty fallen!" was the lament over him of the loyal though injured friend who succeeded to his power. He, who might have been canonized in the catalogue of

the eleventh of Hebrews, is but the prototype of that vision of obduracy and self-inflicted destitution, which none but unbelieving poets of these latter ages have ever thought worthy of aught but the condemnation and abhorrence of mankind.

17. Two questions must be answered before we can apply the lesson of Saul's history to our own circumstances. It is common to contrast Christianity with Judaism, as if the latter were chiefly a system of positive commands, and the former addressed itself to the Reason and natural Conscience; and accordingly, it will perhaps be questioned whether Christians can be exposed to the temptation of wilfulness, that is, disobedience to the external word of God, in any way practically parallel to Saul's trial. And secondly, granting it possible, the warning against wilfulness, contained in his history and that of his nation, may be met by the objection that the Jews were a peculiarly carnal and gross-minded people, so that nothing can be argued concerning our danger at this day, from their being exposed and yielding to the temptation of perversity and presumption.

18. (1.) But such an assumption evidences a great want of fairness towards the ancient people of God, in those who make it, and is evidently perilous in proportion as it is proved to be unfounded. All men, not the Jews only, have a strange propensity, such as Eve evidenced in the beginning, to do what they are told not to do. It is plainly visible in children, and in the common people; and in them we are able to judge what

we all are, before education and habit lay restraints upon
us. Need we even do more than appeal to the events
of the past year, to the conduct of the lower classes
when under that fearful visitation, from which we are
now, as we trust, recovering, in order to detect the
workings of that innate spirit of scepticism and
obduracy which was the enemy of Jewish faith? Of
course, all places did not afford the same evidence of
it; but on the whole there was enough for my present
allusion to it. A suspicion of the most benevolent
exertions in their favour, a jealousy of the interference
of those who knew more than themselves, a perverse
rejection of their services, and a counteraction of their
plans and advice, an unthankful credulity in receiving
all the idle tales told in disparagement of their knowledge and prudence; these were admonitions before
our eyes, not to trust those specious theories which are
built on the supposition, that the actual condition of
the human mind is better now than it was among the
Jews. This is not said without regard to the difference
of guilt in disobeying a Divine and a human command; nor, again, in complaint of the poorer classes,
of whom we are especially bound to be tender, and
who are not the worse merely because they are less
disguised in the expression of their feelings; but as
pointing out for our own instruction the present
existence of a perversity in our common nature, like
that which appears in the history of Israel. Nor,
perhaps, can any one doubt, who examines himself,
that he has within him an unaccountable and instinctive feeling to resist authority as such, which

conscience or the sense of interest is alone able to overcome.

19. Or, again, to take the case of young persons who have not yet taken their place in the serious business of life; consider the false shame they feel at being supposed to be obedient to God or man; their endeavours to be more irreligious than they really can be; their affected indifference to domestic feelings, and the sanctity and the authority of relationship; their adoption of ridicule as an instrument of retaliation on the constraints of duty or necessity. What does all this show us, but that our nature likes its own way, not as thinking it better or safer, but simply because it is its own? In other words, that the principle of Faith is resisted, not only by our attachment to objects of sense and sight, but by an innate rebellious principle, which disobeys as if for the sake of disobedience.

20. (2.) Now if wilfulness be a characteristic of human nature, it is idle to make any such distinction of Dispensations, as will deprive us of the profitableness of the history of Saul; which was the other question just now raised concerning it. Under any circumstances it must be a duty to subdue that which is in itself vicious; and it is no excuse for wilfulness to say that we are not under a positive system of commands, such as the Mosaic, and that there is no room for the sin in Christianity. Rather, it will be our duty to regard ourselves in all our existing religious relations, and not merely according to some abstract views of the Gospel Covenant, and to apply the prin-

ciples of right and wrong, exemplified in the Jewish history, to our changed circumstances on the whole.

21. But, to speak plainly, it may be doubted whether there be any such great difference between the Jewish system and our own, in respect of positive institutions and commandments. Revealed Religion, as such, is of the nature of a positive rule, implying, as it does, an addition, greater or less, to the religion of nature, and the disclosure of facts, which are thus disclosed, because otherwise not discoverable. Accordingly, the difference between the state of Jews and Christians is one simply of degree. We have to practise submission as they had, and we can run counter to the will of God in the very same way as they did, and under the same temptations which overcame them. For instance, the reception of the Catholic faith is a submission to a positive command, as really as was that of the Israelites to the Second Commandment. And the belief in the necessity of such reception, in order to salvation, is an additional instance of submission. Adherence to the Canon of Scripture is a further instance of this obedience of Faith; and St. John marks it as such in the words with which the Canon itself closes, which contain an anathema parallel to that which we use in the Creed. Moreover, the duty of Ecclesiastical Unity is clearly one of positive institution; it is a sort of ceremonial observance, and as such, is the tenure on which the evangelical privileges are chartered to us. The Sacraments, too, are of the same positive character.

22. If these remarks be well founded, it is plain that

instead of our being very differently situated from the Jews, all persons who are subjects of Revealed Religion, coincide in differing from all who are left under the Dispensation of Nature. Revelation puts us on a trial which exists but obscurely in Natural Religion; the trial of obeying for obedience-sake, or on Faith. Deference to the law of Conscience, indeed, is of the nature of Faith; but it is easily perverted into a kind of self-confidence, namely, a deference to our own judgment. Here, then, Revelation provides us with an important instrument for chastening and moulding our moral character, over and above the matter of its disclosures. Christians as well as Jews must submit as little children. This being considered, how strange are the notions of the present day concerning the liberty and irresponsibility of the Christian! If the Gospel be a message, as it is, it ever must be more or less what the multitude of self-wise reasoners declare it shall not be,—a law; it must be of the nature of what they call a form, and a bondage; it must, in its degree, bring darkness, instead of flattering them with the promise of immediate illumination; and must enlighten them only in proportion as they first submit to be darkened. This, then, if they knew their meaning, is the wish of the so-called philosophical Christians, and men of no party, of the present day; namely, that they should be rid altogether of the shackles of a Revelation: and to this assuredly their efforts are tending and will tend,—to identify the Christian doctrine with their own individual convictions, to sink its supernatural character, and to constitute themselves the prophets,

not the recipients, of Divine Truth; creeds and discipline being already in their minds severed from its
substance, and being gradually shaken off by them in
fact, as the circumstances of the times will allow.

23. Let us, then, reflect that, whatever be the trial of
those who have not a Revelation, the trial of those who
have is one of Faith in opposition to self-will. Those
very self-appointed ordinances which are praiseworthy
in a heathen, and the appropriate evidence of his
earnestness and piety, are inexcusable in those to whom
God has spoken. Things indifferent become sins when
they are forbidden, and duties when commanded. The
emblems of the Deity might be invented by Egyptian
faith, but were adopted by Jewish unbelief. The trial
of Abraham, when called on to kill his son, as of Saul
when bid slay the Amalekites, was the duty of quitting
the ordinary rules which He prescribes to our obedience,
upon a positive commandment distinctly conveyed to
them by revelation.

24. And so strong is this tendency of Revealed
Religion to erect positive institutions and laws, that it
absorbs into its province even those temporal ordinances
which are, strictly speaking, exterior to it. It gives to
the laws of man the nature of a divine authority, and
where they exist makes obedience to them a duty. This
is evident in the case of civil government, the forms
and officers of which, when once established, are to be
received for conscience-sake by those who find themselves under them. The same principle is applied in a
more remarkable manner to sanction customs originally
indifferent, in the case of the Rechabites; who were

rewarded with a promise of continuance as a family, on
the ground of their observance of certain discomforts
and austerities, imposed on them by the simple authority
of an ancestor.

25. With these principles fresh in the memory, a
number of reflections crowd upon the mind in surveying the face of society, as at present constituted.
The present open resistance to constituted power, and
(what is more to the purpose) the indulgent toleration
of it, the irreverence towards Antiquity, the unscru-
pulous and wanton violation of the commands and
usages of our forefathers, the undoing of their bene-
factions, the profanation of the Church, the bold transgression of the duty of Ecclesiastical Unity, the avowed
disdain of what is called party religion (though Christ
undeniably made a party the vehicle of His doctrine,
and did not cast it at random on the world, as men
would now have it), the growing indifference to the
Catholic Creed, the sceptical objections to portions of
its doctrine, the arguings and discussings and compar-
ings and correctings and rejectings, and all the train of
presumptuous exercises, to which its sacred articles are
subjected, the numberless discordant criticisms on the
Liturgy, which have shot up on all sides of us; the general irritable state of mind, which is every where to be
witnessed, and craving for change in all things; what
do all these symptoms show, but that the spirit of Saul
still lives?—that wilfulness, which is the antagonist
principle to the zeal of David,—the principle of cleaving
and breaking down all divine ordinances, instead of

building up. And with Saul's sin, Saul's portion awaits his followers,—distraction, aberration; the hiding of God's countenance; imbecility, rashness, and change-ableness in their counsels; judicial blindness, fear of the multitude; alienation from good men and faithful friends; subserviency to their worst foes, the kings of Amalek and the wizards of Endor. So was it with the Jews, who rejected their Messiah only to follow impostors; so is it with infidels, who become the slaves of superstition; and such is ever the righteous doom of those who trust their own wills more than God's word, in one way or other to be led even-tually into a servile submission to usurped authority. As the Apostle says of the Roman Christians, they were but slaves of sin, while they were emancipated from righteousness. "What fruit," he asks, "had ye then in those things whereof ye are now ashamed?"

26. These remarks may at first sight seem irrelevant in the case of those who, like ourselves, are bound by affection and express promises to the cause of Christ's Church; yet it should be recollected that very rarely have its members escaped the infection of the age in which they lived: and there certainly is the danger of our considering ourselves safe, merely because we do not go the lengths of others, and protest against the extreme principles or measures to which they are committed.

SERMON X.

FAITH AND REASON, CONTRASTED AS HABITS OF MIND.

(Preached on the Epiphany, 1839.)

HEB. xi. 1.

" Now Faith is the substance of things hoped for, the evidence of things not seen."

THE subject of Faith is one especially suggested to our minds by the event which we this day commemorate, and the great act of grace of which it was the first-fruits. It was as on this day that the wise men of the East were allowed to approach and adore the infant Saviour, in anticipation of those Gentile multitudes who, when the kingdom of God was preached, were to take possession of it as if by violence, and to extend it to the ends of the earth. To them Christ was manifested as He is to us, and in the same way; not to the eyes of the flesh, but to the illuminated mind, to their Faith. As the manifestation of God accorded to the Jews was circumscribed, and addressed to their senses, so that which is vouchsafed to Christians is universal and spiritual. Whereas the gifts of the Gospel are invisible, Faith is their proper recipient; and whereas its Church is Catholic, Faith is its bond of intercommunion; things external, local, and sensible being no longer objects to dwell upon on their own account, but merely means of conveying onwards the divine gifts from the Giver to their proper home, the heart itself.

2. As, then, Catholicity is the note, so an inward manifestation is the privilege, and Faith the duty, of the Christian Church; or, in the words of the Apostle, "the *Gentiles*" receive "the promise of the *Spirit* through *Faith*."

3. I shall not, then be stepping beyond the range of subjects to which this great Festival draws our attention, if I enter upon some inquiries into the nature of that special Gospel grace, by which Jews and Gentiles apprehend and enjoy the blessings which Christ has purchased for them, and which accordingly is spoken of in the Collect in the service, as the peculiarity of our condition in this life, as Sight will be in the world to come. And in so doing, I shall be pursuing a subject, which is likely to be of main importance in the controversies which lie before us at this day, and upon which I am not speaking now for the first time from this place [1].

4. It is scarcely necessary to prove from Scripture, the especial dignity and influence of Faith, under the Gospel Dispensation, as regards both our spiritual and moral condition. Whatever be the particular faculty or frame of mind denoted by the word, certainly Faith is regarded in Scripture as the chosen instrument connecting heaven and earth, as a novel principle of action most powerful in the influence which it exerts both on

[1] Vide Sermon IV.

the heart and on the Divine view of us, and yet in itself of
a nature to excite the contempt or ridicule of the world.
These characteristics, its apparent weakness, its novelty,
its special adoption, and its efficacy, are noted in such
passages as the following :—" Have faith in God ; for
verily I say unto you, that whosoever shall say unto this
mountain, Be thou removed, and be thou cast into the
sea, and shall not doubt in his heart, but shall believe
that those things which he saith shall come to pass, he
shall have whatsoever he saith. Therefore I say unto
you, what things soever ye desire, when ye pray, believe
that ye receive them, and ye shall have them." And
again : " If thou canst believe, all things are possible
to him that believeth." Again : " The preaching of the
Cross is to them that perish foolishness, but unto us
which are saved it is the power of God. Where is the
wise ? where is the scribe ? where is the disputer of
this world ? For after that in the wisdom of God the
world by wisdom knew not God, it pleased God by the
foolishness of preaching to save them that believe."
Again : " The word is nigh thee, even in thy mouth
and in thy heart, that is, the word of faith which we
preach. . . . Faith cometh by hearing, and hearing by
the word of God." And again : " Yet a little while,
and He that shall come will come, and will not tarry ;
now the just shall live by faith." . . . And then, soon
after, the words of the text : " Now faith is the substance
of things hoped for, the evidence of things not seen [2]."

5. Such is the great weapon which Christianity em-

---

[2] Mark xi. 22—24 ; ix. 23. 1 Cor. i. 18 – 21. Rom. x. 8, 17. Heb.
x. 37, 38.

ploys, whether viewed as a religious scheme, as a social system, or as a moral rule; and what it is described as being in the foregoing texts, it is also said to be expressly or by implication in other passages too numerous to cite. And I suppose that it will not be denied, that the first impression made upon the reader from all these is, that in the minds of the sacred writers, Faith is an instrument of knowledge and action, unknown to the world before, a principle *sui generis,* distinct from those which nature supplies, and in particular (which is the point into which I mean to inquire) independent of what is commonly understood by Reason[3]. Certainly if, after all that is said about Faith in the New Testament, as if it were what may be called a discovery of the Gospel, and a special divine method of salvation; if, after all, it turns out merely to be a believing upon evidence, or a sort of conclusion upon a process of reasoning, a resolve formed upon a calculation, the inspired text is not level to the understanding, or adapted to the instruction, of the unlearned reader. If Faith be such a principle, how is it novel and strange?

6. Other considerations may be urged in support of the same view of the case. For instance: Faith is spoken of as having its life in a certain moral temper[4],

---

[3] ["What is commonly understood by Reason," or "common sense," as that word is often used, is the habit of deciding about religious questions with the off-hand random judgments which are suggested by secular principles; vide supra, Discourse iv. At best, by Reason is usually meant, the faculty of Reason exercising itself explicitly by *à posteriori* or evidential methods.]

[4] [That is, the intellectual principles on which the conclusions are drawn, to which Faith assents, are the consequents of a certain ethical temper, as their *sine quâ non* condition.]

but argumentative exercises are not moral; Faith, then, is not the same method of proof as Reason.

7. Again : Faith is said to be one of the supernatural gifts imparted in the Gospel. "By grace have ye been saved, through faith, and that not of yourselves, it is the gift of God;" but investigation and proof belong to man as man, prior to the Gospel: therefore Faith is something higher than Reason.

8. Again :—That Faith is independent of processes of Reason, seems plain from their respective subject-matters. "Faith cometh by hearing, and hearing by the word of God." It simply accepts testimony. As then testimony is distinct from experience, so is Faith from Reason.

9. And again :—When the Apostles disparage " the wisdom of this world," " disputings," "excellency of speech," and the like, they seem to mean very much what would now be called trains of argument, discussion, investigation,—that is, exercises of Reason.

10. Once more :—Various instances are given us in Scripture of persons making an acknowledgment of Christ and His Apostles upon Faith, which would not be considered by the world as a rational conviction upon evidence. For instance : The lame man who sat at the Beautiful gate was healed on his faith, after St. Peter had but said, "Look on us." And that other lame man at Lystra saw no miracle done by St. Paul, but only heard him preach, when the Apostle, "steadfastly beholding him, and perceiving that he had faith to be healed, said with a loud voice, Stand upright on thy feet." Again, St. Paul at Athens did no miracle, but

preached, and yet "certain men clave unto him and believed." To the same purpose are our Lord's words. when St. John Baptist sent to Him to ask if He were the Christ. He wrought miracles, indeed, to re-assure him, but added, "Blessed is he whosoever shall not be offended in Me." And when St. Thomas doubted of His resurrection, He gave him the sensible proof which he asked, but He added, "Blessed are they that have not seen, and yet have believed." On another occasion He said, "Except ye see signs and wonders, ye will not believe[6]."

11. On the other hand, however, it may be urged, that it is plainly impossible that Faith should be independent of Reason, and a new mode of arriving at truth; that the Gospel does not alter the constitution of our nature, and does but elevate it and add to it; that Sight is our initial, and Reason is our ultimate informant concerning all knowledge. We are conscious that we see; we have an instinctive reliance on our Reason: how can the claims of a professed Revelation be brought home to us as Divine, except through these? Faith, then, must necessarily be resolvable at last into Sight and Reason; unless, indeed, we agree with enthusiasts in thinking that faculties altogether new are implanted in our minds, and that perceptibly, by the grace of the Gospel; faculties which, of course, are known to those who have them without proof; and, to those who have them not, cannot be made known by any. Scripture confirms this representation, as often

---

[6] Acts iii. 4; xiv. 9, 10; xvii. 34. Matt. xi. 6. John xx. 29; iv. 48.

as the Apostles appeal to their miracles, or to the Old Testament. This is an appeal to Reason; and what is recorded, in some instances, was probably or certainly (as it is presumed from the necessity of the case) made in the rest, even when not recorded.

12. Such is the question which presents itself to readers of Scripture, as to the relation of Faith to Reason: and it is usual at this day to settle it in disparagement of Faith,—to say that Faith is but a moral quality, dependent upon Reason,—that Reason judges both of the evidence on which Scripture is to be received, and of the meaning of Scripture; and then Faith follows or not, according to the state of the heart; that we make up our minds by Reason without Faith, and then we proceed to adore and to obey by Faith apart from Reason; that, though Faith rests on testimony, not on reasonings, yet that testimony, in its turn, depends on Reason for the proof of its pretensions, so that Reason is an indispensable preliminary.

13. Now, in attempting to investigate what are the distinct offices of Faith and Reason in religious matters, and the relation of the one to the other, I observe, first, that undeniable though it be, that Reason has a power of analysis and criticism in all opinion and conduct, and that nothing is true or right but what may be justified, and, in a certain sense, proved by it, and undeniable, in consequence, that, unless the doctrines received by Faith are approvable by Reason, they have no claim to be regarded as true,

it does not therefore follow that Faith is actually grounded on Reason in the believing mind itself; unless, indeed, to take a parallel case, a judge can be called the origin, as well as the justifier, of the innocence or truth of those who are brought before him. A judge does not make men honest, but acquits and vindicates them: in like manner, Reason need not be the origin of Faith, as Faith exists in the very persons believing, though it does test and verify it. This, then, is one confusion, which must be cleared up in the question,—the assumption that Reason must be the inward principle of action in religious inquiries or conduct in the case of this or that individual, because, like a spectator, it acknowledges and concurs in what goes on;—the mistake of a critical for a creative power.

14. This distinction we cannot fail to recognize as true in itself, and applicable to the matter in hand. It is what we all admit at once as regards the principle of Conscience. No one will say that Conscience is against Reason, or that its dictates cannot be thrown into an argumentative form; yet who will, therefore, maintain that it is not an original principle, but must depend, before it acts, upon some previous processes of Reason? Reason analyzes the grounds and motives of action: a reason is an analysis, but is not the motive itself. As, then, Conscience is a simple element in our nature, yet its operations admit of being surveyed and scrutinized by Reason; so may Faith be cognizable, and its acts be justified, by Reason, without therefore being, in matter of fact, dependent upon it; and as we reprobate,

under the name of Utilitarianism, the substitution of Reason for Conscience, so perchance it is a parallel error to teach that a process of Reason is the *sine quâ non* for true religious Faith. When the Gospel is said to require a rational Faith, this need not mean more than that Faith is accordant to right Reason in the abstract, not that it results from it in the particular case.

15. A parallel and familiar instance is presented by the generally-acknowledged contrast between poetical or similar powers, and the art of criticism. That art is the sovereign awarder of praise and blame, and con-stitutes a court of appeal in matters of taste; as then the critic ascertains what he cannot himself create, so Reason may put its sanction upon the acts of Faith, without in consequence being the source from which Faith springs.

16. On the other hand, Faith certainly does seem, in matter of fact, to exist and operate quite independently of Reason. Will any one say that a child or uneducated person may not savingly act on Faith, without being able to produce reasons why he so acts? What suffi-cient view has he of the Evidences of Christianity? What logical proof of its divinity? If he has none, Faith, viewed as an internal habit or act, does not depend upon inquiry and examination, but has its own special basis, whatever that is, as truly as Conscience has. We see, then, that Reason may be the judge, without being the origin, of Faith; and that Faith may be justified by Reason, without making use of it. This is what it occurs to mention at first sight.

17. Next, I observe, that, whatever be the real distinction and relation existing between Faith and Reason, which it is not to our purpose at once to determine, the contrast that would be made between them, on a popular view, is this,—that Reason requires strong evidence before it assents, and Faith is content with weaker evidence.

18. For instance : when a well-known infidel of the last century argues, that the divinity of Christianity is founded on the testimony of the Apostles, in opposition to the experience of nature, and that the laws of nature are uniform, those of testimony variable, and scoffingly adds that Christianity is founded on Faith, not on Reason, what is this but saying that Reason is severer in its demands of evidence than Faith ?

19. Again, the founder of the recent Utilitarian School insists, that all evidence for miracles, before it can be received, should be brought into a court of law, and subjected to its searching forms :—this too is to imply that Reason demands exact proofs, but that Faith accepts inaccurate ones.

20. The same thing is implied in the notion which men of the world entertain, that Faith is but credulity, superstition, or fanaticism; these principles being notoriously such as are contented with insufficient evidence concerning their objects. On the other hand, scepticism, which shows itself in a dissatisfaction with evidence of whatever kind, is often called by the name of Reason. What Faith, then, and Reason are, when compared together, may be determined from

their counterfeits, — from the mutual relation of credulity and scepticism, which no one can doubt about.

21. In like manner, when mathematics are said to incline the mind towards doubt and latitudinarianism, this arises, according to the statement of one[6] who felt this influence of the study, from its indisposing us for arguments drawn from mere probabilities.

22. Or, to take particular instances:—When the proof of Infant Baptism is rested by its defenders on such texts as, "Suffer little children to come unto Me[7]," a man of a reasoning turn will object to such an argument as not sufficient to prove the point in hand. He will say that it does not follow that infants ought to be baptized, because they ought to be brought and dedicated to Christ; and that he waits for more decisive evidence.

23. Again, when the religious observance of a Christian Sabbath is defended from the Apostles' observance of it, it may be captiously argued that, considering St. Paul's express declaration, that the Sabbath, as such, is abolished, a mere practice, which happens to be recorded in the Acts, and which, for what we know, was temporary and accidental, cannot restore what was once done away, and introduce a Jewish rite into the Gospel. Religious persons, who cannot answer this objection, are often tempted to impute it to "man's wisdom," "the logic of the schools," "the pride of reason," and the like, and to insist on the necessity of the teachable study of Scrip-

[6] Bishop Watson.　　　　　[7] Matt. xix. 14.

ture as the means of overcoming it. We are not concerned to defend the language they use; but it is
plain that they corroborate what has been laid down,
as implying that Reason requires more evidence for
conviction than Faith.

24. When, then, Reason and Faith are contrasted
together, Faith means easiness, Reason, difficulty of
conviction. Reason is called either strong sense or
scepticism, according to the bias of the speaker; and
Faith, either teachableness or credulity.

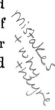

25. The next question, beyond which I shall not
proceed to-day, is this :—If this be so, how is it con-
formable to Reason to accept evidence less than Reason
requires? If Faith be what has been described, it
opposes itself to Reason, as being satisfied with the
less where Reason demands the more. If, then,
Reason be the healthy action of the mind, then Faith
must be its weakness. The answer to this question
will advance us one step farther in our investigation
into the relation existing between Faith and Reason.

26. Faith, then, as I have said, does not demand
evidence so strong as is necessary for what is commonly
considered a rational conviction, or belief on the ground
of Reason; and why? For this reason, because it is
mainly swayed by antecedent considerations. In this
way it is, that the two principles are opposed to one
another : Faith is influenced by previous notices, prepossessions, and (in a good sense of the word) prejudices; but
Reason, by direct and definite proof. The mind that
believes is acted upon by its own hopes, fears, and

existing opinions; whereas it is supposed to reason severely, when it rejects antecedent proof of a fact,— rejects every thing but the actual evidence producible in its favour. This will appear from a very few words.

27. [Faith is a principle of action, and action does not allow time for minute and finished investigations.] We may (if we will) think that such investigations are of high value; though, in truth, they have a tendency to blunt the practical energy of the mind, while they improve its scientific exactness; but, whatever be their character and consequences, they do not answer the needs of daily life. Diligent collection of evidence, sifting of arguments, and balancing of rival testimonies, may be suited to persons who have leisure and opportunity to act when and how they will; they are not suited to the multitude. Faith, then, as being a principle for the multitude and for conduct, is influenced more by what (in language familiar to us of this place) are called εἰκότα than by σημεῖα,—less by evidence, more by previously-entertained principles, views, and wishes.

28. This is the case with all Faith, and not merely religious. We hear a report in the streets, or read it in the public journals. We know nothing of the evidence; we do not know the witnesses, or any thing about them: yet sometimes we believe implicitly, sometimes not; sometimes we believe without asking for evidence, sometimes we disbelieve till we receive it. Did a rumour circulate of a destructive earthquake in Syria or the south of Europe, we should readily credit it; both because it might easily be true, and because it

was nothing to us though it were. Did the report relate to countries nearer home, we should try to trace and authenticate it. We do not call for evidence till antecedent probabilities fail.

29. Again, it is scarcely necessary to point out how much our inclinations have to do with our belief. It is almost a proverb, that persons believe what they wish to be true. They will with difficulty admit the failure of any cherished project, or listen to a messenger of ill tidings. It may be objected, indeed, that great desire of an object sometimes makes us incredulous that we have attained it. Certainly ; but this is only when we consider its attainment improbable, as well as desirable. Thus St. Thomas doubted of the Resurrection; and thus Jacob, especially as having already been deceived by his children, believed not the news of Joseph's being governor of Egypt. "Jacob's heart fainted, for he believed them not . . . but when he saw the waggons which Joseph had sent to carry him, the spirit of Jacob their father revived."

30. The case is the same as regards preconceived opinions. Men readily believe reports unfavourable to persons they dislike, or confirmations of theories of their own. "Trifles light as air" are all that the predisposed mind requires for belief and action.

31. Such are the inducements to belief which prevail with all of us, by a law of our nature, and whether they are in the particular case reasonable or not. (When the probabilities we assume do not really exist, or our wishes are inordinate, or our opinions are wrong, our Faith degenerates into weakness, extravagance, super-

stition, enthusiasm, bigotry, prejudice, as the case
may be; but when our prepossessions are unexceptionable, then we are right in believing or not believing,
not indeed without, but upon slender evidence.

32. Whereas Reason then (as the word is commonly
used) rests on the evidence, Faith is influenced by
presumptions; and hence, while Reason requires
rigid proofs, Faith is satisfied with vague or defective
ones.

33. It will serve to bring out this doctrine into a
more tangible form, to set down some inferences and
reflections to which it leads, themselves not unimpor-
tant.

34. (1.) First, then, I would draw attention to the
coincidence, for such it would seem to be, of what has
been said, with St. Paul's definition of Faith in the
text. He might have defined it " reliance on the word
of another," or "acceptance of a divine message," or
" submission of the intellect to mysteries," or in other
ways equally true and more theological; but instead of
such accounts of it, he adopts a definition bearing upon
its nature, and singularly justifying the view which has
been here taken of it. " Faith," he says, " is the substance" or realizing " of things hoped for." It is the
reckoning that to be, which it hopes or wishes to be;
not " the realizing of things proved by evidence." Its
desire is its main evidence; or, as the Apostle expressly
goes on to say, it makes its own evidence, " being the
evidence of things not seen." And this is the cause, as
is natural, why Faith seems to the world so irrational,

as St. Paul says in other Epistles. Not that it has no
grounds in Reason, that is, in evidence ; but because it
is satisfied with so much less than would be necessary,
were it not for the bias of the mind, that to the world
its evidence seems like nothing.

35. (2.) Next it is plain in what sense Faith is a
moral principle. It is created in the mind, not so much
by facts, as by probabilities ; and since probabilities
have no definite ascertained value, and are reducible to
no scientific standard, what are such to each individual,
depends on his moral temperament. A good and a bad
man will think very different things probable. In the
judgment of a rightly disposed mind, objects are desirable and attainable which irreligious men will consider
to be but fancies. Such a correct moral judgment and
view of things is the very medium in which the argument for Christianity has its constraining influence ; a
faint proof under circumstances being more availing
than a strong one, apart from those circumstances.

36. This holds good as regards the matter as well
as the evidence of the Gospel. It is difficult to say
where the evidence, whether for Scripture or the Creed,
would be found, if it were deprived of those adven-
titious illustrations which it extracts and absorbs from
the mind of the inquirer, and which a merciful Providence places there for that very purpose. Texts have
their illuminating power, from the atmosphere of habit,
opinion, usage, tradition, through which we see them.
On the other hand, irreligious men are adequate judges
of the value of mere evidence, when the decision turns
upon it ; for evidence is addressed to the Reason, com-

pels the Reason to assent so far as it is strong, and
allows the Reason to doubt or disbelieve so far as it is
weak. The blood on Joseph's coat of many colours
was as perceptible to enemy as to friend; miracles
appeal to the senses of all men, good and bad; and,
while their supernatural character is learned from that
experience of nature which is common to the just and
to the unjust, the fact of their occurrence depends on
considerations about testimony, enthusiasm, imposture,
and the like, in which there is nothing inward, nothing
personal. It is a sort of proof which a man does not
make for himself, but which is made for him. It exists
independently of him, and is apprehended from its own
clear and objective character. It is its very boast that
it does but require a candid hearing; nay, it especially
addresses itself to the unbeliever, and engages to convert him as if against his will. There is no room for
choice; there is no merit, no praise or blame, in believing or disbelieving; no test of character in the one
or the other. But a man *is* responsible for his faith,
because he is responsible for his likings and dislikings,
his hopes and his opinions, on all of which his faith
depends. And whereas unbelievers do not see this
distinction, they persist in saying that a man is as
little responsible for his faith as for his bodily functions;
that both are from nature; that the will cannot make a
weak proof a strong one; that if a person thinks a
certain reason goes only a certain way, he is dishonest
in attempting to make it go farther; that if he is after
all wrong in his judgment, it is only his misfortune,
not his fault; that he is acted on by certain principles

from without, and must obey the laws of evidence, which are necessary and constant. But in truth, though a given evidence does not vary in force, the antecedent probability attending it does vary without limit, according to the temper of the mind surveying it.

37. (3.) Again: it is plain from what has been said, why our great divines, Bull and Taylor, not to mention others, have maintained that justifying faith is *fides formata charitate,* or in St. Paul's words, πίστις δι' ἀγάπης ἐνεργουμένη. For as that faith, which is not moral, but depends upon evidence, is *fides formata ratione,*— dead faith, which an infidel may have; so that which justifies or is acceptable in God's sight, lives in, and from, a desire after those things which it accepts and confesses.

38. (4.) And here, again, we see what is meant by saying that Faith is a supernatural principle. The laws of evidence are the same in regard to the Gospel as to profane matters. If they were the sole arbiters of Faith, of course Faith could have nothing supernatural in it. But love of the great Object of Faith, watchful attention to Him, readiness to believe Him near, easiness to believe Him interposing in human affairs, fear of the risk of slighting or missing what may really come from Him; these are feelings not natural to fallen man, and they come only of supernatural grace; and these are the feelings which make us think evidence sufficient, which falls short of a proof in itself. The natural man has no heart for the promises of the Gospel, and dissects its evidence without reverence, without hope, without suspense, without misgivings

and, while he analyzes that evidence perhaps more philosophically than another, and treats it more luminously, and sums up its result with the precision and propriety of a legal tribunal, he rests in it as an end, and neither attains the farther truths at which it points, nor inhales the spirit which it breathes.

39. (5.) And this remark bears upon a fact which has sometimes perplexed Christians,—that those philosophers [8], ancient and modern, who have been eminent in physical science, have not unfrequently shown a tendency to infidelity. The system of physical causes is so much more tangible and satisfying than that of final, that unless there be a pre-existent and independent interest in the inquirer's mind, leading him to dwell on the phenomena which betoken an Intelligent Creator, he will certainly follow out those which terminate in the hypothesis of a settled order of nature and self-sustained laws. It is indeed a great question whether Atheism is not as philosophically consistent with the phenomena of the physical world, taken by themselves [9], as the doctrine of a creative and governing Power. But, however this be, the practical safeguard against Atheism in the case of scientific inquirers is the inward need and desire, the inward

[8] Vide Bacon, de Augm. Scient. § 5.

[[9] "*Physical* phenomena, *taken by themselves ;*" that is, apart from psychological phenomena, apart from moral considerations, apart from the moral principles by which they must be interpreted, and apart from that idea of God which wakes up in the mind under the stimulus of intellectual training. The question is, whether physical phenomena logically *teach* us, or on the other hand logically *remind* us of the Being of a God. In either case, if they do not bring to us this cardinal truth, we are, in St. Paul's words, "without excuse."]

experience of that Power, existing in the mind before and independently of their examination of His material world.

40. (6.) And in this lies the main fallacy of the celebrated argument against miracles, already referred to, of a Scotch philosopher, whose depth and subtlety all must acknowledge. Let us grant (at least for argument's sake) that judging from the experience of life, it is more likely that witnesses should deceive, than that the laws of nature should be suspended. Still there may be considerations distinct from this view of the question which turn the main probability the other way,—viz. the likelihood, *à priori*, that a Revelation should be given. Here, then, we see how Faith is and is not according to Reason; taken together with the antecedent probability that Providence will reveal Himself to mankind, such evidence of the fact, as is otherwise deficient, may be enough for conviction, even in the judgment of Reason. But it need not be enough, apart from that probability. That is, Reason, weighing evidence only, or arguing from external experience, is counter to Faith; but, admitting the legitimate influence and logical import of the moral feelings, it concurs with it.

41. (7.) Hence it would seem as though Paley had hardly asked enough in the Introduction to his work on the Evidences, when he says of the doctrine of a future state and of a revelation relating to it, " that it is not necessary for our purpose that these propositions be capable of proof, or even that, by arguments drawn from the light of nature, they can be made out to be

probable; it is enough that we are able to say concerning them, that they are not so violently improbable," that the propositions or the facts connected with them ought to be rejected at first sight. This acute and ingenious writer here asks leave to do only what the Utilitarian writer mentioned in a former place demands should be done, namely, to bring his case (as it were) into court; as if trusting to the strength of his evidence, dispensing with moral and religious considerations on one side or the other, and arguing from the mere phenomena of the human mind, that is, the inducements, motives, and habits according to which man acts. I will not say more of such a procedure than that it seems to me dangerous. As miracles, according to the common saying, are not wrought to convince Atheists, and, when they claim to be evidence of a Revelation, presuppose the being of an Intelligent Agent to whom they may be referred, so Evidences in general are grounded on the admission that the doctrine they are brought to prove is, not merely not inconsistent, but actually accordant with the laws of His moral governance. Miracles, though they contravene the physical

laws of the universe, tend to the due fulfilment of its moral laws. And in matter of fact, when they were wrought, they addressed persons who were already believers, not in the mere probability, but even in the truth of supernatural revelations. This appears from the preaching of our Lord and His Apostles, who are accustomed to appeal to the religious feelings of their hearers; and who, though they might fail with the many, did thus persuade those who were persuaded—

not, indeed, the sophists of Athens or the politicians of
Rome, yet men of very different states of mind one from
another, the pious, the superstitious, and the dissolute,
different, indeed, but all agreeing in this, in the acknowledgment of truths beyond this world, whether
or not their knowledge was clear, or their lives consistent,—the devout Jew, the proselyte of the gate,
the untaught fisherman, the outcast Publican, and the
pagan idolater.

42. (8.) And last of all, we here see what divines mean,
who have been led to depreciate what are called the
Evidences of Religion. The last century, a time
when love was cold, is noted as being especially the
Age of Evidences; and now, when more devout and
zealous feelings have been excited, there is, I need
scarcely say, a disposition manifested in various quar-
ters, to think lightly, as of the eighteenth century,
so of its boasted demonstrations. I have not here to
make any formal comparison of the last century with
the present, or to say whether they are nearer the
truth, who in these matters advance with the present
age, or who loiter behind with the preceding. I will
only state what seems to me meant when persons
disparage the Evidences,—viz. they consider that, as
a general rule, religious minds embrace the Gospel
mainly on the great antecedent probability of a Revelation, and the suitableness of the Gospel to their
needs; on the other hand, that on men of irreligious
minds Evidences are thrown away. Further, they
perhaps would say, that to insist much on matters
which are for the most part so useless for any prac-

tical purpose, draws men away from the true view of Christianity, and leads them to think that Faith is mainly the result of argument, that religious Truth is a legitimate matter of disputation, and that they who reject it rather err in judgment than commit sin. They think they see in the study in question a tendency to betray the sacredness and dignity of Religion, when those who profess themselves its champions allow themselves to stand on the same ground as philosophers of the world, admit the same principles, and only aim at drawing different conclusions.

43. For is not this the error, the common and fatal error, of the world, to think itself a judge of Religious Truth without preparation of heart? "I am the good Shepherd, and know My sheep, and am known of Mine." "He goeth before them, and the sheep follow Him, for they know His voice." "The pure in heart shall see God:" "to the meek mysteries are revealed;" "he that is spiritual judgeth all things." "The darkness comprehendeth it not." Gross eyes see not; heavy ears hear not. But in the schools of the world the ways towards Truth are considered high roads open to all men, however disposed, at all times. Truth is to be approached without homage. Every one is considered on a level with his neighbour; or rather the powers of the intellect, acuteness, sagacity, subtlety, and depth, are thought the guides into Truth. Men consider that they have as full a right to discuss religious subjects, as if they were themselves religious. They will enter upon the most sacred points of Faith at the moment, at their pleasure,—if it so happen, in

a careless frame of mind, in their hours of recre-
ation, over the wine cup. Is it wonderful that they
so frequently end in becoming indifferentists, and
conclude that Religious Truth is but a name, that all
men are right and all wrong, from witnessing externally
the multitude of sects and parties, and from the clear
consciousness they possess within, that their own inquiries end in darkness?

44. Yet, serious as these dangers may be, it does
not therefore follow that the Evidences may not be of
great service to persons in particular frames of mind.
Careless persons may be startled by them as they
might be startled by a miracle, which is no necessary
condition of believing, notwithstanding. Again, they
often serve as a test of honesty of mind; their rejection
being the condemnation of unbelievers. Again, religious persons sometimes get perplexed and lose their
way; are harassed by objections; see difficulties which
they cannot surmount; are a prey to subtlety of mind
or over-anxiety. Under these circumstances the varied
proofs of Christianity will be a stay, a refuge, an
encouragement, a rallying point for Faith, a gracious
economy; and even in the case of the most established
Christian they are a source of gratitude and reverent
admiration, and a means of confirming faith and hope.
Nothing need be detracted from the use of the Evidences on this score; much less can any sober mind
run into the wild notion that actually no proof at all is
implied in the maintenance, or may be exacted for
the profession of Christianity. I would only maintain
that that proof need not be the subject of analysis,

or take a methodical form, or be complete and symmetrical, in the believing mind; and that probability is its life. I do but say that it is antecedent probability that gives meaning to those arguments from facts which are commonly called the Evidences of Revelation; that, whereas mere probability proves nothing, mere facts persuade no one; that probability is to fact, as the soul to the body; that mere presumptions may have no force, but that mere facts have no warmth. A mutilated and defective evidence suffices for persuasion where the heart is alive; but dead evidences, however perfect, can but create a dead faith.

45. To conclude: It will be observed, I have not yet said what Reason really is, or what is its relation to Faith, but have merely contrasted the two together, taking Reason in the sense popularly ascribed to the word. Nor do I aim at more than ascertaining the sense in which the words Faith and Reason are used by Christian and Catholic writers. If I shall succeed in this, I shall be content, without attempting to defend it. Half the controversies in the world are verbal ones; and could they be brought to a plain issue, they would be brought to a prompt termination. Parties engaged in them would then perceive, either that in substance they agreed together, or that their difference was one of first principles. This is the great object to be aimed at in the present age, though confessedly a very arduous one. We need not dispute, we need not prove,—we need but define. At all events, let us, if we can, do this first of all; and then see who are left

for us to dispute with, what is left for us to prove. Controversy, at least in this age, does not lie between the hosts of heaven, Michael and his Angels on the one side, and the powers of evil on the other; but it is a sort of night battle, where each fights for himself, and friend and foe stand together. When men understand what 'each other mean, they see, for the most part, that controversy is either superfluous or hopeless.

SERMON XI.

THE NATURE OF FAITH IN RELATION TO REASON.

(Preached January 13, 1839.)

1 Cor. i. 27.

*" God hath chosen the foolish things of the world to confound the wise,
and God hath chosen the weak things of the world to confound the
things which are mighty."*

1. IT is usual at this day to speak as if Faith were
simply of a moral nature, and depended and followed
upon a distinct act of Reason beforehand,—Reason
warranting, on the ground of evidence, both ample and
carefully examined, that the Gospel comes from God,
and *then* Faith embracing it. On the other hand, the
more Scriptural representation seems to be this, which
is obviously more agreeable to facts also, that, instead
of there being really any such united process of reasoning first, and then believing, the act of Faith is sole
and elementary, and complete in itself, and depends on
no process of mind previous to it: and this doctrine is
borne out by the common opinion of men, who, though
they contrast Faith and Reason, yet rather consider
Faith to be weak Reason, than a moral quality or act
following upon Reason. The Word of Life is offered to
a man; and, on its being offered, he has Faith in it.

Why ? On these two grounds,—the word of its human messenger, and the likelihood of the message. And why does he feel the message to be probable ? Because he has a love for it, his love being strong, though the testimony is weak. He has a keen sense of the intrinsic excellence of the message, of its desirableness, of its likeness to what it seems to him Divine Goodness would vouchsafe did He vouchsafe any, of the need of a Revelation, and its probability. Thus Faith is the reasoning of a religious mind, or of what Scripture calls a right or renewed heart, which acts upon presumptions rather than evidence, which speculates and ventures on the future when it cannot make sure of it.

2. Thus, to take the instance of St. Paul preaching at Athens : he told his hearers that he came as a messenger from that God whom they worshipped already, though ignorantly, and of whom their poets spoke. He appealed to the conviction that was lodged within them of the spiritual nature and the unity of God; and he exhorted them to turn to Him who had appointed One to judge the whole world hereafter. This was an appeal to the antecedent probability of a Revelation, which would be estimated variously according to the desire of it existing in each breast. Now, what was the evidence he gave, in order to concentrate those various antecedent presumptions, to which he referred, in behalf of the message which he brought ? Very slight, yet something ; not a miracle, but his own word that God had raised Christ from the dead ; very like the evidence given to the mass of men now, or

rather not so much. No one will say it was strong
evidence; yet, aided by the novelty, and what may be
called originality, of the claim, its strangeness and
improbability considered as a mere invention, and the
personal bearing of the Apostle, and supported by the
full force of the antecedent probabilities which existed,
and which he stirred within them, it was enough. It
was enough, for some did believe,—enough, not indeed
in itself, but enough for those who had love, and therefore were inclined to believe. To those who had no
fears, wishes, longings, or expectations, of another
world, he was but " a babbler;" those who had such,
or, in the Evangelist's words in another place, were
" ordained to eternal life," " clave unto him, and believed."

3. This instance, then, seems very fully to justify
the view of Faith which I have been taking, that it is
an act of Reason, but of what the world would call weak,
bad, or insufficient Reason; and that, because it rests
on presumption more, and on evidence less. On the
other hand, I conceive that this passage of Scripture
does not fit in at all with the modern theory now in esteem
that Faith is a mere moral act, dependent on a previous
process of clear and cautious Reason. If so, one would
think that St. Paul had no claim upon the faith of his
hearers, till he had first wrought a miracle, such as
Reason might approve, in token that his message was
to be handed over to the acceptance of Faith.

4. Now, that this difference of theories as regards
the nature of religious Faith is not a trifling one, is
evident, perhaps, from the conclusions which I drew

from it last week, which, if legitimate, are certainly important: and as feeling it to be a serious difference, I now proceed to state distinctly what I conceive to be the relation of Faith to Reason. I observe, then, as follows :—

5. We are surrounded by beings which exist quite independently of us,—exist whether we exist, or cease to exist, whether we have cognizance of them or no. These we commonly separate into two great divisions, material and immaterial. Of the material we have direct knowledge through the senses; we are sensible of the existence of persons and things, of their properties and modes, of their relations towards each other, and the courses of action which they carry on. Of all these we are directly cognizant through the senses; we see and hear what passes, and that immediately. As to immaterial beings, that we have faculties analogous to sense by which we have direct knowledge of their presence, does not appear, except indeed as regards our own soul and its acts. But so far is certain at least, that we are not conscious of possessing them; and we account it, and rightly, to be enthusiasm to profess such consciousness. At times, indeed, that consciousness has been imparted, as in some of the appearances of God to man contained in Scripture: but, in the ordinary course of things, whatever direct intercourse goes on between the soul and immaterial beings, whether we perceive them or not, and are influenced by them or not, certainly we have no consciousness of that perception or influence, such as our senses convey to us in the perception of

things material. The senses, then, are the only instruments which we know to be granted to us for
direct and immediate acquaintance with things external
to us.   Moreover, it is obvious that even our senses
convey us but a little way out of ourselves, and introduce us to the external world only under circumstances,
under conditions of time and place, and of certain media
through which they act.   We must be near things to
touch them ; we must be interrupted by no simultaneous
sounds to hear them; we must have light to see them ;
we can neither see, hear, nor touch things past or future.

6. Now, Reason is that faculty of the mind by which
this deficiency is supplied; by which knowledge of
things external to us, of beings, facts, and events, is
attained beyond the range of sense.   It ascertains for
us not natural things only, or immaterial only, or
present only, or past, or future; but, even if limited
in its power, it is unlimited in its range, viewed as a
faculty, though, of course, in individuals it varies in
range also.   It reaches to the ends of the universe,
and to the throne of God beyond them; it brings us
knowledge, whether clear or uncertain, still knowledge, in whatever degree of perfection, from every
side; but, at the same time, with this characteristic,
that it obtains it indirectly, not directly.

7. Reason does not really perceive any thing; but
it is a faculty of proceeding from things that are per-
ceived to things which are not; the existence of which
it certifies to us on the hypothesis of something else
being known to exist, in other words, being assumed
to be true.

8. Such is Reason, simply considered; and hence the fitness of a number of words which are commonly used to denote it and its acts. For instance: its act is usually considered a process, which, of course, a progress of thought from one idea to the other must be; an exercise of mind, which perception through the senses can hardly be called; or, again, an investigation, or an analysis; or it is said to compare, discriminate, judge, and decide: all which words imply, not simply assent to the reality of certain external facts, but a search into grounds, and an assent upon grounds. It is, then, the faculty of gaining knowledge upon grounds given; and its exercise lies in asserting one thing, because of some other thing; and, when its exercise is conducted rightly, it leads to knowledge; when wrongly, to apparent knowledge, to opinion, and error.

9. Now, if this be Reason, an act or process of Faith, simply considered, is certainly an exercise of Reason; whether a right exercise or not is a farther question; and, whether so to call it, is a sufficient account of it, is a farther question. It is an acceptance of things as real, which the senses do not convey, upon certain previous grounds; it is an instrument of indirect knowledge concerning things external to us,—the process being such as the following: "I assent to this doctrine as true, because I have been taught it;" or, "because superiors tell me so;" or, "because good men think so;" or, "because very different men think so;" or, "because all men;" or, "most men;" or, "because it is established;" or, "because persons whom I trust

say that it was once guaranteed by miracles;" or,
"because one who is said to have wrought miracles,"
or "who says he wrought them," "has taught it;" or,
"because I have seen one who saw the miracles;" or,
"because I saw what I took to be a miracle;" or for
all or some of these reasons together. Some such
exercise of Reason is the act of Faith, considered in its
nature.

10. On the other hand, Faith plainly lies exposed
to the popular charge of being a faulty exercise of
Reason, as being conducted on insufficient grounds;
and, I suppose, so much must be allowed on all hands,
either that it is illogical, or that the mind has some
grounds which are not fully brought out, when the
process is thus exhibited. In other words, that when
the mind savingly believes, the reasoning which that
belief involves, if it be logical, does not merely proceed
from the actual evidence, but from other grounds
besides.

11. I say, there is this alternative in viewing the
particular process of Reason which is involved in Faith;
—to say either that the process is illogical, or the subject-matter more or less special and recondite; the act
of inference faulty, or the premisses undeveloped; that
Faith is weak, or that it is unearthly. Scripture says
that it is unearthly, and the world says that it is weak.

12. This, then, being the imputation brought against
Faith, that it is the reasoning of a weak mind, whereas
it is in truth the reasoning of a divinely enlightened
one, let me now, in a few words, attempt to show the
analogy of this state of things, with what takes place in

regard to other exercises of Reason also; that is, I shall attempt to show that Faith is not the only exercise of Reason, which, when critically examined, would be called unreasonable, and yet is not so.

13. (1.) In truth, nothing is more common among men of a reasoning turn than to consider that no one reasons well but themselves. All men of course think that they themselves are right and others wrong, who differ from them; and so far all men must find fault with the reasonings of others, since no one proposes to act without reasons of some kind. Accordingly, so far as men are accustomed to analyze the opinions of others and to contemplate their processes of thought, they are tempted to despise them as illogical. If any one sets about examining why his neighbours are on one side in political questions, not on another; why for or against certain measures, of a social, economical, or civil nature; why they belong to this religious party, not to that; why they hold this or that doctrine; why they have certain tastes in literature; or why they hold certain views in matters of opinion; it is needless to say that, if he measures their grounds merely by the reasons which they produce, he will have no difficulty in holding them up to ridicule, or even to censure.

14. And so again as to the deductions made from definite facts common to all. From the sight of the same sky one may augur fine weather, another bad; from the signs of the times one the coming in of good, another of evil; from the same actions of individuals one infers moral greatness, another depravity or perversity, one simplicity, another craft; upon the same evidence

P

one justifies, another condemns. The miracles of
Christianity were in early times imputed by some to
magic, others they converted; the union of its professors was ascribed to seditious and traitorous aims by
some, while others it moved to say, " See how these
Christians love one another." The phenomena of the
physical world have given rise to a variety of theories,
that is, of alleged facts, at which they are supposed to
point; theories of astronomy, chemistry, and physiology;
theories religious and atheistical. The same events are
considered to prove a particular providence, and not ;
to attest the divinity of one religion or of another.
The downfall of the Roman Empire was to Pagans a
refutation, to Christians an evidence, of Christianity.
Such is the diversity with which men reason, showing
us that Faith is not the only exercise of Reason, which
approves itself to some and not to others, or which is,
in the common sense of the word, irrational.

15. Nor can it fairly be said that such varieties do
arise from deficiency in the power of reasoning in the
multitude; and that Faith, such as I have described it, is
but proved thereby to be a specimen of such deficiency.
This is what men of clear intellects are not slow to
imagine. Clear, strong, steady intellects, if they are
not deep, will look on these differences in deduction
chiefly as failures in the reasoning faculty, and will
despise them or excuse them accordingly. Such are
the men who are commonly latitudinarians in religion
on the one hand, or innovators on the other; men of
exact or acute but shallow minds, who consider all men
wrong but themselves, yet think it no matter though

they be; who regard the pursuit of truth only as a syllogistic process, and failure in attaining it as arising merely from a want of mental conformity with the laws on which just reasoning is conducted. But surely there is no greater mistake than this. For the experience of life contains abundant evidence that in practical matters, when their minds are really roused, men commonly are not bad reasoners. Men do not mistake when their interest is concerned. They have an instinctive sense in which direction their path lies towards it, and how they must act consistently with self-preservation or self-aggrandisement. And so in the case of questions in which party spirit, or political opinion, or ethical principle, or personal feeling, is concerned, men have a surprising sagacity, often unknown to themselves, in finding their own place. However remote the connexion between the point in question and their own creed, or habits, or feelings, the principles which they profess guide them unerringly to their legitimate issues; and thus it often happens that in apparently indifferent practices or usages or sentiments, or in questions of science, or politics, or literature, we can almost prophesy beforehand, from their religious or moral views, where certain persons will stand, and often can defend them far better than they defend themselves. The same thing is proved from the internal consistency of such religious creeds as are allowed time and space to develope freely; such as Primitive Christianity, or the Medieval system, or Calvinism—a consistency which nevertheless is wrought out in and through the rude and inaccurate minds of the multitude. Again, it is

proved from the uniformity observable in the course of
the same doctrine in different ages and countries,
whether it be political, religious, or philosophical; the
laws of Reason forcing it on into the same developments, the same successive phases, the same rise, and
the same decay, so that its recorded history in one
century will almost suit its prospective course in the
next.

16. All this shows, that in spite of the inaccuracy in
expression, or (if we will) in thought, which prevails in
the world, men on the whole do not reason incorrectly.
If their reason itself were in fault, they would reason
each in his own way : whereas they form into schools,
and that not merely from imitation and sympathy, but
certainly from internal compulsion, from the constraining influence of their several principles. They may
argue badly, but they reason well; that is, their professed grounds are no sufficient measures of their real
ones. And in like manner, though the evidence with
which Faith is content is apparently inadequate to its
purpose, yet this is no proof of real weakness or imperfection in its reasoning. It seems to be contrary to
Reason, yet is not ; it is but independent of and distinct
from what are called philosophical inquiries, intellectual
systems, courses of argument, and the like.

17. So much on the general phenomena which attend
the exercise of this great faculty, one of the characteristics of human over brute natures. Whether we
consider processes of Faith or other exercise of Reason,
men advance forward on grounds which they do not,
or cannot produce, or if they could, yet could not prove

to be true, on latent or antecedent grounds which they take for granted.

18. (2.) Next, let it be observed, that however full and however precise our producible grounds may be, however systematic our method, however clear and tangible our evidence, yet when our argument is traced down to its simple elements, there must ever be something assumed ultimately which is incapable of proof, and without which our conclusion will be as illogical as Faith is apt to seem to men of the world.

19. To take the case of actual evidence, and that of the strongest kind. Now, whatever it be, its cogency must be a thing taken for granted; so far it is its own evidence, and can only be received on instinct or prejudice. For instance, we trust our senses, and that in spite of their often deceiving us. They even contradict each other at times, yet we trust them. But even were they ever consistent, never unfaithful, still their fidelity would not be thereby proved. We consider that there is so strong an antecedent probability that they are faithful, that we dispense with proof. We take the point for granted; or, if we have grounds for it, these either lie in our secret belief in the stability of nature, or in the preserving presence and uniformity of Divine Providence,—which, again, are points assumed. As, then, the senses may and do deceive us, and yet we trust them from a secret instinct, so it need not be weakness or rashness, if upon a certain presentiment of mind we trust to the fidelity of testimony offered for a Revelation.

20. Again: we rely implicitly on our memory, and

that, too, in spite of its being obviously unstable and treacherous. And we trust to memory for the truth of most of our opinions; the grounds on which we hold them not being at a given moment all present to our minds. We trust to memory to inform us what we do hold and what we do not. It may be said, that without such assumption the world could not go on: true; and in the same way the Church could not go on without Faith. Acquiescence in testimony, or in evidence not stronger than testimony, is the only method, as far as we see, by which the next world can be revealed to us.

21. The same remarks apply to our assumption of the fidelity of our reasoning powers; which in certain instances we implicitly believe, though we know they have deceived us in others.

22. Were it not for these instincts, it cannot be doubted but our experience of the deceivableness of Senses, Memory, and Reason, would perplex us much as to our practical reliance on them in matters of this world. And so, as regards the matters of another, they who have not that instinctive apprehension of the Omnipresence of God and His unwearied and minute Providence which holiness and love create within us, must not be surprised to find that the evidence of Christianity does not perform an office which was never intended for it,—viz. that of recommending itself as well as the Revelation. Nothing, then, which Scripture says about Faith, however startling it may be at first sight, is inconsistent with the state in which we find ourselves by nature with reference to the acquisition of know-

ledge generally,—a state in which we must assume something to prove anything, and can gain nothing without a venture.

23. (3.) To proceed. Next let it be considered, that the following law seems to hold in our attainment of knowledge, that according to its desirableness, whether in point of excellence, or range, or intricacy, so is the subtlety of the evidence on which it is received. We are so constituted, that if we insist upon being as sure as is conceivable, in every step of our course, we must be content to creep along the ground, and can never soar. If we are intended for great ends, we are called to great hazards; and, whereas we are given absolute certainty[1] in nothing, we must in all things choose between doubt and inactivity, and the conviction that we are under the eye of One who, for whatever reason, exercises us with the less evidence when He might give us the greater. He has put it into our hands, who loves us; and He bids us examine it, indeed, with our best judgment, reject this and accept that, but still all the while as loving Him in our turn; not coldly and critically, but with the thought of His presence, and the reflection that perchance by the defects of the evidence He is trying our love of its matter; and that perchance it is a law of His Providence to speak less loudly the more He promises. For instance, the touch is the most certain and cautious,

[1] Here, by "absolute certainty in nothing," is meant, as I believe, "proofs such as absolutely to make doubt impossible;" and by "between doubt and inactivity," is meant, not formal doubt, but a state of mind which recognizes the possibility of doubting. Vide *infra* xiv. 34]

but it is the most circumscribed of our senses, and reaches but an arm's length. The eye, which takes in a far wider range, acts only in the light. Reason, which extends beyond the province of sense or the present time, is circuitous and indirect in its convey-ance of knowledge, which, even when distinct, is traced out pale and faint, as distant objects on the horizon. And Faith, again, by which we get to know divine things, rests on the evidence of testimony, weak in proportion to the excellence of the blessing attested. And as Reason, with its great conclusions, is con-fessedly a higher instrument than Sense with its secure premisses, so Faith rises above Reason, in its subject-matter, more than it falls below it in the obscurity of its process. And it is, I say, but agree-able to analogy, that Divine Truth should be attained by so subtle and indirect a method, a method less tangible than others, less open to analysis, reducible but partially to the forms of Reason, and the ready sport of objection and cavil.

24. (4.) Further, much might be observed concern-ing the special delicacy and abstruseness of such reasoning processes as attend the acquisition of all higher knowledge. It is not too much to say that there is no one of the greater achievements of the Reason, which would show to advantage, which would be apparently justified and protected from criticism, if thrown into the technical forms which the science of argument requires. The most remarkable victories of genius, remarkable both in their originality and the confidence with which they have been pursued, have

been gained, as though by invisible weapons, by ways of thought so recondite and intricate that the mass of men are obliged to take them on trust, till the event or other evidence confirms them. Such are the methods which penetrating intellects have invented in mathematical science, which look like sophisms till they issue in truths[2]. Here, even in the severest of disciplines, and in absolutely demonstrative processes, the instrument of discovery is so subtle, that technical expressions and formulæ are of necessity substituted for it, to thread the labyrinth withal, by way of tempering its difficulties to the grosser reason of the many. Or, let it be considered how rare and immaterial (if I may use the words) is metaphysical proof : how difficult to embrace, even when presented to us by philosophers in whose clearness of mind and good sense we fully confide; and what a vain system of words without ideas such men seem to be piling up, while perhaps we are obliged to confess that it must be we who are dull, not they who are fanciful; and that, whatever be the character of their investigations, we want the vigour or flexibility of mind to judge of them. Or let us attempt to ascertain the passage of the mind, when slight indications in things present are made the informants of what is to be. Consider the preternatural sagacity with which a great general knows what his friends and enemies are about, and what will be the

[2 "The principle of concrete reasoning," which leads to Faith, "is parallel to the method of proof, which is the foundation of modern mathematical science, as contained in the celebrated Lemma, with which Newton opens his *Principia*." Essay on Assent, viii. 2, 3.]

final result, and where, of their combined movements, —and then say whether, if he were required to argue the matter in word or on paper, all his most brilliant conjectures might not be refuted, and all his producible reasons exposed as illogical.

25. And, in an analogous way, Faith is a process of the Reason, in which so much of the grounds of infer- ence cannot be exhibited, so much lies in the character of the mind itself, in its general view of things, its estimate of the probable and the improbable, its im- pressions concerning God's will, and its anticipations derived from its own inbred wishes, that it will ever seem to the world irrational and despicable;—till, that is, the event confirms it. The act of mind, for instance, by which an unlearned person savingly believes the Gospel, on the word of his teacher, may be analogous to the exercise of sagacity in a great statesman or general, supernatural grace doing for the uncultivated reason what genius does for them.

26. (5.) Now it is a singular confirmation of this view of the subject, that the reasonings of inspired men in Scripture, nay, of God Himself, are of this recondite nature; so much so, that irreverent minds scarcely hesitate to treat them with the same contempt which they manifest towards the faith of ordinary Christians. St. Paul's arguments have been long ago abandoned even by men who professed to be defenders of Christianity. Nor can it be said surely that the line of thought (if I may dare so to speak), on which some of our Ever-blessed Saviour's discourses proceed, is more intelligible to our feeble minds. And here, more-

over, let it be noted that, supposing the kind of reasoning which we call Faith to be of the subtle character which I am maintaining, and the instances of professed reasoning found in Scripture to be of a like subtlety, light is thrown upon another remarkable circumstance, which no one can deny, and which some have made an objection,—I mean, the indirectness of the Scripture proof on which the Catholic doctrines rest. It may be, that such a peculiarity in the inspired text is the proper correlative of Faith; such a text the proper matter for Faith to work upon; so that a Scripture such as we have, and not such as the Pentateuch was to the Jews, may be implied in our being under Faith and not under the Law.

27. (6.) Lastly, it should be observed that the analogy which I have been pursuing extends to moral actions, and their properties and objects, as well as to intellectual exercises. According as objects are great, the mode of attaining them is extraordinary; and again, according as it is extraordinary, so is the merit of the action. Here, instead of going to Scripture, or to a religious standard, let me appeal to the world's judgment in the matter. Military fame, for instance, power, character for greatness of mind, distinction in experimental science, are all sought and attained by risks and adventures. Courage does not consist in calculation, but in fighting against chances. The statesman whose name endures, is he who ventures upon measures which seem perilous, and yet succeed, and can be only justified on looking back upon them. Firmness and greatness of soul are shown, when a ruler

stands his ground on his instinctive perception of a
truth which the many scoff at, and which seems failing.
The religious enthusiast bows the hearts of men to a
voluntary obedience, who has the keenness to see, and
the boldness to appeal to, principles and feelings deep
buried within them, which they know not themselves,
which he himself but by glimpses and at times realizes,
and which he pursues from the intensity, not the
steadiness of his view of them. And so in all things,
great objects exact a venture, and a sacrifice is the
condition of honour. And what is true in the world,
why should it not be true also in the kingdom of God ?
We must " launch out into the deep, and let down our
nets for a draught;" we must in the morning sow our
seed, and in the evening withhold not our hand, for we
know not whether shall prosper, either this or that.
" He that observeth the wind shall not sow, and he that
regardeth the clouds shall not reap." He that fails
nine times and succeeds the tenth, is a more honourable man than he who hides his talent in a napkin; and
so, even though the feelings which prompt us to see
God in all things, and to recognize supernatural works
in matters of the world, mislead us at times, though
they make us trust in evidence which we ought not to
admit, and partially incur with justice the imputation of
credulity, yet a Faith which generously apprehends
Eternal Truth, though at times it degenerates into
superstition, is far better than that cold, sceptical,
critical tone of mind, which has no inward sense of
an overruling, ever-present Providence, no desire to
approach its God, but sits at home waiting for the

fearful clearness of His visible coming, whom it might seek and find in due measure amid the twilight of the present world.

28. To conclude: such is Faith as contrasted with Reason;—what it is contrasted with Superstition, how separate from it, and by what principles and laws restrained from falling into it, is a most important question, without settling which any view of the subject of Faith is of course incomplete; but which it does not fall within my present scope to consider.

SERMON XII.

LOVE THE SAFEGUARD OF FAITH AGAINST SUPERSTITION.

(Preached on Whit-Tuesday, May 21, 1839.)

JOHN x. 4, 5.

" The sheep follow Him, for they know His voice. And a stranger will they not follow, but will flee from him, for they know not the voice of strangers."

1. FAITH, considered as an exercise of Reason, has this characteristic,—that it proceeds far more on antecedent grounds than on evidence; it trusts much to presumptions, and in doing this lies its special merit. Thus it is distinguished from Knowledge in the ordinary sense of that word. We are commonly said to know a thing when we have ascertained it by the natural methods given us for ascertaining it. Thus we know mathematical truths, when we are possessed of demonstrative evidence concerning them; we know things present and material by our senses. We know the events of life by moral evidence; we know things past or things invisible, by reasoning from certain present consequences of the facts, such as testimony borne to them. When, for instance, we have ascertained the fact of a

miracle by good testimony, the testimony of men who
neither deceive nor are deceived, we may be said to know
the fact; for we are possessed of those special grounds,
of that distinct warrant in its behalf, which the nature of
the case assigns and allows. These special grounds are
often called the Evidence; and when we believe in
consequence of them, we are said to believe upon
Reason.

2. By the exercise of Reason, indeed, is properly
meant any process or act of the mind, by which, from
knowing one thing it advances on to know another;
whether it be true or false Reason, whether it proceed
from antecedent probabilities, by demonstration, or on
evidence. And in this general sense it includes of
course Faith, which is mainly an anticipation or presumption; but in its more popular sense (in which, as
in former Discourses, I shall here for the most part use
it) it is contrasted with Faith, as meaning in the main
such inferences concerning facts, as are derived from
the facts in question themselves, that is from Evidences, and which lead consequently to Knowledge.

3. Faith, then, and Reason, are popularly contrasted
with one another; Faith consisting of certain exercises
of Reason which proceed mainly on presumption, and
Reason of certain exercises which proceed mainly upon
proof. Reason makes the particular fact which is to
be ascertained the point of primary importance, contemplates it, inquires into its evidence, not of course
excluding antecedent considerations, but not beginning
with them. Faith, on the other hand, begins with its
own previous knowledge and opinions, advances and

decides upon antecedent probabilities, that is, on grounds which do not reach so far as to touch precisely the desired conclusion, though they tend towards it, and may come very near it. It acts, before actual certainty or knowledge[1], on grounds which, for the most part, near as they may come, yet in themselves stand clear of the definite thing which is its object. Hence it is said, and rightly, to be a venture, to involve a risk; or again, to be against Reason, to triumph over Reason, to surpass or outstrip Reason, to attain what Reason falls short of, to effect what Reason finds beyond its powers; or again, to be a principle above or beyond argument, not to be subject to the rules of argument, not to be capable of defending itself, to be illogical, and the like.

4. This is a view of Faith on which I have insisted before now; and though it is a subject which at first sight is deficient in interest, yet I believe it will be found to repay attention, as bearing immediately on practice. It is, moreover, closely connected with the doctrine laid down in the text, and with the great revealed truth which we commemorate at this Season, and with a view to which the Gospel for the day, of which the text forms a part, has been selected.

5. To maintain that Faith is a judgment about facts in matters of conduct, such, as to be formed, not so much from the impression legitimately made upon the mind by those facts, as from the reaching forward of the mind itself towards them,—that it is a presumption, not a proving,—may sound paradoxical, yet

[1 This is what may be called the *pietas fidei*.]

surely is borne out by the actual state of things as they come before us every day. Can it, indeed, be doubted that the great majority of those who have sincerely and deliberately given themselves to religion, who take it for their portion, and stake their happiness upon it, have done so, not on an examination of evidence, but from a spontaneous movement of their hearts towards it ? They go out of themselves to meet Him who is unseen, and they discern Him in such symbols of Him as they find ready provided for them. Whether they examine afterwards the evidence on which their faith may be justified or not, or how far soever they do so, still their faith does not originate in the evidence, nor is it strong in proportion to their knowledge of the evidence ; but, though it may admit of being strengthened by such knowledge, yet it may be quite as strong without it as with it. They believe on grounds within themselves, not merely or mainly on the external testimony on which Religion comes to them.

6. As to the multitude of professed Christians, they indeed believe on mere custom, or nearly so. Not having their hearts interested in religion, they may fairly be called mere hereditary Christians. I am not speaking of these, but of the serious portion of the community; and I say, that they also, though not believing merely because their fathers believed, but with a faith of their own, yet, for that very reason, believe on something distinct from evidence—believe with a faith more personal and living than evidence could create. Mere evidence would but lead to passive

opinion and knowledge; but anticipations and presumptions are the creation of the mind itself; and the
faith which exists in them is of an active nature,
whether in rich or poor, learned or unlearned, young
or old. They have heard or recollect nothing of "in-
terruptions of the course of nature," "sensible miracles," "men neither deceivers nor deceived," and
other similar topics; but they feel that the external
religion offered them elicits into shape, and supplies
the spontaneous desires and presentiments of their
minds; certain, as they are, that some religion must
be from God, though not absolutely certain or able to
prove, at starting, น ฯ, nor asking themselves, whether
some other form is not more simply from Him than
that which is presented to them.

7. The same view of Faith, as being a presumption,
is also implied in our popular mode of regarding it.
It is commonly and truly said, that Faith is a test of
a man's heart. Now, what does this really mean, but
that it shows what he thinks likely to be?—and what he
thinks likely, depends surely on nothing else than the
general state of his mind, the state of his convictions,
feelings, tastes, and wishes. A fact is asserted, and is
thereby proposed to the acceptance or rejection of those
who hear it. Each hearer will have his own view concerning it, prior to the evidence; this view will result
from the character of his mind; nor commonly will it
be reversed by any ordinary variation in the evidence.
If he is indisposed to believe, he will explain away very
strong evidence; if he is disposed, he will accept very
weak evidence. On the one hand, he will talk of its

being the safer side to believe; on the other hand, that he does not feel that he can go so far as to close with what is offered him. That the evidence is something, and not every thing; that it tells a certain way, yet might be more; he will hold, in either case: but then follows the question, what is to come of the evidence, being what it is, and this he decides according to (what is called) the state of his heart.

8. I do not mean that there is no extent or deficiency of evidence sufficient to convince him against his will, or at least to silence him; but commonly the evidence for and against religion, whether true religion or false religion, in matter of fact, is not of this overpowering nature. Neither do I mean that the evidence does not bear one way more than another, or have a determinate meaning (for Christianity and against Naturalism, for the Church and against every other religious body), but that, as things are, amid the engagements, the confusion, and the hurry of the world, and, considering the private circumstances of most minds, few men are in a condition to weigh things in an accurate balance, and to decide, after calm and complete investigations of the evidence. Most men must and do decide by the principles of thought and conduct which are habitual to them; that is, the antecedent judgment, with which a man approaches the subject of religion, not only acts as a bearing this way or that,—as causing him to go out to meet the evidence in a greater or less degree, and nothing more,—but, further, it practically colours the evidence, even in a case in which he has recourse to evidence, and interprets it for him.

2

9. This is the way in which judgments are commonly formed concerning facts alleged or reported in political and social matters, and for the same reason, because it cannot be helped. Act we must, yet seldom indeed is it that we have means of examining into the evidence of the statements on which we are forced to act. Hence statements are often hazarded by persons interested, for the very purpose of bringing out the public mind on some certain point, ascertaining what it thinks, and feeling how their way es, and what courses are feasible and safe. And, in lil manner, startling or unexpected reports are believed or disbelieved, and acted on in this way or that, according as the hearer is or is not easy of belief, or desirous of the event, or furnished with precedents, or previously informed. And so in religious matters, on hearing or apparently witnessing a supernatural occurrence, men judge of it this way or that, according as they are credulous or not, or wish it to be true or not, or are influenced by such or such views of life, or have more or less knowledge on the subject of miracles. We decide one way or another, according to the position of the alleged fact, relatively to our existing state of religious knowledge and feeling.

10. I am not saying that such religious judgments are parallel to those which we form in daily and secular matters, as regards their respective chances of turning out correct in the event. That is another matter. Reports in matters of this world are many, and our resources of mind for the discrimination of them very insufficient. Religions are few, and the moral powers

by which they are to be accepted or rejected, strong and correspondent. It does not follow, then, because even the most sagacious minds are frequently wrong in their antecedent judgments in matters of this world, that therefore even common minds need be wrong in similar judgments about the personal matters of the world unseen. It does not follow, because, in the insignificant matters of this world, *a priori* judgments run counter to judgments on evidence, that therefore, in the weightier matters of the next, a merciful Providence may not have so ordered the relation between our minds and His revealed will, that presumption, which is the method of the many, may lead to the same conclusions as examination, which is the method of the few. But this is not the point. I am not speaking of the trustworthiness of Faith, but of its nature: it is generally allowed to be a test of moral character. Now, I say that it is a test, as matters of this world show, only so far as it goes upon presumptions, whatever follows from this as to the validity of its inferences, which is another matter. As far, then, as its being a test of moral character is of the essence of religious Faith, so far its being an antecedent judgment or presumption is of its essence. On the other hand, when we come to what is called Evidence, or, in popular language, exercises of Reason, prejudices and mental peculiarities are excluded from the discussion; we descend to grounds common to all; certain scientific rules and fixed standards for weighing testimony, and examining facts, are received. Nothing can be urged, or made to tell, but what all feel, all comprehend, all

can put into words; current language becomes the
measure of thought; only such conclusions may be
drawn as can produce their reasons; only such reasons
are in point as can be exhibited in simple propositions;
the multiform and intricate assemblage of considerations, which really lead to judgment and action, must
be attenuated or mutilated into a major and a minor
premiss.   Under such circumstances, there is as little
virtue or merit in deciding aright as in working a
mathematical problem correctly; as little guilt in deciding wrongly as in mistakes in accounts, or in a faulty
memory in history.

11. And, again: — As Faith may be viewed as
opposed to Reason, in the popular sense of the latter
word, it must not be overlooked that Unbelief is
opposed to Reason also.   Unbelief, indeed, considers
itself especially rational, or critical of evidence; but it
criticizes the evidence of Religion, only because it does
not like it, and really goes upon presumptions and prejudices as much as Faith does, only presumptions of an
opposite nature.   This I have already implied.   It
considers a religious system so improbable, that it will
not listen to the evidence of it; or, if it listens, it
employs itself in doing what a believer could do, if he
chose, quite as well, what he is quite as well aware can
be done; viz., in showing that the evidence might be
more complete and unexceptionable than it is.   On
this account it is that unbelievers call themselves
rational; not because they decide by evidence, but
because, after they have made their decision, they
merely occupy themselves in sifting it.   This surely is

quite plain, even in the case of Hume, who first asks, "What have we to oppose to such a cloud of witnesses," in favour of certain alleged miracles he mentions, "but the absolute impossibility or miraculous nature of the events which they relate? And this surely," he adds, "in the eyes of all reasonable people, will alone be regarded as a sufficient refutation;" that is, the antecedent improbability is a sufficient refutation of the evidence. And next, he scoffingly observes, that "our most holy Religion is founded on Faith, not on Reason;" and that "mere Reason is insufficient to convince us of its veracity." As if his infidelity were "founded on Reason," in any more exact sense; or presumptions on the side of Faith could not have, and presumptions on the side of unbelief might have, the nature of proof.

12. Such, then, seems to be the state of the case, when we carefully consider it. Faith is an exercise of presumptive reasoning, or of Reason proceeding on antecedent grounds: such seems to be the fact, whatever comes of it. Let us take things as we find them: let us not attempt to distort them into what they are not. True philosophy deals with facts. We cannot make facts. All our wishing cannot change them. We must use them. If Revelation has always been offered to mankind in one way, it is in vain to say that it ought to have come to us in another. If children, if the poor, if the busy, can have true Faith, yet cannot weigh evidence, evidence is not the simple foundation on which Faith is built. If the great bulk of serious men believe, not because they have examined evidence, but

because they are disposed in a certain way,—because they are "ordained to eternal life," this must be God's order of things. Let us attempt to understand it. Let us not disguise it, or explain it away. It may have difficulties; if so, let us own them. Let us fairly meet them: if we can, let us overcome them.

13. Now, there is one very serious difficulty in the view which I have taken of Faith, which most persons will have anticipated before I refer to it; that such a view may be made an excuse for all manner of prejudice and bigotry, and leads directly to credulity and super-stition; and, on the other hand, in the case of unbelief, that it affords a sort of excuse for impenetrable ob-duracy. Antecedent probabilities may be equally avail-able for what is true, and what pretends to be true, for a Revelation and its counterfeit, for Paganism, or Ma-hometanism, or Christianity. They seem to supply no intelligible rule what is to be believed, and what not; or how a man is to pass from a false belief to a true. If a claim of miracles is to be acknowledged because it happens to be advanced, why not in behalf of the miracles of India, as well as of those of Palestine? If the abstract probability of a Revelation be the measure of genuineness in a given case, why not in the case of Mahomet, as well as of the Apostles? How are we to manage (as I may say) the Argument from Presump-tion in behalf of Christianity, so as not to carry it out into an argument against it?

14. This is the difficulty. It is plain that some safe-guard of Faith is needed, some corrective principle

which will secure it from running (as it were) to seed, and becoming superstition or fanaticism. All parties who have considered the subject seem to agree in thinking some or other corrective necessary. And here reasoners of a school which has been in fashion of late years have their answer ready, and can promptly point out what they consider the desired remedy. What, according to them, forms the foundation of Faith, is also its corrective. "Faith is built upon Reason[2], and Reason is its safeguard. Cultivate the Reason, and in the same degree you lead men both to the acknowledgment, and also to the sober use of the Gospel. Their religion will be rational, inasmuch as they know why they believe, and what. The young, the poor, the ignorant, those whose reason is undeveloped, are the victims of an excessive faith. Give them, then, education; open their minds; enlighten them; enable them to reflect, compare, investigate, and infer; draw their attention to the Evidences of Christianity. While, in this way, you bring them into the right path, you also obviate the chance of their wandering from it; you tend to prevent enthusiasm and superstition, while you are erecting a bulwark against infidelity."

15. This, or something like this, is often maintained, and, if correctly, it must be confessed, nothing can be more extravagant than to call Faith an exercise or act of Reason, as I have done, when, in fact, it needs Reason; such language does but tend to break down the partition-wall which separates Faith from Super-

[2] On processes of a logical or explicit character.

stition, and to allow it to dissipate itself in every variety of excess, and to throw itself away upon the most unworthy and preposterous objects.

16. This is what, perhaps, will be objected; and yet I am not unwilling to make myself responsible for the difficulty in question, by denying that any intellectual act is necessary for right Faith besides itself; that it need be much more than a presumption[3], or that it need be fortified and regulated by investigation; by denying, that is, that Reason is the safeguard of Faith. What, then, is the safeguard, if Reason is not? I shall give an answer, which may seem at once common-place and paradoxical, yet I believe is the true one. The safeguard of Faith is a right state of heart. This it is that gives it birth; it also disciplines it. This is what protects it from bigotry, credulity, and fanaticism. It is holiness, or dutifulness, or the new creation, or the spiritual mind, however we word it, which is the quickening and illuminating principle of true faith, giving it eyes, hands, and feet. It is Love which forms it out of the rude chaos into an image of Christ; or, in scholastic language, justifying Faith, whether in Pagan, Jew, or Christian, is *fides formata charitate*.

17. "Verily, verily, I say unto you," says the Divine Speaker, "I am the Door of the sheep. . . . . I am the Good Shepherd, and know My sheep, and am known of Mine."

18. "Ye believe not, because ye are not of My sheep,

[3 It is a presumption, not as being a mere conjecture, but because the mind cannot master its own reasons and anticipates in its conclusions a logical exposition of them.]

as I said unto you. My sheep hear My voice, and I
know them, and they follow Me; and I give unto them
eternal Life, and they shall never perish, neither shall
any one pluck them out of My hand."

19. " He that entereth in by the door is the Shepherd of the sheep. To Him the porter openeth, and
the sheep hear His voice, and He calleth His own sheep
by name, and leadeth them out. And when He putteth
forth His own sheep, He goeth before them, and the
sheep follow Him, for they know His voice. And a
stranger will they not follow, but will flee from Him,
for they know not the voice of strangers."

20. What is here said about exercises of Reason, in
order to believing? What is there not said of sympathetic feeling, of newness of spirit, of love? It was
from lack of love towards Christ that the Jews discerned not in Him the Shepherd of their souls. " Ye
believe not, because ye are not of My sheep. My sheep
hear My voice, and follow Me." It was the regenerate
nature sent down from the Father of Lights which
drew up the disciples heavenward,—which made their
affections go forth to meet the Bridegroom, and fixed
those affections on Him, till they were as cords of love
staying the heart upon the Eternal. " All that the
Father giveth Me, shall come to Me. No man can
come unto Me, except the Father which hath sent Me
draw him. It is written in the' Prophets, And they
shall be all taught of God. Every man, therefore, that
hath heard and hath learned of the Father, cometh unto
Me." It is the new life, and not the natural reason,
which leads the soul to Christ. Does a child trust his

parents because he has proved to himself that they are such, and that they are able and desirous to do him good, or from the instinct of affection? We *believe*, because we *love* [4]. How plain a truth! What gain is it to be wise above that which is written? Why, O men, deface with your minute and arbitrary philosophy the simplicity, the reality, the glorious liberty of the inspired teaching? Is this your godly jealousy for Scripture? this your abhorrence of human additions?

21. It is the doctrine, then, of the text, that those who believe in Christ, believe because they know Him to be the Good Shepherd; and they know Him by His voice; and they know His voice, because they are His sheep; that they do not follow strangers and robbers, because they know not the voice of strangers: moreover, that they know and follow Christ, upon His loving them. "I am come that they might have life. . . . . The hireling fleeth, because he is a hireling, and careth not for the sheep." The divinely-enlightened mind sees in Christ the very Object whom it desires to love and worship,—the Object correlative of its own affections; and it trusts Him, or believes, from loving Him.

22. The same doctrine is contained in many other places, as in the second chapter of St. Paul's First Epistle to the Corinthians. In this passage, doubtless, there are one or two expressions, which, taken by themselves, admit, and may well be taken to include, another interpretation: as a whole, however, it dis-

[4 This means, not love precisely, but the virtue of religiousness, under which may be said to fall the *pia affectio*, or *voluntas credendi*.]

tinctly teaches the nothingness of natural Reason [5], and the all-sufficiency of supernatural grace in the conversion of the soul. " And I, brethren, when I came to you, came not with excellency of speech or of wisdom," (with discussion, argument, elaborate proof, cumulation of evidence,) "declaring unto you the testimony of God. For I determined not to know any thing among you, save Jesus Christ, and Him crucified. . . . . And my speech and my preaching was not with enticing words of man's wisdom," not with the reasonings of the schools, " but in demonstration of the Spirit, and of power," with an inward and spiritual conviction, " that your Faith should not stand in the wisdom of men," natural Reason, " but in the power of God," His regenerating and renewing influences. " But the natural man receiveth not the things of the Spirit of God, for they are foolishness unto him; neither can he know them, because they are spiritually discerned : but he that is spiritual judgeth all things, yet he himself is judged of no man. For who hath known the mind of the Lord, that he may instruct Him? But we have the mind of Christ." Here a certain moral state, and not evidence, is made the means of gaining the Truth, and the beginning of spiritual perfection.

23. In like manner St. John : "They went out from us, but they were not of us; for if they had been of us, they would no doubt have continued with us; but they went out, that they might be made manifest that they

[5 That is the nothingness of Reason, not when viewed as a personal act, instinctive, unconscious, presumptive, and having, as its condition, a certain ethical character, but as an appreciation of explicit evidences.]

were not all of us. But ye have an unction from the Holy One, and ye know all things." If this unction and this knowledge which God the Holy Ghost bestows, be a moral gift, (as who will deny?) then also must our departing from Christ arise from the want of a moral gift, and our adhering to Him must be the consequence of a moral gift.

24. Again:—"The anointing which ye have received of Him abideth in you, and ye need not that any man teach you, but as the same anointing teacheth you of all things, and is true and is no lie, and even as it hath taught you, ye shall abide in Him[6]." Surely the faculty by which we know the Truth is here represented to us, not as a power of investigation, but as a moral perception.

25. If this, then, is the real state of the case (as I do think would be granted by all of us, if, discarding systems, we allowed Scripture to make its legitimate and full impression upon our minds), if holiness, dutifulness, or love, however we word it, and not Reason, is the eye of Faith, the discriminating principle which keeps it from fastening on unworthy objects, and degenerating into enthusiasm or superstition, it now follows, to attempt to analyze the process by which it does so. I mean, let us examine *how* it does so, *what* in the actual course of thinking and determining is the mode by which Love does regulate as well as animate Faith, guiding it in a clear and high path, neither enervated by excitement, nor depressed by bondage, nor distorted by extravagance. For till we

[6] 1 Cor. ii. 1 2. 4. 14—16.   1 John ii. 19 20—27.

have done this in some good measure, it is plain that we have made little advance towards grasping the meaning of the Scripture statements on the subject. I will make an endeavour this way, as far as time permits, and so bring my present remarks to an end.

26. Right Faith is the faith of a right mind. Faith is an intellectual act; right Faith is an intellectual act, done in a certain moral disposition. Faith is an act of Reason, viz. a reasoning upon presumptions; right Faith is a reasoning upon holy, devout, and enlightened presumptions. Faith ventures and hazards; right Faith ventures and hazards deliberately, seriously, soberly, piously, and humbly, counting the cost and delighting in the sacrifice. As far as, and wherever Love is wanting, so far, and there, Faith runs into excess or is perverted. The grounds of Faith, when animated by the spirit of love and purity, are such as these :—that a Revelation is very needful for man ; that it is earnestly to be hoped for from a merciful God ; that it is to be expected ; nay, that of the two it is more probable that what professes to be a Revelation should be or should contain a Revelation, than that there should be no Revelation at all ; that, if Almighty God interposes in human affairs, His interposition will not be in opposition to His known attributes, or to His dealings in the world, or to certain previous revelations of His will ; that it will be in a way worthy of Him ; that it is likely to bear plain indications of His hand ; that it will be for great ends, specified or signified ; and moreover, that such and such ends are in their nature great,

such and such a message important, such and such means worthy, such and such circumstances congruous. I consider that under the guidance of such anticipations and calculations as these, which Faith—not mere Faith, but Faith working by Love—suggests, the honest mind may, under ordinary circumstances, be led, and practically is led, into an acceptable, enlightened, and saving apprehension of Divine Truth without that formal intimacy and satisfaction with the special evidence existing for the facts believed, which is commonly called Reasoning, or the use of Reason, and which results in knowledge. Some instances will serve to explain how:—

27. (1.) Superstition, in its grossest form, is the worship of evil spirits. What the Gentiles sacrifice is done (we are told) "to devils, not to God;" their table is "the table of devils." "They offered their sons and their daughters unto devils[7]." It is needless to say, that the view above taken of the nature of Religious Faith has no tendency towards such impieties. Faith, indeed, considered as a mere abstract principle, certainly does tend to humble the mind before any thing which comes with a profession of being supernatural; not so the Faith of a religious mind, a right religious Faith, which is instinct with Love towards God and towards man. Love towards man will make it shrink from cruelty; love towards God from false worship. This is idolatry, to account creatures as the primary and independent sources of providence and the ultimate objects of our devotion. I say, the principle of Love,

[7] 1 Cor. x. 20. Ps. cvi. 37.

acting not by way of inquiry or argument, but spontaneously and as an instinct, will cause the mind to recoil from cruelty, impurity, and the assumption of divine power, though coming with ever so superhuman a claim, real or professed. And though there are cases in which such a recoil is erroneous, as arising from partial views or misconceptions, yet on the whole it will be found a correct index of the state of the case, and a safe direction for our conduct.

28. (2.) Again: another kind of Superstition, as the word is usually understood, is the payment of religious honour to things forbidden. Such were some of the idolatries to which the Israelites surrendered themselves, as the worship of the golden calf. Moreover, when a ritual has directly been given from heaven, what is not commanded may be accounted forbidden, except a power of making additions has been granted; it being the same undutifulness to supersede or alter the revealed manner of approaching God, as to adopt means actually unlawful. Such might be the continued worship of the Brazen Serpent, which, though at a certain juncture an ordained symbol and instrument of God, nevertheless, in a rigid system of rites, such as the Mosaic, could not be honoured in continuance at the people's will, especially with self-devised rites, without great undutifulness, or lack of love. On the other hand, Nebuchadnezzar's homage to Daniel, when the king "fell on his face and worshipped him, and commanded that they should offer an oblation and sweet odours unto him," was accepted by the Prophet, as coming from a heathen, to whom such works of reverence had not been forbidden by any

[UNIV. S.] R

imposed ritual, and who on the other hand could not mean to acknowledge Daniel as the very source of prophetic knowledge, both because the Prophet had himself just declared that there was a "God in heaven that revealeth secrets, and maketh known to the king Nebuchadnezzar what shall be in the latter days," and also because the king himself, while commanding the oblation, proceeds to say, "Of a truth it is that your God is a God of gods, and a Lord of kings, and a Revealer of secrets, seeing thou couldest reveal this secret." Nebuchadnezzar then (it would seem) did not stop short of God; but honoured Daniel as God's visible emblem, and that without any revealed prohibition of his doing so. And if so, his faith did not evince any deficiency of love, or any superstition.

29. (3.) Here we may lay it down as a principle, that what is superstition in Jew or Christian is not necessarily such in heathen; or what in Christian is not in Jew. Faith leads the mind to communion with the invisible God; its attempts at approaching and pleasing Him are acceptable or not, according as they are or are not self-willed; and they are self-willed when they are irrespective of God's revealed will. It was a superstition in the Israelites, and not faith, to take the Ark to battle uncommanded, and they were punished with the loss of it. It was no superstition in the Philistines, abundantly superstitious and wicked as they otherwise were, to yoke the kine to the Ark, and to leave them to themselves to see what they would do; thus making trial of the Ark's sacredness. It was a trial which

could but be unsuccessful, but might give them assurance; and whatever of heathen irreverence there was in the circumstances of the action, yet still it was to a certain extent a tacit, or (if we will) an unwilling, acknowledgment of the God of Israel. Again, sacrifices of blood were not necessarily superstitious in heathen; they would be most superstitious and profane in Christians, as being superseded by the great Atonement made once for all, and the continual Memory of it in Holy Communion. On the other hand, the Sign of the Cross in Baptism would be superstitious, unless the Church had "power to decree rites and ceremonies in the worship of God."

30. (4.) Again: when the barbarous people of Melita saw the viper fasten upon St. Paul's hand, first they considered him a murderer, then a god. What is to be said of their conduct? Plainly it evinced Faith; but was it healthy Faith or perverted? On the one hand, they had a sense of the probability of supernatural interference such, as to lead them to accept this occurrence as more than ordinary, while they doubted and wavered in their interpretation of it according as circumstances varied. Faith accepted it as supernatural; and in matter of fact they were not wrong in the main point. They judged rightly in thinking that God's presence was in some immediate way with St. Paul; Reason, following upon Faith, attempted to deduce from it. Their reasoning was wrong, their faith was right. But did it not involve Superstition? We must distinguish here. It is no refinement, surely, to say that they were not superstitious, though their con-

duct, viewed in itself, was such. Their reasoning was superstitious in *our* idea of Superstition; I mean, with our superior knowledge of religious truth, *we* are able to say that they were seeing in things visible what was not there, and drawing conclusions which were not valid; but it needs to be proved that they acted preposterously or weakly under their circumstances. I am speaking, be it observed, of their incidental reasoning; and concerning this I say that it does not become us, who are blessed with light, which gives us freedom from the creature by telling us definitely where are the paths and dwelling-places of God in the visible world, to despise those who were " seeking Him, if haply they might feel after Him and find Him." Superstition is a faith which falls below that standard of religion which God has given, whatever it is. We are accustomed naturally and fairly to define, according to our own standard, what things are abstractedly superstitious and what are not; but we have no right to apply this standard, in particular cases, to other men whose circumstances are different from our own.

31. (5.) The woman with the issue of blood, who thought to be healed by secretly touching our Lord's garment, may perhaps be more correctly called superstitious than the barbarians of Melita. Yet it is remarkable that even she was encouraged by our Lord, and that on the very ground of her faith. In His judgment, then, a religious state of mind, which is not free from Superstition, may still be Faith,—nay, and high Faith. "Daughter," He said, "be of good comfort; thy faith hath made thee whole; go in peace, and be whole

of thy plague." I have said that she showed a more
superstitious temper than the people of Melita, inasmuch as what she did was inconsistent with what she
knew. Her faith did not rise to the standard of her
own light. She knew enough of the Good Shepherd to
have directed her faith to Him as the one source of all
good, instead of which she lingered in the circumstances
and outskirts of His Divine Perfections. She in effect
regarded the hem of His garment as an original principle of miraculous power, and thereby placed herself
almost in the position of those who idolize the creature.
Yet even this seems to have arisen from great humble-
ness of mind: like the servants of the ruler of the
synagogue, who were then standing by, she feared probably to "trouble the Master" with her direct intercession; or like the Apostles on a subsequent occasion,
who rebuked those who brought children for His touch,
she was unwilling to interrupt Him; or she was full of
her own unworthiness, like the centurion who prayed
that Christ would not condescend to enter his roof, but
would speak the word instead, or send a messenger.
She thought that a little one, such as herself, might
come in for the crumbs from His table by chance, and
without His distinct bidding, by the perpetual operation
and spontaneous exuberance of those majestic general
laws on which He wrought miracles. In all this,—in
her faith and her humility, her faith tinged with superstition, her abject humility,—she would seem to resemble such worshippers in various ages and countries
in the Christian Church, as have impaired their simple
veneration of the Invisible, by an undue lingering of

mind upon the outward emblems which they have considered He had blessed.

32. (6.) One more instance shall be added,—that of the Prophet from Judah, who had a message brought him by a lying Prophet in the name of the Lord, bidding him go home with him. Had he not been a Prophet himself, had he known for certain the other to have been a Prophet; nay, or even considering that that other called himself such, and that prophets then were in Israel, there would have been nothing very superstitious or wrong in his yielding to his solicitations. But of course the character of the act was quite changed, considering his own commission, and the express directions which had been given him how to conduct himself in the apostate land. If he went back with his seducer merely to refresh himself, as it would appear, of course neither Faith nor Superstition had any thing to do with his conduct, which was a mere yielding to temptation; but if he did suppose that he was thereby commending himself to God, he showed credulousness, not Faith.

33. And here we see why it is not Faith, but credulousness and superstition, to listen to idle tales of apparitions, charms, omens, and the like, which may be current even in a Christian land; viz. because we have already received a Revelation. The miracles, which we believe, indispose us to believe the report of other miracles which are external to the revealed system. We have found the Christ, we are not seeking. And much more, if the doctrine put forth in the professed revelation of to-day contradicts or invalidates the doctrine of those

revelations which have been received from the beginning. Hence we are expressly warned in Scripture,
that though an Angel from heaven preach unto us any
other Gospel than that we have received, he must be
pronounced anathema.

34. And this was the sin of the Judaizers, that having
received the Spirit, they went back for perfection to
the rites of the Law then abolished. In like manner
the Israelites had been warned by Moses: "If there
arise among you a prophet, or a dreamer of dreams, and
giveth thee a sign or a wonder, and the sign or the
wonder come to pass whereof he spake unto thee,
saying, Let us go after other gods, which thou hast not
known, and let us serve them; thou shalt not hearken
unto the words of that prophet or that dreamer of
dreams, for the Lord your God proveth you, to know
whether ye love the Lord your God with all your heart
and with all your soul." *(*And hence it was a point of
especial moment with St. Paul to prove that the Gospel
was not an annulling of the Law, but its fulfilment,
built upon it and intended by it; and that in the rejection
of the Jews and the calling of the Gentiles, the old
Church as well as the old Commandment was still
preserved.

35. And thus, even in the case of the heathen, the
Apostle was anxious to pay due respect to the truths
which they already admitted, and to show that the
Gospel was rather the purification, explanation, development, and completion of those scattered verities of
Paganism than their abrogation. "Whom therefore ye
ignorantly worship," he says, "Him declare I unto you."

In other words, it was not his method to represent the faith, to which he exhorted his hearers, as a state of mind utterly alien from their existing knowledge, their convictions, and their moral character. He drew them on, not by unsettling them, but through their own system, as far as might be,—by persuasives of a positive nature, and which, while fitted to attract by their innate truth and beauty, excluded by their very presence whatever in Paganism was inconsistent with them. What they already were, was to lead them on, as by a venture, to what they were not; what they knew was to lead them on, upon presumptions, to what they as yet knew not. Neither of Jew nor of Gentile did he demand Faith in his message, on the bare antecedent ground that God was every where, and therefore, if so be, might be with himself in particular who spoke to them; nor, again, did he appeal merely to his miraculous powers; but he looked at men steadfastly, to see whether they had "faith to be healed;" he appealed to that whole body of opinion, affection, and desire, which made up, in each man, his moral self; which, distinct from all guesses and random efforts, set him forward steadily in one direction,—which, if it was what it should be, would respond to the Apostle's doctrine, as the strings of one instrument vibrate with another,—which, if it was not, would either not accept it, or not abide in it. He taught men, not only that Almighty God was, and was every where, but that He had certain moral attributes; that He was just, true, holy, and merciful; that His representative was in their hearts; that He already dwelt in them as a lawgiver and a judge, by a sense of right and a conscience of sin ; and that what he himself was then bringing them fulfilled what was thus begun in them by nature, by tokens so like the truth, as to constrain all who loved God under the Religion of Nature to believe in Him as revealed in the Gospel.

36. Such, then, under all circumstances, is real Faith ; a presumption, yet not a mere chance conjecture, —a reaching forward, yet not of excitement or of passion,—a moving forward in the twilight, yet not without clue or direction ;—a movement from something known to something unknown, but kept in the narrow path of truth by the Law of dutifulness which inhabits it, the Light of heaven which animates and guides it,— and which, whether feeble and dim as in the Heathen, or bright and vigorous as in the Christian, whether merely the awakening and struggling conscience, or the "affection of the Spirit," whether as a timid hope, or in the fulness of love, is, under every Dispensation, the one acceptable principle commending us to God for the merits of Christ. And it becomes superstition or credulity, enthusiasm or fanaticism, or bigotry, in pro- portion as it emancipates itself from this spirit of wisdom and understanding, of counsel and ghostly strength, of knowledge and true godliness, and holy fear. And thus I would answer the question how it may be secured from excess, without the necessity of employing what is popularly called Reason for its protection,—I mean processes of investigation, discrimination, discussion, argument, and inference. It is itself an intellectual act.

and it takes its character from the moral state of the
agent.   It is perfected, not by intellectual cultivation,
but by obedience.   It does not change its nature or its
function, when thus perfected.   It remains what it is in
itself, an initial principle of action; but it becomes
changed in its quality, as being made spiritual.   It is
as before a presumption, but the presumption of a
serious, sober, thoughtful, pure, affectionate, and devout
mind.   It acts, because it is Faith; but the direction,
firmness, consistency, and precision of its acts, it gains
from Love.

37. Let these remarks suffice, insufficient as they are
in themselves, on the relation and distinction between
Faith and Superstition.   Other important questions,
however, remain, which have a claim on the attention
of all who would gain clear notions on an important
and difficult subject.

SERMON XIII.

(Preached on St. Peter's Day, 1840.)

1 PET. iii. 15.

" Sanctify the Lord God in your hearts ; and be ready always to give
an answer to every man that asketh you a reason of the hope that is
in you, with meekness and fear."

ST. PETER'S faith was one of his characteristic
graces. It was ardent, keen, watchful, and prompt.
It dispensed with argument, calculation, deliberation,
and delay, whenever it heard the voice of its Lord
and Saviour: and it heard that voice even when its
accents were low, or when it was unaided by the testimony of the other senses. When Christ appeared
walking on the sea, and said, "It is I," Peter answered
Him, and said, "Lord, if it be Thou, bid me come unto
Thee on the water." When Christ asked His disciples
who He was, " Simon Peter answered and said," as we
read in the Gospel for this day, "Thou art the Christ,
the Son of the Living God," and obtained our Lord's
blessing for such clear and ready Faith. At another
time, when Christ asked the Twelve whether they would

leave Him as others did, St. Peter said, "Lord, to whom shall we go? Thou hast the words of eternal life; and we believe and are sure that Thou art the Christ, the Son of the Living God." And after the Resurrection, when he heard from St. John that it was Christ who stood on the shore, he sprang out of the boat in which he was fishing, and cast himself into the sea, in his impatience to come near Him. Other instances of his faith might be mentioned. If ever Faith forgot self, and was occupied with its Great Object, it was the faith of Peter. If in any one Faith appears in contrast with what we commonly understand by Reason, and with Evidence, it so appears in the instance of Peter. When he reasoned, it was at times when Faith was lacking. "When he saw the wind boisterous, he was afraid;" and Christ in consequence called him, "Thou of little faith." When He had asked, "Who touched Me?" Peter and others reasoned, "Master," said they, "the multitude throng Thee, and press Thee, and sayest Thou, Who touched Me?" And in like manner, when Christ said that he should one day follow Him in the way of suffering, "Peter said unto Him, Lord, *why* cannot I follow Thee now?"—and we know how his faith gave way soon afterwards.

2. Faith and Reason, then, stand in strong contrast in the history of Peter: yet it is Peter, and he not the fisherman of Galilee, but the inspired Apostle, who in the text gives us a precept which implies, in order to its due fulfilment, a careful exercise of our Reason, an exercise both upon Faith, considered as an act or habit of mind, and upon the Object of it. We are not only

to "sanctify the Lord God in our hearts," not only to prepare a shrine within us in which our Saviour Christ may dwell, and where we may worship Him; but we are so to understand what we do, so to master our thoughts and feelings, so to recognize what we believe, and how we believe, so to trace out our ideas and impressions, and to contemplate the issue of them, that we may be "ready *always* to give an answer to *every* man that asketh us an account of the hope that is in us." In these words, I conceive, we have a clear warrant, or rather an injunction, to cast our religion into the form of Creed and Evidences.

3. It would seem, then, that though Faith is the characteristic of the Gospel, and Faith is the simple lifting of the mind to the Unseen God, without conscious reasoning or formal argument, still the mind may be allowably, nay, religiously engaged, in reflecting upon its own Faith; investigating the grounds and the Object of it, bringing it out into words, whether to defend, or recommend, or teach it to others. And St. Peter himself, in spite of his ardour and earnestness, gives us in his own case some indications of such an exercise of mind. When he said, "Thou art the Christ, the Son of the Living God," he cast his faith, in a measure, into a dogmatic form: and when he said, "To whom shall we go? Thou hast the words of eternal life," he gave "an account of the hope that was in him," or grounded his faith upon Evidence.

4. Nothing would be more theoretical and unreal than to suppose that true Faith cannot exist except when moulded upon a Creed, and based upon Evidence;

yet nothing would indicate a more shallow philosophy than to say that it ought carefully to be disjoined from dogmatic and argumentative statements. To assert the latter is to discard the science of theology from the service of Religion; to assert the former, is to maintain that every child, every peasant, must be a theologian. Faith cannot exist without grounds or without an object; but it does not follow that all who have faith should recognize, and be able to state what they believe, and why. Nor, on the other hand, because it is not identical with its grounds, and its object, does it therefore cease to be true Faith, on its recognizing them. In proportion as the mind reflects upon itself, it will be able "to give an account" of what it believes and hopes; as far as it has not thus reflected, it will not be able. Such knowledge cannot be wrong, yet cannot be necessary, as long as reflection is at once a natural faculty of our souls, yet not an initial faculty. Scripture gives instances of Faith in each of these states, when attended by a conscious exercise of Reason, and when not. When Nicodemus said, "No man can do these miracles that Thou doest, except God be with him," he investigated. When the Scribe said, "There is One God, and there is none other but He; and to love Him with all the heart . . . . . is more than all whole burnt offerings and sacrifices," his belief was dogmatical. On the other hand, when the cripple at Lystra believed, on St. Paul's preaching, or the man at the Beautiful gate believed in the Name of Christ, their faith was independent not of objects or grounds (for that is impossible,) but of perceptible, recognized, producible objects and grounds: they believed, they could not say what or why. True Faith, then, admits, but does not require, the exercise of what is commonly understood by Reason.

5. I hope it will not seem any want of reverence towards a great Apostle, who reigns with Christ in heaven, if, instead of selecting one of the many lessons to which his history calls our attention, or of the points of doctrine in it which might so profitably be enlarged upon, I employ his Day to continue a subject to which I have already devoted such opportunities of speaking from this place, as have from time to time occurred, though it be but incidentally connected with him. Such a continuation of subject has some sanction in the character of our first Lessons for Holy days, which, for the most part, instead of being appropriate to the particular Festivals on which they are appointed, are portions of a course, and connected with those which are assigned to others. And I will add that, if there is a question, the intrusion of which may be excused in the present age, and to which the mind is naturally led on the Days commemorative of the first Founders of the Church, it is the relation of Faith to Reason under the Gospel; and the means whereby, and the grounds whereon, and the subjects wherein, the mind is bound to believe and acquiesce, in matters of religion.

6. In the Epistle for this Day we have an account of St. Peter, when awakened by the Angel, obeying him implicitly, yet not understanding, while he obeyed. He girt himself, and bound on his sandals, and cast his garment about him, and " went out and followed

him;" yet "wist not that it was true which was done by the Angel, but thought he saw a vision." Afterwards, when he "was come to himself, he said, Now I know of a surety, that the Lord hath sent His Angel, and hath delivered me." First he acted spontaneously, then he contemplated his own acts. This may be taken as an illustration of the difference between the more simple faculties and operations of the mind, and that process of analyzing and describing them, which takes place upon reflection. We not only feel, and think, and reason, but we know that we feel, and think, and reason; not only know, but can inspect and ascertain our thoughts, feelings, and reasonings: not only ascertain, but describe. Children, for a time, do not realize even their material frames, or (as I may say) count their limbs; but, as the mind opens, and is cultivated, they turn their attention to soul as well as body; they contemplate all they are, and all they do; they are no longer beings of impulse, instinct, conscience, imagination, habit, or reason, merely; but they are able to reflect upon their own mind as if it were some external object; they reason upon their reasonings. This is the point on which I shall now enlarge.

7. Reason, according to the simplest view of it, is the faculty of gaining knowledge without direct perception, or of ascertaining one thing by means of another. In this way it is able, from small beginnings, to create to itself a world of ideas, which do or do not correspond to the things themselves for which they stand, or are true or not, according as it is exercised soundly or otherwise. One fact may suffice for a whole

theory; one principle may create and sustain a system; one minute token is a clue to a large discovery. The mind ranges to and fro, and spreads out, and advances forward with a quickness which has become a proverb, and a subtlety and versatility which baffle investigation. It passes on from point to point, gaining one by some indication; another on a probability; then availing itself of an association; then falling back on some received law; next seizing on testimony; then committing itself to some popular impression, or some inward instinct, or some obscure memory; and thus it makes progress not unlike a clamberer on a steep cliff, who, by quick eye, prompt hand, and firm foot, ascends how he knows not himself, by personal endowments and by practice, rather than by rule, leaving no track behind him, and unable to teach another. It is not too much to say that the stepping by which great geniuses scale the mountains of truth is as unsafe and precarious to men in general, as the ascent of a skilful mountaineer up a literal crag. It is a way which they alone can take; and its justification lies in their success. And such mainly is the way in which all men, gifted or not gifted, commonly reason,—not by rule, but by an inward faculty.

8. Reasoning, then, or the exercise of Reason, is a living spontaneous energy within us, not an art. But when the mind reflects upon itself, it begins to be dissatisfied with the absence of order and method in the exercise, and attempts to analyze the various processes which take place during it, to refer one to another, and to discover the main principles on which they are conducted, as it might contemplate and investigate its

faculty of memory or imagination. The boldest, simplest, and most comprehensive theory which has been invented for the analysis of the reasoning process, is the well-known science for which we are indebted to Aristotle, and which is framed upon the principle that every act of reasoning is exercised upon neither more nor less than three terms. Short of this, we have many general words in familiar use to designate particular methods of thought, according to which the mind reasons (that is, proceeds from truth to truth), or to designate particular states of mind which influence its reasonings. Such methods are antecedent probability, analogy, parallel cases, testimony, and circumstantial evidence; and such states of mind are prejudice, deference to authority, party spirit, attachment to such and such principles, and the like. In like manner we distribute the Evidences of Religion into External and Internal; into à *priori* and à *posteriori*; into Evidences of Natural Religion and of Revealed; and so on. Again, we speak of proving doctrines either from the nature of the case, or from Scripture, or from history; and of teaching them in a dogmatic, or a polemical, or a hortatory way. In these and other ways we instance the reflective power of the human mind, contemplating and scrutinizing its own acts.

9. Here, then, are two processes, distinct from each other,—the original process of reasoning, and next, the process of investigating our reasonings. All men reason, for to reason is nothing more than to gain truth from former truth, without the intervention of sense, to which brutes are limited; but all men do not reflect

upon their own reasonings, much less reflect truly and accurately, so as to do justice to their own meaning; but only in proportion to their abilities and attainments. In other words, all men have a reason, but not all men can give a reason. We may denote, then, these two exercises of mind as reasoning and arguing, or as conscious and unconscious reasoning, or as Implicit Reason and Explicit Reason. And to the latter belong the words, science, method, development, analysis, criticism, proof, system, principles, rules, laws, and others of a like nature.

10. That these two exercises are not to be confounded together would seem too plain for remark, except that they have been confounded. Clearness in argument certainly is not indispensable to reasoning well. Accuracy in stating doctrines or principles is not essential to feeling and acting upon them. The exercise of analysis is not necessary to the integrity of the process analyzed. The process of reasoning is complete in itself, and independent. The analysis is but an account of it; it does not make the conclusion correct; it does not make the inference rational. It does not cause a given individual to reason better. It does but give him a sustained consciousness, for good or for evil, that he is reasoning. How a man reasons is as much a mystery as how he remembers. He remembers better and worse on different subject-matters, and he reasons better and worse. Some men's reason becomes genius in particular subjects, and is less than ordinary in others. The gift or talent of reasoning may be distinct in different subjects, though the process of reasoning is the same. Now a

s 2

good arguer or clear speaker is but one who excels in analyzing or expressing a process of reason, taken as his subject-matter. He traces out the connexion of facts, detects principles, applies them, supplies deficiencies, till he has reduced the whole into order. But his talent of reasoning, or the gift of reason as possessed by him, may be confined to such an exercise, and he may be as little expert in other exercises, as a mathematician need be an experimentalist; as little creative of the reasoning itself which he analyzes, as a critic need possess the gift of writing poems.

11. But if reasoning and arguing be thus distinct, what is to be thought of assertions such as the following? Certainly, to say the least, they are very inaccurately worded, and may lead, as they have led, to great error.

12. Tillotson[1], for instance, says: "Nothing ought to be received as a divine doctrine and revelation, *without good evidence* that it is so: that is, without some *argument* sufficient to *satisfy* a prudent and considerate man[2]." Again: "Faith . . . is an assent of the mind to something as revealed by God: now all assent must be *grounded upon evidence;* that is, no man can believe any thing, unless he have, or think he hath, some *reason* to do so. For to be confident of a thing without reason is not faith, but a presumptuous persuasion and obstinacy of mind[3]." Such assertions either have an untrue meaning, or are unequal to the inferences which the writers proceed to draw from them.

[1] Of course the statements of these various authors are true and important in their own place and from their own point of view.]
Serm. vol. ii. p. 260.   [3] Serm. vol. iv. p. 42.

13. In like manner Paley and others[4] argue that miracles are not improbable unless a Revelation is improbable, on the ground that there is no other conceivable way of ascertaining a Revelation; that is, they would imply the necessity of a conscious investigation and verification of its claims, or the possession of grounds which are satisfactory in argument; whereas considerations which seem weak and insufficient in an explicit form may lead, and justly lead, us by an implicit process to a reception of Christianity; just as a peasant may from the look of the sky foretell tomorrow's weather, on grounds which, as far as they are producible, an exact logician would not scruple to pronounce inaccurate and inconsequent. "In what way," he asks, "can a Revelation be made," that is, as the context shows, be ascertained, "but by miracles? In none which we are able to conceive."

14. Again: another writer says, "There are but two ways by which God could reveal His will to mankind; either by an immediate influence on the mind of every individual of every age, or by selecting some particular persons to be His instruments . . . . and for this purpose vested by Him with such powers as *might carry the strongest evidence* that they were really divine teachers[5]." On the other hand, Bishop Butler tells us that it is impossible to decide what evidence will be afforded of a Revelation, supposing it made; and certainly it might have been given without any supernatural display at all, being left (as it is in a manner even now)

---

[4] Prepar. Consid. p. 3; vide also Farmer on Miracles, p. 539.
[5] Douglas, Criterion, pp. 21, 22.

to be received or rejected by each man according as
his heart sympathized in it, that is, on the influence of
reasons, which, though practically persuasive, are weak
when set forth as the argumentative grounds of conviction.

15. Faith, then, though in all cases a reasonable
process, is not necessarily founded on investigation,
argument, or proof; these processes being but the explicit form which the reasoning takes in the case of
particular minds. Nay, so far from it, that the opposite
opinion has, with much more plausibility, been advanced, viz. that Faith is not even compatible with
these processes. Such an opinion, indeed, cannot be
maintained, particularly considering the light which
Scripture casts upon the subject, as in the text; but
it may easily take possession of serious minds. When
they witness the strife and division to which argument
and controversy minister, the proud self-confidence
which is fostered by strength of the reasoning powers,
the laxity of opinion which often accompanies the study
of the Evidences, the coldness, the formality, the secular
and carnal spirit which is compatible with an exact
adherence to dogmatic formularies; and on the other
hand, when they recollect that Scripture represents
religion as a divine life, seated in the affections and
manifested in spiritual graces, no wonder that they
are tempted to rescue Faith from all connexion with
faculties and habits which may exist in perfection
without Faith, and which too often usurp from Faith its
own province, and profess to be a substitute for it.   I
repeat, such a persuasion is extreme, and will not main-

tain itself, and cannot be acted on, for any long time; it being as paradoxical to prohibit religious inquiry and inference, as to make it imperative. Yet we should not dismiss the notice of it, on many accounts, without doing justice to it; and therefore I propose now, before considering⁶ some of the uses of our critical and analytical powers, in the province of Religion, to state certain of the inconveniences and defects; an undertaking which will fully occupy what remains of our time this morning.

16. Inquiry and argument may be employed, first, in ascertaining the divine origin of Religion, Natural and Revealed; next, in interpreting Scripture; and thirdly, in determining points of Faith and Morals; that is, in the Evidences, Biblical Exposition, and Dogmatic Theology. In all three departments there is, first of all, an exercise of implicit reason, which is in its degree common to all men; for all men gain a certain impression, right or wrong, from what comes before them, for or against Christianity, for or against certain interpretations of Scripture, for or against certain doctrines. This impression, made upon their minds, whether by the claim itself of Revealed Religion, or by its documents, or by its teaching, it is the object of science to analyze, verify, methodize, and exhibit. We believe certain things, on certain grounds, through certain informants; and the analysis of these three, the why, the how, and the what, seems pretty nearly to constitute the science of divinity.

[⁶ Vide Sermons xiv. and xv.]

17. (1.) By the Evidences of Religion I mean the systematic analysis of all the grounds on which we believe Christianity to be true. I say "all," because the word Evidence is often restricted to denote only such arguments as arise out of the thing itself which is to be proved; or, to speak more definitely, facts and circumstances which presuppose the point under inquiry as a condition of their existence, and which are weaker or stronger arguments, according as that point approaches more or less closely to be a necessary condition of them. Thus blood on the clothes is an evidence of a murderer, just so far as a deed of violence is necessary to the fact of the stains, or alone accounts for them. Such are the Evidences as drawn out by Paley and other writers; and though only a secondary part, they are popularly considered the whole of the Evidences, because they can be exhibited and studied with far greater ease than antecedent considerations, presumptions, and analogies, which, vague and abstruse as they are, still are more truly the grounds on which religious men receive the Gospel; but on this subject something has been said on a former occasion.

18. (2.) Under the science of Interpretation is of course included all inquiry into its principles; the question of mystical interpretation, the theory of the double sense, the doctrine of types, the phraseology of prophecy, the drift and aim of the several books of Scripture; the dates when, the places where, and persons by and to whom they were written; the comparison and adjustment of book with book; the uses

of the Old Testament; the relevancy of the Law to
Christians and its relation to the Gospel; and the
historical fulfilment of prophecy.   And previous to
such inquiries are others still more necessary, such as
the study of the original languages in which the sacred
Volume is written.

19. (3.) Under Dogmatic Theology must be included,
not only doctrine, such as that of the Blessed Trinity,
or the theory of Sacramental Influence, or the settle-
ment of the Rule of Faith, but questions of morals and
discipline also.

20. Now, in considering the imperfections and defects incident to such scientific exercises, we must carefully exempt from our remarks all instances of them
which have been vouchsafed to us from above, and
therefore have a divine sanction; and that such instances do exist, is the most direct and satisfactory
answer to any doubts which religious persons may
entertain, of the lawfulness of employing science in the
province of Faith at all.   Of such analyses and deter-
minations as are certainly from man, we are at liberty
to dispute both the truth and the utility: but what
God has done is perfect, that is, perfect according to
its subject-matter.   Whether in the department of evidence, Scripture interpretation, or dogmatic teaching,
what He has spoken must be received, not criticized ;—
and in saying this, I have not to assign the limits or
the channels of God's communications.   Whether He
speaks only by Scripture, or by private and personal
suggestion, or by the first ages, or by Tradition, or by
the Church collective, or by the Church in Council, or

by the Chair of Saint Peter, are questions about which Christians may differ without interfering with the principle itself, that what God has given is true, and what He has not given may, if so be, be not true. What He has not given by His appointed methods, whatever they be, may be venerable for its antiquity, or authoritative as held by good men, or safer to hold as held by many, or necessary to hold because it has been subscribed, or persuasive from its probability, or expedient from its good effects; but after all, except that all good things are from God, it is, as far as we know, a human statement, and is open to criticism, because the work of man. To such human inferences and propositions I confine myself in the remarks that follow.

21. Now the great practical evil of method and form in matters of religion,—nay, in all moral matters,—is obviously this:—their promising more than they can effect. At best the science of divinity is very imperfect and inaccurate, yet the very name of science is a profession of accuracy. Other and more familiar objections readily occur; such as its leading to familiarity with sacred things, and consequent irreverence; its fostering formality; its substituting a sort of religious philosophy and literature for worship and practice; its weakening the springs of action by inquiring into them; its stimulating to controversy and strife; its substituting, in matters of duty, positive rules which need explanation for an instinctive feeling which commands the mind; its leading the mind to mistake system for truth, and to suppose that an hypothesis is real because it is consistent: but all such objections, though important,

rather lead us to a cautious use of science than to a distrust of it in religious matters. But its insufficiency in so high a province is an evil which attaches to it from first to last, an inherent evil which there are no means of remedying, and which, perhaps, lies at the root of those other evils which I have just been enumerating. To this evil I shall now direct my attention, having already incidentally referred to it in some of the foregoing remarks.

22. No analysis is subtle and delicate enough to represent adequately the state of mind under which we believe, or the subjects of belief, as they are presented to our thoughts. The end proposed is that of delineating, or, as it were, painting what the mind sees and feels : now let us consider what it is to portray duly in form and colour things material, and we shall surely understand the difficulty, or rather the impossibility, of representing the outline and character, the hues and shades, in which any intellectual view really exists in the mind, or of giving it that substance and that exactness in detail in which consists its likeness to the original, or of sufficiently marking those minute differences which attach to the same general state of mind or tone of thought as found in this or that individual respectively. It is probable that a given opinion, as held by several individuals, even when of the most congenial views, is as distinct from itself as are their faces. Now how minute is the defect in imitation which hinders the likeness of a portrait from being successful! how easy is it to recognize who is intended by it, without allowing that really he is represented ! Is it

not hopeless, then, to expect that the most diligent and anxious investigation can end in more than in giving some very rude description of the living mind, and its feelings, thoughts, and reasonings? And if it be difficult to analyze fully any state, or frame, or opinion of our own minds, is it a less difficulty to delineate, as Theology professes to do, the works, dealings, providences, attributes, or nature of Almighty God?

23. In this point of view we may, without irreverence, speak even of the words of inspired Scripture as imperfect and defective; and though they are not subjects for our judgment (God forbid), yet they will for that very reason serve to enforce and explain better what I would say, and how far the objection goes. Inspiration is defective, not in itself, but in consequence of the medium it uses and the beings it addresses. It uses human language, and it addresses man; and neither can man compass, nor can his hundred tongues utter, the mysteries of the spiritual world, and God's appointments in this. This vast and intricate scene of things cannot be generalized or represented through or to the mind of man; and inspiration, in undertaking to do so, necessarily lowers what is divine to raise what is human. What, for instance, is the mention made in Scripture of the laws of God's government, of His providences, counsels, designs, anger, and repentance, but a gracious mode (the more gracious because necessarily imperfect) of making man contemplate what is far beyond him[7]? Who shall give method to what is infinitely complex, and measure to the unfathomable? We are as worms

[7 Vide Hist. of the Arians, p. 77. Edit. 3.]

in an abyss of divine works ; myriads upon myriads of years would it take, were our hearts ever so religious, and our intellects ever so apprehensive, to receive from without the just impression of those works as they really are, and as experience would convey them to us :— sooner, then, than we should know nothing, Almighty God has condescended to speak to us so far as human thought and language will admit, by approximations, in order to give us practical rules for our own conduct amid His infinite and eternal operations.

24. And herein consists one great blessing of the Gospel Covenant, that in Christ's death on the Cross, and in other parts of that all-gracious Economy, are concentrated, as it were, and so presented to us those attributes and works which fill eternity. And with a like graciousness we are also told, in human language, things concerning God Himself, concerning His Son and His Spirit, and concerning His Son's incarnation, and the union of two natures in His One Person— truths which even a peasant holds implicitly, but which Almighty God, whether by His Apostles, or by His Church after them, has vouchsafed to bring together and methodize, and to commit to the keeping of science.

25. Now all such statements are likely at first to strike coldly or harshly upon religious ears, when taken by themselves, for this reason if for no other,—that they express heavenly things under earthly images, which are infinitely below the reality. This applies especially to the doctrine of the Eternal Sonship of our Lord and Saviour, as all know who have turned their minds to the controversies on the subject.

26. Again, it may so happen, that statements are only possible in the case of certain aspects of a doctrine, and that these seem inconsistent with each other, or mysteries, when contrasted together, apart from what lies between them; just as if one were shown the picture of a little child and an old man, and were told that they represented the same person,—a statement which would be incomprehensible to beings who were unacquainted with the natural changes which take place, in the course of years, in the human frame.

27. Or doctrinal statements may be introduced, not so much for their own sake, as because many consequences flow from them, and therefore a great variety of errors may, by means of them, be prevented. Such is the doctrine that our Saviour's personality is in His Godhead, not in His manhood; that He has taken the manhood into God. It is evident that such statements, being made for the sake of something beyond, when viewed apart from their end, or in themselves, are abrupt, and may offend hearers.

28. Again, so it is, however it be explained, that frequently we do not recognize our sensations and ideas, when put into words ever so carefully. The representation seems out of shape and strange, and startles us, even though we know not how to find fault with it. This applies, at least in the case of some persons, to portions of the received theological analysis of the impression made upon the mind by the Scripture notices concerning Christ and the Holy Spirit. In like manner, such phrases as "good works are a condition of eternal life," or "the salvation of the regenerate ulti-

mately depends upon themselves,"—though unexceptionable, are of a nature to offend certain minds.

29. This difficulty of analyzing our more recondite feelings happily and convincingly, has a most important influence upon the science of the Evidences. Defenders of Christianity naturally select as reasons for belief, not the highest, the truest, the most sacred, the most intimately persuasive, but such as best admit of being exhibited in argument; and these are commonly not the real reasons in the case of religious men.

30. Nay, they are led for the same reason, to select such arguments as all will allow; that is, such as depend on principles which are a common measure for all minds. A science certainly is, in its very nature, public property; when, then, the grounds of Faith take the shape of a book of Evidences, nothing properly can be assumed but what men in general will grant as true; that is, nothing but what is on a level with all minds, good and bad, rude and refined.

31. Again, as to the difficulty of detecting and expressing the real reasons on which we believe, let this be considered,—how very differently an argument strikes the mind at one time and another, according to its particular state, or the accident of the moment. At one time it is weak and unmeaning,—at another, it is nothing short of demonstration. We take up a book at one time, and see nothing in it; at another, it is full of weighty remarks and precious thoughts. Sometimes a statement is axiomatic,—sometimes we are at a loss to see what can be said for it. Such, for instance, are the following, many like which are found in contro-

versy;—that true saints cannot but persevere to the end; or that the influences of the Spirit cannot but be effectual; or that there must be an infallible Head of the Church on earth; or that the Roman Church, extending into all lands, is the Catholic Church; or that a Church, which is Catholic abroad, cannot be schismatical in England; or that, if our Lord is the Son of God, He must be God; or that a Revelation is probable; or that, if God is All-powerful, He must be also All-good. Who shall analyze the assemblage of opinions in this or that mind, which occasions it almost instinctively to reject or to accept each of these and similar positions? Far be it from me to seem to insinuate that they are *but* opinions, neither true nor false, and approving themselves or not, according to the humour or prejudice of the individual: so far from it, that I would maintain that the recondite reasons which lead each person to take or decline them, are just the most important portion of the considerations on which his conviction depends; and I say so, by way of showing that the science of controversy, or again the science of Evidences, has done very little, since it cannot analyze and exhibit these momentous reasons; nay, so far has done worse than little, in that it professes to have done much, and leads the student to mistake what are but secondary points in debate, as if they were the most essential.

32. It often happens, for the same reason, that controversialists or philosophers are spoken of by this or that person as unequal, sometimes profound, sometimes weak. Such cases of inequality, of course, do occur;

but we should be sure, when tempted so to speak, that the fault is not with ourselves, who have not entered into an author's meaning, or analyzed the implicit reasonings along which his mind proceeds in those parts of his writings which we not merely dissent from (for that we have a right to do), but criticize as inconsecutive.

33. These remarks apply especially to the proofs commonly brought, whether for the truth of Christianity, or for certain doctrines from texts of Scripture. Such alleged proofs are commonly strong or slight, not in themselves, but according to the circumstances under which the doctrine professes to come to us, which they are brought to prove; and they will have a great or small effect upon our minds, according as we admit those circumstances or not. Now, the admission of those circumstances involves a variety of antecedent views, presumptions, implications, associations, and the like, many of which it is very difficult to detect and analyze. One person, for instance, is convinced by Paley's argument from the Miracles, another is not; and why? Because the former admits that there is a God, that He governs the world, that He wishes the salvation of man, that the light of nature is not sufficient for man, that there is no other way of introducing a Revelation but miracles, and that men, who were neither enthusiasts nor impostors, could not have acted as the Apostles did, unless they had seen the miracles which they attested; the other denies some one, or more, of these statements, or does not feel the force of some other principle more recondite and latent

still than any of these, which is nevertheless necessary to the validity of the argument.

34. Further, let it be considered, that, even as regards what are commonly called Evidences, that is, arguments *à posteriori*, conviction for the most part follows, not upon any one great and decisive proof or token of the point in debate, but upon a number of very minute circumstances together, which the mind is quite unable to count up and methodize in an argumentative form. Let a person only call to mind the clear impression he has about matters of every day's occurrence, that this man is bent on a certain object, or that that man was displeased, or another suspicious; or that one is happy, and another unhappy; and how much depends in such impressions on manner, voice, accent, words uttered, silence instead of words, and all the many subtle symptoms which are felt by the mind, but cannot be contemplated; and let him consider how very poor an account he is able to give of his impression, if he avows it, and is called upon to justify it. This, indeed, is meant by what is called moral proof, in opposition to legal. We speak of an accused person being guilty without any doubt, even though the evidences of his guilt are none of them broad and definite enough in themselves to admit of being forced upon the notice of those who will not exert themselves to see them.

35. Now, should the proof of Christianity, or the Scripture proof of its doctrines, be of this subtle nature, of course it cannot be exhibited to advantage in argument: and even if it be not such, but contain strong

and almost legal evidences, still there will always be a temptation in the case of writers on Evidence, or on the Scripture proof of doctrine, to over-state and exaggerate, or to systematize in excess; as if they were making a case in a court of law, rather than simply and severely analyzing, as far as is possible, certain existing reasons why the Gospel is true, or why it should be considered of a certain doctrinal character. It is hardly too much to say, that almost all reasons formally adduced in moral inquiries, are rather specimens and symbols of the real grounds, than those grounds themselves. They do but approximate to a representation of the general character of the proof which the writer wishes to convey to another's mind. They cannot, like mathematical proof, be passively followed with an attention confined to what is stated, and with the admission of nothing but what is urged. Rather, they are hints towards, and samples of, the true reasoning, and demand an active, ready, candid, and docile mind, which can throw itself into what is said, neglect verbal difficulties, and pursue and carry out principles. This is the true office of a writer, to excite and direct trains of thought; and this, on the other hand, is the too common practice of readers, to expect every thing to be done for them,—to refuse to think,—to criticize the letter, instead of reaching forwards towards the sense,—and to account every argument as unsound which is illogically worded.

36. Here is the fertile source of controversy, which may undoubtedly be prolonged without limit by those who desire it, while words are incomplete exponents of

ideas, and complex reasons demand study, and involve prolixity. They, then, who wish to shorten the dispute, and to silence a captious opponent, look out for some strong and manifest argument which may be stated tersely, handled conveniently, and urged rhetorically; some one reason, which bears with it a show of vigour and plausibility, or a profession of clearness, simplicity, or originality, and may be easily reduced to mood and figure. Hence the stress often laid upon particular texts, as if decisive of the matter in hand : hence one disputant dismisses all parts of the Bible which relate to the Law,—another finds the high doctrines of Christianity revealed in the Book of Genesis,— another rejects certain portions of the inspired volume, as the Epistle of St. James,—another gives up the Apocrypha,—another rests the defence of Revelation on Miracles only, or the Internal Evidence only,— another sweeps away all Christian teaching but Scripture,—one and all from impatience at being allotted, in the particular case, an evidence which does little more than create an impression on the mind; from dislike of an evidence, varied, minute, complicated, and a desire of something producible, striking, and decisive.

37. Lastly, since a test is in its very nature of a negative character, and since argumentative forms are mainly a test of reasoning, so far they will be but critical, not creative. They will be useful in raising objections, and in ministering to scepticism; they will pull down, and will not be able to build up.

38. I have been engaged in proving the following

points : that the reasonings and opinions which are in-volved in the act of Faith are latent and implicit; that the mind reflecting on itself is able to bring them out into some definite and methodical form; that Faith, however, is complete without this reflective faculty, which, in matter of fact, often does interfere with it, and must be used cautiously.

39. I am quite aware that I have said nothing but what must have often passed through the minds of others ; and it may be asked whether it is worth while so diligently to traverse old ground. Yet perhaps it is never without its use to bring together in one view, and steadily contemplate truths, which one by one may be familiar notwithstanding.

40. May we be in the number of those who, with the Blessed Apostle whom we this day commemorate, employ all the powers of their minds to the service of their Lord and Saviour, who are drawn heavenward by Hiswonder-working grace, whose hearts are filled with His love, who reason in His fear, who seek Him in the way of His commandments, and who thereby believe on Him to the saving of their souls !

SERMON XIV.

WISDOM, AS CONTRASTED WITH FAITH AND WITH BIGOTRY.

(Preached on Whit-Tuesday, 1841.)

1 Cor. ii. 15.

" He that is spiritual iudgeth all things, yet he himself is judged of no man."

THE gift to which this high characteristic is ascribed by the Apostle is Christian Wisdom, and the Giver is God the Holy Ghost. "We speak wisdom," he says, shortly before the text, "among them that are perfect, yet not the wisdom of this world . . . but we speak the wisdom of God in a mystery, even the hidden wisdom." And after making mention of the heavenly truths which Wisdom contemplates, he adds: "God hath revealed them unto us by His Spirit . . . we have received, not the spirit of the world, but the Spirit which is of God."

2. In a former verse St. Paul contrasts this divine Wisdom with Faith. "My speech and my preaching was not with enticing words of man's wisdom, but in demonstration of the Spirit and of power, that your faith should not stand in the wisdom of men, but in

the power of God.   Howbeit, we speak wisdom among
them that are perfect."   Faith, then, and Wisdom, are
distinct, or even opposite gifts.   Wisdom belongs to
the perfect, and more especially to preachers of the
Gospel; and Faith is the elementary grace which is
required of all, especially of hearers.   The two are introduced again in a later chapter of the same Epistle :
" To one is given by the Spirit the word of Wisdom, to
another the word of Knowledge by the same Spirit, to
another Faith by the same Spirit."   Such are the two
gifts which will be found to lie at the beginning and
at the end of our new life, both intellectual in their
nature, and both divinely imparted; Faith being an
exercise of the Reason, so spontaneous, unconscious, and
unargumentative, as to seem at first sight even to be
a moral act, and Wisdom being that orderly and mature
development of thought, which in earthly language
goes by the name of science and philosophy.

3. In like manner, in the Services of this sacred
Season, both these spiritual gifts are intimated, and
both referred to the same heavenly source.   The Collect virtually speaks of Faith, when it makes mention
of Almighty God's " teaching the hearts of His faithful
people by the sending to them the light of His Holy
Spirit;" and of the Wisdom of the perfect, when it
prays God, that " by the same Spirit " we may " have a
right judgment in all things."

4. Again, in the Gospel for Whitsunday, the gift of
Wisdom is surely implied in Christ's promise, that the
Comforter should teach the Apostles " all things," and
"bring all things to their remembrance whatsoever He

had said unto them;" and in St. Paul's exhortation,
which we read yesterday, "In malice be children, but
in understanding be men." Again, a cultivation of the
reasoning faculty, near akin to Philosophy or Wisdom,
is surely implied in the precepts, of which we have
heard, or shall hear, from the same Apostle and St.
John to-day, about "proving all things," and "holding
fast that which is good," and about "trying the spirits
whether they are of God."

5. Again, other parts of our Whitsun Services speak
of exercises of Reason more akin to Faith, as being
independent of processes of investigation or discussion.
In Sunday's Gospel our Lord tells us, "He that loveth
Me shall be loved of My Father, and I will love him,
and will manifest Myself to him. . . . If a man love
Me, he will keep My words, and My Father will love
him, and We will come unto him, and make Our abode
with him." This manifestation is doubtless made to
us through our natural faculties; but who will maintain
that even so far as it is addressed to our Reason, it
comes to us in forms of argument? Again, in the
Gospel for yesterday, "He that doeth truth cometh to
the light," and on the contrary, "Light is come into
the world, and men loved darkness rather than light,
because their deeds were evil; for every one that doeth
evil hateth the light." Men do not choose light or
darkness without Reason, but by an instinctive Reason,
which is prior to argument and proof. And in the
Gospel for to-day, "The sheep hear His voice, and He
calleth His own sheep by name, and leadeth them out.
The sheep follow Him, for they know His voice, and a

stranger will they not follow, for they know not the voice of strangers." The sheep could not tell *how* they knew the Good Shepherd; they had not analyzed their own impressions or cleared the grounds of their know-ledge, yet doubtless grounds there were : they, however, acted spontaneously on a loving Faith.

6. In proceeding, then, as I shall now do, to inquire into the nature of Christian Wisdom, as a habit or faculty of mind distinct from Faith, the mature fruit of Reason, and nearly answering to what is meant by Philosophy, it must not be supposed that I am denying its spiritual nature or its divine origin. Almighty God influences us and works in us, through our minds, not without them or in spite of them ; as at the fall we did not become other beings than we had been, but forfeited gifts which had been added to us on our creation, so under the Gospel we do not lose any part of the nature in which we are born, but regain what we have lost. We are what we were, and something more. And what is true of God's dealings with our minds generally, is true in particular as regards our reasoning powers. His grace does not supersede, but uses them, and renews them by using. We gain Truth by reasoning, whether implicit or explicit, in a state of nature : we gain it in the same way in a state of grace. Both Faith and Wisdom, the elementary and the perfecting gift of the Holy Spirit, are intellectual habits, and involve the exercise of Reason, and may be examined and defined as any other power of the mind, and are subject to perversion and error, and may be fortified by rules, just as if they were not instruments in the hands of

the Most High. It is no derogation, then, from the
divine origin of Christian Wisdom, to treat it in its
human aspect, to show what it consists in, and what
are its counterfeits and perversions; to determine, for
instance, that it is much the same as Philosophy, and
that its perversions are such as love of system, theorizing, fancifulness, dogmatism, and bigotry,—as we
shall be led to do. And now to enter upon our
subject.

7. The words philosophy, a philosophical spirit, enlargement or expansion of mind, enlightened ideas, a
wise and comprehensive view of things, and the like,
are, I need hardly say, of frequent occurrence in the
literature of this day, and are taken to mean very much
the same thing. That they are always used with a
definite meaning, or with any meaning at all, will be
maintained by no one; that so many persons, and many
of them men of great ability, should use them absolutely
with no meaning whatever, and yet should lay 'such
stress and rest so much upon them, is, on the other
hand, not to be supposed. Yet their meaning certainly
requires drawing out and illustrating. Perhaps it will
be best ascertained by setting down some cases, which
are commonly understood, or will be claimed, as instances of this process of mental growth or enlargement, in the sense in which the words are at present
used.

8. I suppose that, when a person whose experience
has hitherto been confined to our own calm and unpre-
tending scenery, goes for the first time into parts where

physical nature puts on her wilder and more awful forms, whether at home or abroad, as especially into mountainous districts,—or when one who has ever lived in a quiet village comes for the first time to a great metropolis,—he will have a sensation of mental enlarge‧ ment, as having gained a range of thoughts to which he was before a stranger.

9. Again, the view of the heavens, which the telescope opens upon us, fills and possesses the mind, and is called an enlargement, whatever is meant by the term.

10. Again, the sight of an assemblage of beasts of prey and other foreign animals, their strangeness and startling novelty, the originality (if I may use the term) and mysteriousness of their forms, and gestures, and habits, and their variety and independence of one another, expand the mind, not without its own conscious- ness; as if knowledge were a real opening, and as if an addition to the external objects presented before it were an addition to its inward powers.

11. Hence physical science, generally, in all its depart- ments, as bringing before us the exuberant riches, the active principles, yet the orderly course of the universe, is often set forth even as the only true philosophy, and will be allowed by all persons to have a certain power of elevating and exciting the mind, and yet to exercise a tranquillizing influence upon it.

12. Again, the knowledge of history, and again, the knowledge of books generally—in a word, what is meant by education, is commonly said to enlighten and enlarge the mind, whereas ignorance is felt to

involve a narrow range and a feeble exercise of its powers.

13. Again, what is called seeing the world, entering into active life, going into society, travelling, acquaintance with the various classes of the community, coming into contact with the principles and modes of thought of separate parties, interests, or nations, their opinions, views, aims, habits, and manners, their religious creeds and forms of worship,—all this exerts a perceptible effect upon the mind, which it is impossible to mistake, be it good or be it bad, and which is popularly called its enlargement or enlightenment.

14. Again, when a person for the first time hears the arguments and speculations of unbelievers, and feels what a very novel light they cast upon what he has hitherto accounted most sacred, it cannot be denied that, unless he is shocked and closes his ears and heart to them, he will have a sense of expansion and elevation.

15. Again, sin brings with it its own enlargement of mind, which Eve was tempted to covet, and of which she made proof. This, perhaps, in the instance of some sins, to which the young are especially tempted, is their great attraction and their great recompense. They excite the curiosity of the innocent, and they intoxicate the imagination of their miserable victims, whose eyes seem opened upon a new world, from which they look back upon their state of innocence with a sort of pity and contempt, as if it were below the dignity of men.

16. On the other hand, religion has its own enlarge-

ment. It is often remarked of uneducated persons, who hitherto have lived without seriousness, that on their turning to God, looking into themselves, regulating their hearts, reforming their conduct, and studying the inspired Word, they seem to become, in point of intellect, different beings from what they were before. Before, they took things as they came, and thought no more of one thing than of another. But now every event has a meaning; they form their own estimate of whatever occurs; they recollect times and seasons; and the world, instead of being like the stream which the countryman gazed on, ever in motion and never in progress, is a various and complicated drama, with parts and with an object.

17. Again, those who, being used to nothing better than the divinity of what is historically known as the nonconformist school,—or, again, of the latitudinarian, —are introduced to the theology of the early Church, will often have a vivid sense of enlargement, and will feel they have gained something, as becoming aware of the existence of doctrines, opinions, trains of thought, principles, aims, to which hitherto they have been strangers.

18. And again, such works as treat of the Ministry of the Prophets under the various divine Dispensations, of its nature and characteristics, why it was instituted and what it has effected; the matter, the order, the growth of its disclosures; the views of divine Providence, of the divine counsels and attributes which it was the means of suggesting; and its contrast with the pretences to prophetical knowledge which the

world furnishes in mere political partisans or popular fortune-tellers; such treatises, as all will admit, may fitly be said to enlarge the mind.

19. Once more, such works as Bishop Butler's Analogy, which carry on the characteristic lineaments of the Gospel Dispensation into the visible course of things, and, as it were, root its doctrines into nature and society, not only present before the mind a large view of the matters handled, but will be commonly said, and surely, as all will feel, with a true meaning, to enlarge the mind itself which is put in possession of them.

20. These instances show beyond all question that what is called Philosophy, Wisdom, or Enlargement of mind, has some intimate dependence upon the acquisition of Knowledge; and Scripture seems to say the same thing. "God gave Solomon," says the inspired writer, "wisdom and understanding, exceeding much, and largeness of heart even as the sand that is on the sea shore. . . . And he spake three thousand proverbs, and his songs were a thousand and five. And he spake of trees, from the cedar-tree that is in Lebanon, even unto the hyssop that springeth out of the wall. He spake also of beasts and of fowl, and of creeping things and of fishes." And again, when the Queen of Sheba came, " Solomon told her all her questions; there was not any thing hid from the king, which he told her not." And in like manner St. Paul, after speaking of the Wisdom of the perfect, calls it a revelation, a knowledge, of the things of God, such as the natural man " discerneth " not. And in another

Epistle, evidently speaking of the same Wisdom, he prays that his brethren may be given to "comprehend with all saints what is the breadth and length and depth and height, and to know the love of Christ which passeth knowledge, that they might be filled with all the fulness of God."

21. However, a very little consideration will make it plain also, that knowledge itself, though a condition of the mind's enlargement, yet, whatever be its range, is not that very thing which enlarges it. Rather the foregoing instances show that this enlargement consists in the comparison of the subjects of knowledge one with another. We feel ourselves to be ranging freely, when we not only learn something, but when we also refer it to what we knew before. It is not the mere addition to our knowledge which is the enlargement, but the change of place, the movement onwards, of that moral centre, to which what we know and what we have been acquiring, the whole mass of our knowledge, as it were, gravitates. And therefore a philosophical cast of thought, or a comprehensive mind, or wisdom in conduct or policy, implies a connected view of the old with the new; an insight into the bearing and influence of each part upon every other; without which there is no whole, and could be no centre. It is the knowledge, not only of things, but of their mutual relations. It is organized, and therefore living knowledge.

22. A number of instances might readily be supplied in which knowledge is found apart from this analytical

treatment of the matter of it, and in which it is never associated with Philosophy, or considered to open, enlarge, and enlighten the mind.

23. For instance, a great memory is never made synonymous with Wisdom, any more than a dictionary would be called a treatise. There are men who contemplate things both in the mass and individually, but not correlatively, who accumulate facts without forming judgments, who are satisfied with deep learning or extensive information. They may be linguists, antiquarians, annalists, biographers, or naturalists; but, whatever their merits, which are often very great, they have no claim to be considered philosophers.

24. To the same class belong persons, in other respects very different, who have seen much of the world, and of the men who, in their own day, have played a conspicuous part in it, who are full of information, curious and entertaining, about men and things, but who having lived under the influence of no very clear or settled principles, speak of every one and every thing as mere facts of history, not attempting to illustrate opinions, measures, aims, or policy,—not discussing or teaching, but conversing.

25. Or take, what is again a very different instance, the case of persons of little intellect, and no education, who perhaps have seen much of foreign countries, and who receive in a passive, otiose, unfruitful way, the various facts which are forced upon them. Seafaring men, for example, range from one end of the earth to the other; but the multiplicity of phenomena which they have encountered, forms no harmonious and con-

sistent picture upon their imagination : they see, as it
were, the tapestry of human life on the wrong side of it.
They sleep, and they rise up, and they find themselves
now in Europe, now in Asia; they see visions of great
cities and wild regions; they are in the marts of
commerce, or amid the islands of the ocean ; they gaze
on the Andes, or they are ice-bound; and nothing
which meets them carries them on to any idea beyond
itself. Nothing has a meaning, nothing has a history,
nothing has relations. Every thing stands by itself,
and comes and goes in its turn, like the shifting sights
of a show, leaving the beholder where he was. Or,
again, under other circumstances, every thing seems
to such persons strange, monstrous, miraculous, and
awful; as in fable, to Ulysses and his companions in
their wanderings.

26. Or, again, the censure often passed on what is
called undigested reading, shows us that knowledge
without system is not Philosophy. Students who store
themselves so amply with literature or science, that no
room is left for determining the respective relations
which exist between their acquisitions, one by one, are
rather said to load their minds than to enlarge them.

27. Scepticism, in religious matters, affords another
instance in point. Those who deliberately refuse to form
a judgment upon the most momentous of all subjects;
who are content to pass through life in ignorance, why
it is given, or by whom, or to what it leads; and who
bear to be without tests of truth and error in conduct,
without rule and measure for the principles, persons,
and events, which they encounter daily,—these men,

though they often claim, will not by any Christian be granted, the name of philosophers.

28. All this is more than enough to show that some analytical process, some sort of systematizing, some insight into the mutual relations of things, is essential to that enlargement of mind or philosophical temper, which is commonly attributed to the acquisition of knowledge. In other words, Philosophy is Reason exercised upon Knowledge; for, from the nature of the case, where the facts are given, as is here supposed, Reason is synonymous with analysis, having no office beyond that of ascertaining the relations existing between them. Reason is the power of proceeding to new ideas by means of given ones. Where but one main idea is given, it can employ itself in developing this into its consequences. Thus, from scanty data, it often draws out a whole system, each part with its ascertained relations, collateral or lineal, towards the rest, and all consistent together, because all derived from one and the same origin. And should means be found of ascertaining directly some of the facts which it has been deducing by this abstract process, then their coincidence with its *à priori* judgments will serve to prove the accuracy of its deductions. Where, however, the facts or doctrines in question are all known from the first, there, instead of advancing from idea to idea, Reason does but connect fact with fact; instead of discovering, it does but analyze; and what was, in the former case, the tracing out of inferences, becomes a laying down of relations.

29. Philosophy, then, is Reason exercised upon

Knowledge; or the Knowledge not merely of things in general, but of things in their relations to one another. It is the power of referring every thing to its true place in the universal system,—of understanding the various aspects of each of its parts,—of comprehending the exact value of each,—of tracing each backwards to its beginning, and forward to its end,—of anticipating the separate tendencies of each, and their respective checks or counteractions; and thus of accounting for anomalies, answering objections, supplying deficiencies, making allowance for errors, and meeting emergencies. It never views any part of the extended subject-matter of knowledge, without recollecting that it is but a part, or without the associations which spring from this recollection. It makes every thing lead to every thing else; it communicates the image of the whole body to every separate member, till the whole becomes in imagination like a spirit, every where pervading and penetrating its component parts, and giving them their one definite meaning. Just as our bodily organs, when mentioned, recall to mind their function in the body, as the word creation suggests the idea of a Creator, as subjects that of a sovereign, so in the mind of a philosopher, the elements of the physical and moral world, sciences, arts, pursuits, ranks, offices, events, opinions, individualities, are all viewed, not in themselves, but as relative terms, suggesting a multitude of correlatives, and gradually, by successive combinations, converging one and all to their true centre. Men, whose minds are possessed by some one object, take exaggerated views of its importance, are feverish in their

pursuit of it, and are startled or downcast on finding
obstacles in the way of it; they are ever in alarm or
in transport. And they, on the contrary, who have no
firm grasp of principles, are perplexed and lose their
way every fresh step they take; they do not know
what to think or say of new phenomena which meet
them, of whatever kind; they have no view, as it may
be called, concerning persons, or occurrences, or facts,
which come upon them suddenly; they cannot form a
judgment, or determine on a course of action; and
they ask the opinion or advice of others as a relief to
their minds. But Philosophy cannot be partial,
cannot be exclusive, cannot be impetuous, cannot
be surprised, cannot fear, cannot lose its balance,
cannot be at a loss, cannot but be patient, collected,
and majestically calm, because it discerns the whole in
each part, the end in each beginning, the worth of
each interruption, the measure of each delay, because
it always knows where it is, and how its path lies from
one point to another. There are men who, when in
difficulties, by the force of genius, originate at the
moment vast ideas or dazzling projects; who, under
the impulse of excitement, are able to cast a light,
almost as if from inspiration, on a subject or course of
action which comes before them; who have a sudden
presence of mind equal to any emergency, rising with
the occasion, and an undaunted heroic bearing, and an
energy and keenness, which is but sharpened by opposition. Faith is a gift analogous to this thus far, that
it acts promptly and boldly on the occasion, on slender
evidence, as if guessing and reaching forward to the

truth, amid darkness or confusion; but such is not the
Wisdom of the perfect. Wisdom is the clear, calm, accurate vision, and comprehension of the whole course, the
whole work of God; and though there is none who
has it in its fulness but He who "searcheth all things,
yea, the deep things of" the Creator, yet "by that
Spirit" they are, in a measure, "revealed unto us."
And thus, according to that measure, is the text fulfilled, that "he that is spiritual judgeth all things, yet he
himself is judged by no man." Others understand him
not, master not his ideas, fail to combine, harmonize, or
make consistent, those distinct views and principles
which come to him from the Infinite Light, and are
inspirations of the breath of God. He, on the contrary, compasses others, and locates them, and anticipates their acts, and fathoms their thoughts, for, in the
Apostle's language, he "hath the mind of Christ," and
all things are his, "whether Paul, or Apollos, or
Cephas, or the world, or life, or death, or things present, or things to come." Such is the marvellousness
of the Pentecostal gift, whereby we "have an unction
from the Holy One, and know all things."

30. Now, this view of the nature of Philosophy leads
to the following remark : that, whereas no arguments
in favour of Religion are of much account but such as
rest on a philosophical basis, Evidences of Religion, as
they are called, which are truly such, must consist
mainly in such investigations into the relation of idea
to idea, and such developments of system, as have been
described, if Philosophy lie in these abstract exercises
of Reason. Such, for instance, is the argument from

analogy, or from the structure of prophecy, or from the
needs of human nature; or from the establishment and
history of the Catholic Church. From which it follows,
first, that what may be called the rhetorical or forensic
Evidences,—I mean those which are content with the
proof of certain facts, motives, and the like, such as,
that a certain miracle must have taken place, or
a certain prophecy must have been both written
before, and fulfilled in, a certain event; these, whatever their merits, which I have no wish to disparage,
are not philosophical. And next, it follows that Evidences in general are not the essential groundwork of
Faith, but its reward; since Wisdom is the last gift of
the Spirit, and Faith the first.

31. In the foregoing observations I have, in fact,
been showing,—in prosecution of a line of thought to
which I have before now drawn attention,—what is the
true office, and what the legitimate bounds, of those
abstract exercises of Reason which may best be described by the name of systematizing. They are in
their highest and most honourable place, when they
are employed upon the vast field of Knowledge, not in
conjecturing unknown truths, but in comparing, adjusting, connecting, explaining facts and doctrines ascer
tained. Such a use of Reason is Philosophy; such em
ployment was it to which the reason of Newton dedicated
itself; and the reason of Butler; and the reason of
those ancient Catholic Divines, nay, in their measure,
of those illustrious thinkers of the middle ages, who
have treated of the Christian Faith on system, Atha-

nasius, Augustine, Aquinas.   But where the exercise
of Reason much outstrips our Knowledge; where
Knowledge is limited, and Reason active; where ascertained truths are scanty, and courses of thought
abound; there indulgence of system is unsafe, and may
be dangerous.   In such cases there is much need of
wariness, jealousy of self, and habitual dread of presumption, paradox, and unreality, to preserve our deductions within the bounds of sobriety, and our guesses
from assuming the character of discoveries.   System,
which is the very soul, or, to speak more precisely,
the formal cause of Philosophy, when exercised upon
adequate knowledge, does but make, or tend to make,
theorists, dogmatists, philosophists, and sectarians,
when or so far as Knowledge is limited or incomplete.

32. This statement, which will not be questioned,
perhaps, in the abstract, requires to be illustrated in
detail, and that at a length inconsistent with my present
limits.   At the risk, however, of exceeding them, I will
attempt so much as this,—to show that Faith, distinct
as it is from argument, discussion, investigation, philosophy, nay, from Reason altogether, in the popular
sense of the word, is at the same time perfectly distinct
also from narrowness of mind in all its shapes, though
sometimes accidentally connected with it in particular
persons.   I am led to give attention to this point from
its connexion with subjects, of which I have already
treated on former occasions.

33. It is as if a law of the human mind, ever to do
things in one and the same way.   It does not vary in
its modes of action, except by an effort; but, if left to

itself, it becomes almost mechanical, as a matter of course. Its doing a thing in a certain way to-day, is the cause of its doing it in the same way to-morrow. The order of the day perpetuates itself. This is, in fact, only saying that habits arise out of acts, and that character is inseparable from our moral nature. Not only do our features and make remain the same day after day, but we speak in the same tone, adopt the same phrases and turns of thought, fall into the same expressions of countenance, and walk with the same gait as yesterday. And, besides, we have an instinctive love of order and arrangement; we think and act by rule, not only unconsciously, but of set purpose. Method approves itself to us, and aids us in various ways, and to a certain point is pleasant, and in some respects absolutely necessary. Even sceptics cannot proceed without elementary principles, though they would fain dispense with every yoke and bond. Even the uneducated have their own rude modes of classifying, not the less really such, because fantastic or absurd; children too, amid their awe at all that meets them, yet in their own thoughts unconsciously subject these wonders to a law. Poets, while they disown philosophy, frame an ideal system of their own; and naturalists invent, if they do not find, orders and *genera*, to assist the memory. Latitudinarians, again, while they profess charity towards all doctrines, nevertheless count it heresy to oppose the principle of latitude. Those who condemn persecution for religious opinions, in self-defence persecute those who advocate it. Few of those who maintain that the exercise of private judgment upon Scripture leads to the attainment of Gospel truth, can tolerate the Socinian and Pelagian, who in their own inquiries have taken pains to conform to this rule. Thus, what is invidiously called dogmatism and system, in one shape or other, in one degree or another, is, I may say, necessary to the human mind; we cannot reason, feel, or act, without it; it forms the stamina of thought, which, when it is removed, languishes, and droops. Sooner than dispense with principles, the mind will take them at the hand of others, will put up with such as are faulty or uncertain;—and thus much Wisdom, Bigotry, and Faith, have in common. Principle is the life of them all; but Wisdom is the application of adequate principles to the state of things as we find them, Bigotry is the application of inadequate or narrow principles, while Faith is the maintenance of principles, without caring to apply or adjust them. Thus they differ; and this distinction will serve to enable us to contrast Bigotry and Faith with Wisdom, as I proposed.

34. Now, certainly, Faith may be confused with Bigotry, with dogmatism, positiveness, and kindred habits of mind, on several plausible grounds; for, what is Faith but a reaching forth after truth amid darkness, upon the warrant of certain antecedent notions or spontaneous feelings? It is a presumption about matters of fact, upon principle rather than on knowledge; and what is Bigotry also but this? And, further still, its grounds being thus conditional, what does it issue in? in the absolute acceptance of a certain message or doctrine as divine; that is, it starts from probabilities, yet

it ends in peremptory statements, if so be, mysterious,
or at least beyond experience. It believes an informant
amid doubt, yet accepts his information without doubt.
Such is the *primâ facie* resemblance between two habits
of mind, which nevertheless are as little to be confused
as the Apostles with their Jewish persecutors, as a few
words may suffice to show.

35. Now, in the first place, though Faith be a presumption of facts under defective knowledge, yet, be it
observed, it is altogether a practical principle. It
judges and decides because it cannot help doing so, for
the sake of the man himself, who exercises it—not in the
way of opinion, not as aiming at mere abstract truth, not
as teaching some theory or view. It is the act of a mind
feeling that it is its duty any how, under its particular
circumstances, to judge and to act, whether its light be
greater or less, and wishing to make the most of that
light and acting for the best. Its knowledge, then,
though defective, is not insufficient for the purpose for
which it uses it, for this plain reason, because (such is
God's will) it has no more. The servant who hid his
Lord's money was punished; and we, since we did not
make our circumstances, but were placed in them, shall
be judged, not by them, but by our use of them. A
view of duty, such as this, may lead us to wrong acts,
but not to act wrongly. Christians have sometimes
inflicted death from a zeal not according to knowledge;
and sometimes they have been eager for the toleration
of heresy from an ill-instructed charity. Under such
circumstances a man's error may be more acceptable to
God than his truth; for his truth, it may be, but evi-

dences clearness of intellect, whereas his error proceeds
from conscientiousness; though whence it proceeds,
and what it evidences, in a particular case, must be left
to the Searcher of hearts.

36. Faith, then, though a presumption, has this
peculiarity, that it is exercised under a sense of personal responsibility. It is when our presumptions take
a wide range, when they affect to be systematical and
philosophical, when they are indulged in matters of
speculation, not of conduct, not in reference to self,
but to others, then it is that they deserve the name of
bigotry and dogmatism. For in such a case we make
a wrong use of such light as is given us, and mistake what
is "a lantern unto our feet" for the sun in the heavens.

37. Again, it is true that Faith as well as Bigotry
maintains dogmatic statements which go beyond its
knowledge. It uses words, phrases, propositions, it
accepts doctrines and practices, which it but partially
understands, or not at all. Now, so far indeed as these
statements do not relate to matters of this world, but
to heavenly things, of course they are no evidence of
Bigotry. As the widest experience of life would not
tend to remove the mysteriousness of the doctrine of
the Holy Trinity, so even the narrowest does not deprive us of the right of asserting it. Much knowledge
and little knowledge leave us very much as we were,
in a matter of this kind. But the case is very different
when positions are in question of a social or moral
character, which claim to be rules or maxims for political combination or conduct, for the well-being of
the world, or for the guidance of public opinion. Yet

many such positions Faith certainly does accept; and
thus it seems to place the persons who act upon it in
the very position of the bigoted, theoretical, and unreal;
who use words beyond their depth, or avow sentiments
to which they have no right, or enunciate general
principles on defective knowledge.   Questions, for instance, about the theory of government, national duties,
the establishment of Religion, its relations to the State,
the treatment of the poor, and the nature of the Christian Church : these, and other such, may, it cannot be
denied, be peremptorily settled, on religious grounds,
by persons whose qualifications are manifestly unequal
to so great an undertaking, who have not the knowledge, penetration, subtlety, calmness, or experience,
which are a claim upon our attention, and who in consequence are, at first sight, to say the least, very like
bigots and partisans.

38. Now that Faith may run into Bigotry, or may
be mixed with Bigotry in matter of fact in this instance
or that, of course I do not deny; at the same time the
two habits of mind, whatever be their resemblance,
differ in their dogmatism, in this :—Bigotry professes
to understand what it maintains, though it does not;
it argues and infers, it disowns Faith, and makes a
show of Reason instead of it.   It persists, not in abandoning argument, but in arguing only in one way.   It
takes up, not a religious, but a philosophical position;
it lays claim to Wisdom, whereas Faith from the first
makes men willing, with the Apostle, to be fools for
Christ's sake.   Faith sets out with putting reasoning
aside as out of place, and proposes instead simple

obedience to a revealed command. Its disciples represent that they are neither statesmen nor philosophers;
that they are not developing principles or evolving
systems; that their ultimate end is not persuasion,
popularity, or success; that they are but doing God's
will, and desiring His glory. They profess a sincere
belief that certain views which engage their minds
come from God; that they know well that they are
beyond them; that they are not able to enter into
them, or to apply them as others may do; that, understanding them but partially themselves, they are not
sanguine about impressing them on others; that a
divine blessing alone can carry them forward; that
they look for that blessing; that they feel that God
will maintain His own cause; that *that* belongs to Him,
not to them[1]; that if their cause is God's cause, it will
be blessed, in His time and way; that if it be not, it
will come to nought; that they securely wait the
issue; that they leave it to the generation to come;
that they can bear to seem to fail, but cannot bear to
be "disobedient to a heavenly vision;" that they think
that God has taught them and put a word in their
mouths; that they speak to acquit their own souls;
that they protest in order to be on the side of God's
host, of the glorious company of the Apostles, the
goodly fellowship of the Prophets, the noble army of
Martyrs, in order to be separate from the congregation
of His enemies. "Blessed is the man that hath not
walked in the counsel of the ungodly, nor stood in the
way of sinners, and hath not sat in the seat of the

[1] Dan. iii. 17, 18.

scornful." They desire to gain this blessedness; and
though they have not the capacity of mind to embrace,
nor the keenness to penetrate and analyze the contents
of this vast world, nor the comprehensive faculty which
resolves all things into their true principles, and
connects them in one system, though they can neither
answer objections made to their doctrines, nor say for
certain whither they are leading them, yet profess them
they can and must. Embrace them they can, and go
out, not knowing whither they go. Faith, at least,
they may have; Wisdom, if so be, they have not; but
Faith fits them to be the instruments and organs, the
voice and the hands and the feet of Him who is
invisible, the Divine Wisdom in the Church,—who
knows what they know not, understands their words,
for they are His own, and directs their efforts to His
own issues, though they see them not, because they
dutifully place themselves upon His path. This is what
they will be found to profess; and their state is that of
the multitude of Christians in every age, nay even in
the Apostolic, when, for all the supernatural illumination of such as St. Paul, " God chose the foolish things
of the world to confound the wise, and the weak things
of the world to confound the things which were mighty,
and base things of the world, and things which were
despised, yea, and things which were not, to bring to
nought things that were, that no flesh should glory in
His presence."

39. Such a view of things is not of a nature to be affected by what is external to it. It did not grow out
of knowledge, and an increase or loss of knowledge

cannot touch it. The revolution of kingdoms, the rise
or the fall of parties, the growth of society, the discoveries of science, leave it as they found it. On God's
word does it depend; that word alone can alter it. And
thus we are introduced to a distinct peculiarity of Faith;
for considering that Almighty God often speaks, nay is
ever speaking in one way or another, if we would watch
for His voice, Faith, while it is so stable, is necessarily
a principle of mental growth also, in an especial way;
according, that is, as God sees fit to employ it. "I
will stand upon my watch," says the prophet, "and set
me upon the tower, and will watch to see what He will
say unto me;" and though since Christ came no new
revelation has been given, yet much even in the latter
days has been added in the way of explaining and
applying what was given once for all. As the world
around varies, so varies also, not the principles of the
doctrine of Christ, but the outward shape and colour
which they assume. And as Wisdom only can apply
or dispense the Truth in a change of circumstances, so
Faith alone is able to accept it as one and the same
under all its forms. And thus Faith is ever the means
of learning something new, and in this respect differs
from Bigotry, which has no element of advance in it,
and is under a practical persuasion that it has nothing
to learn. To the narrow-minded and the bigoted the
history of the Church for eighteen centuries is unintel-
ligible and useless; but where there is Faith, it is full
of sacred principles, ever the same in substance, ever
varying in accidentals, and is a continual lesson of
"the manifold Wisdom of God."

40. Moreover, though Faith has not the gift of tracing out and connecting one thing with another, which Wisdom has, and Bigotry professes to have, but is an isolated act of Reason upon any matter in hand, as it comes; yet on this very account it has as wide a range as Wisdom, and a far wider one than can belong to any narrow principle or partial theory, and is able to take discursive views, though not systematic. There is no subject which Faith working by Love may not include in its province, on which it may not have a judgment, and to which it may not do justice, though it views each point by itself, and not as portions of a whole. Hence, unable as Faith is to analyze its grounds, or to show the consistency of one of its judgments with another, yet every one of these has its own place, and corresponds to some doctrine or precept in the philosophical system of the Gospel, for they are all the instincts of a pure mind, which steps forward truly and boldly, and is never at fault. Whatever be the subject-matter and the point in question, sacred or profane, Faith has a true view of it, and Wisdom can have no more; nor does it become truer because it is held in connexion with other opinions, or less true because it is not. And thus, since Faith is the characteristic of all Christians, a peasant may take the same view of human affairs in detail as a philosopher; and we are often perplexed whether to say that such persons are intellectually gifted or not. They have clear and distinct opinions; they know what they are saying; they have something to say about any subject; they do not confuse points of primary with those of secondary import-

ance; they never contradict themselves: on the other hand they are not aware that there is any thing extra-ordinary about their judgments; they do not connect any two judgments together; they do not recognize any common principles running through them; they forget the opinions they have expressed, together with the occasion; they cannot defend themselves; they are easily perplexed and silenced; and, if they set themselves to reason, they use arguments which appear to be faulty, as being but types and shadows of those which they really feel, and attempts to analyze that vast system of thought which is their life, but not their instrument.

41. It is the peculiarity, then, of Faith, that it forms its judgment under a sense of duty and responsibility, with a view to personal conduct, according to revealed directions, with a confession of ignorance, with a care-lessness about consequences, in a teachable and humble spirit, yet upon a range of subjects which Philosophy itself cannot surpass. In all these respects it is con-trasted with Bigotry. Men of narrow minds, far from confessing ignorance and maintaining Truth mainly as a duty, profess, as I observed just now, to understand the subjects which they take up and the principles which they apply to them. They do not see difficulties. They consider that they hold their doctrines, whatever they are, at least as much upon Reason as upon Faith; and they expect to be able to argue others into a belief of them, and are impatient when they cannot. They consider that the premisses with which they start just prove the conclusions which they draw, and nothing else. They think that their own views are exactly fitted

to solve all the facts which are to be accounted for, to
satisfy all objections, and to moderate and arbitrate between all parties. They conceive that they profess just
the truth which makes all things easy. They have their
one idea or their favourite notion, which occurs to them
on every occasion. They have their one or two topics,
which they are continually obtruding, with a sort of
pedantry, being unable to discuss, in a natural uncon-
strained way, or to let their thoughts take their course,
in the confidence that they will come safe home at the
last. Perhaps they have discovered, as they think, the
leading idea, or simple view, or sum and substance of
the Gospel; and they insist upon this or that isolated
tenet, selected by themselves or by others not better
qualified, to the disparagement of the rest of the revealed scheme. They have, moreover, clear and decisive explanations always ready of the sacred mysteries
of Faith; they may deny those mysteries or retain them,
but in either case they think their own to be the rational
view and the natural explanation of them, and all minds
feeble or warped or disordered which do not acknowledge this. They profess that the inspired writers were
precisely of their particular creed, be it a creed of to-
day, or yesterday, or of a hundred years since; and
they do not shrink from appealing to the common sense
of mankind at large to decide this point. Then their
proof of doctrines is as meagre as their statement of
them. They are ready with the very places of Scripture,—one, two, or three,—where it is to be found;
they profess to say just what each passage and verse
means, what it cannot mean, and what it must mean.

To see in it less than they see is, in their judgment, to explain away; to see more, is to gloss over. To proceed to other parts of Scripture than those which they happen to select, is, they think, superfluous, since they have already adduced the very arguments sufficient for a clear proof; and if so, why go beyond them? And again, they have their own terms and names for every thing; and these must not be touched any more than the things which they stand for. Words of parties or politics, of recent date and unsatisfactory origin, are as much a portion of the Truth in their eyes, as if they were the voice of Scripture or of Holy Church. And they have their forms, ordinances, and usages, which are as sacred to them as the very Sacraments given us from heaven.

42. Narrow minds have no power of throwing themselves into the minds of others. They have stiffened in one position, as limbs of the body subjected to confinement, or as our organs of speech, which after a while cannot learn new tones and inflections. They have already parcelled out to their own satisfaction the whole world of knowledge; they have drawn their lines, and formed their classes, and given to each opinion, argument, principle, and party, its own locality; they profess to know where to find every thing; and they cannot learn any other disposition. They are vexed at new principles of arrangement, and grow giddy amid cross divisions; and, even if they make the effort, cannot master them. They think that any one truth excludes another which is distinct from it, and that every opinion is contrary to their own opinions which is not included

in them. They cannot separate words from their own ideas, and ideas from their own associations; and if they attain any new view of a subject, it is but for a moment. They catch it one moment, and let it go the next; and then impute to subtlety in it, or obscurity in its expression, what really arises from their own want of elasticity or vigour. And when they attempt to describe it in their own language, their nearest approximation to it is a mistake; not from any purpose to be unjust, but because they are expressing the ideas of another mind, as it were, in translation.

43. It is scarcely necessary to observe upon the misconceptions which such persons form of foreign habits of thought, or again of ancient faith or philosophy; and the more so because they are unsuspicious of their own deficiency. Thus we hear the Greek Fathers, for instance, sometimes called Arminians, and St. Augustine Calvinistic; and that not analogously, but as if each party really answered to the title given to it. And again an inquiry is made whether Christians in those early days held this or that point of doctrine, which may be in repute in particular sects or schools now; as, for instance, whether they upheld the union of Church and State, or the doctrine of assurance. It is plain that to answer either in the affirmative or negative would be to misrepresent them; yet the persons in question do not contemplate more than such an absolute alternative.

44. Nor is it only in censure and opposition that narrowness of view is shown; it lies quite as often in approval and partisanship. None are so easily deceived

by others as they who are pre-occupied with their own
notions. They are soon persuaded that another agrees
with them, if he disagrees with their opponents. They
resolve his ideas into their own, and, whatever words
he may use to clear his meaning, even the most distinct and forcible, these fail to convey to them any new
view, or to open to them his mind.

45. Again, if those principles are narrow which
claim to interpret and subject the whole world of knowledge, without being adequate to the task, one of the
most striking characteristics of such principles will be
the helplessness which they exhibit, when new materials
or fields of thought are opened upon them. True philosophy admits of being carried out to any extent; it
is its very test, that no knowledge can be submitted to
it with which it is not commensurate, and which it cannot annex to its territory. But the theory of the narrow
or bigoted has already run out within short limits, and
a vast and anxious region lies beyond, unoccupied and
in rebellion. Their " bed is shorter than that a man
can stretch himself on it; and the covering narrower,
than that he can wrap himself in it." And then
what is to be done with these unreclaimed wastes ?—
the exploring of them must in consequence be forbidden, or even the existence denied. Thus, in the
present day, there are new sciences, especially physical,
which we all look at with anxiety, feeling that our views,
as we at present hold them, are unequal to them, yet
feeling also that no truth can really exist external to
Christianity. Another striking proof of narrowness of
mind among us may be drawn from the alteration of

feeling with which we often regard members of this or that communion, before we know them and after. If our theory and our view of facts agreed together, they could not lead to opposite impressions about the same matters. And another instance occurs daily : true Catholicity is commensurate with the wants of the human mind; but persons are often to be found who are surprised that they cannot persuade all men to follow them, and cannot destroy dissent, by preaching a portion of the Divine system, instead of the whole of it.

46. Under these circumstances, it is not wonderful that persons of narrow views are often perplexed, and sometimes startled and unsettled, by the difficulties of their position. What they did not know, or what they knew but had not weighed, suddenly presses upon their notice. Then they become impatient that they cannot make their proofs clear, and try to make a forcible riddance of objections. They look about for new arguments, and put violence on Scripture or on history. They show a secret misgiving about the truth of their principles, by shrinking from the appearance of defeat or from occasional doubt within. They become alarmists, and they forget that the issue of all things, and the success of their own cause (if it be what they think it), is sealed and secured by Divine promise; and sometimes, in this conflict between broad fact and narrow principle, the hard material breaks their tools ; they are obliged to give up their principles. A state of uncertainty and distress follows, and, in the end, perhaps, bigotry is supplanted by general scepticism. They who thought their own ideas could measure all

things, end in thinking that even a Divine Oracle is unequal to the task.

47. In these remarks, it will be observed that I have been contrasting Faith and Bigotry as habits of mind entirely distinct from each other. They are so; but it must not be forgotten, as indeed I have already observed, that, though distinct in themselves, they may and do exist together in the same person. No one so imbued with a loving Faith but has somewhat, perhaps, of Bigotry to unlearn; no one so narrow-minded, and full of self, but is influenced, it is to be hoped, in his degree, by the spirit of Faith.

48. Let us ever make it our prayer and our endeavour, that we may know the whole counsel of God, and grow unto the measure of the stature of the fulness of Christ; that all prejudice, and self-confidence, and hollowness, and unreality, and positiveness, and partisanship, may be put away from us under the light of Wisdom, and the fire of Faith and Love; till we see things as God sees them, with the judgment of His Spirit, and according to the mind of Christ.

SERMON XV.

THE THEORY OF DEVELOPMENTS IN RELIGIOUS
DOCTRINE.

(Preached on the Purification, 1843.)

LUKE ii. 19.

"But Mary kept all these things, and pondered them in her heart."

LITTLE is told us in Scripture concerning the Blessed
Virgin, but there is one grace of which the Evangelists make her the pattern, in a few simple sentences,
—of Faith. Zacharias questioned the Angel's message, but "Mary said, Behold the handmaid of the
Lord; be it unto me according to thy word." Accordingly Elisabeth, speaking with an apparent allusion
to the contrast thus exhibited between her own highly-
favoured husband, righteous Zacharias, and the still
more highly-favoured Mary, said, on receiving her salu-
tation, "Blessed art thou among women, and blessed
is the fruit of thy womb; Blessed is she that believed,
for there shall be a performance of those things which
were told her from the Lord."

2. But Mary's faith did not end in a mere acquiescence in Divine providences and revelations : as the
text informs us, she "pondered" them. When the

shepherds came, and told of the vision of Angels which they had seen at the time of the Nativity, and how one of them announced that the Infant in her arms was "the Saviour, which is Christ the Lord," while others did but wonder, "Mary kept all these things, and pondered them in her heart." Again, when her Son and Saviour had come to the age of twelve years, and had left her for awhile for His Father's service, and had been found, to her surprise, in the Temple, amid the doctors, both hearing them and asking them questions, and had, on her addressing Him, vouchsafed to justify His conduct, we are told, "His mother kept all these sayings in her heart." And accordingly, at the marriage-feast in Cana, her faith anticipated His first miracle, and she said to the servants, "Whatsoever He saith unto you, do it."

3. Thus St. Mary is our pattern of Faith, both in the reception and in the study of Divine Truth. She does not think it enough to accept, she dwells upon it; not enough to possess, she uses it; not enough to assent, she developes it; not enough to submit the Reason, she reasons upon it; not indeed reasoning first, and believing afterwards, with Zacharias, yet first believing without reasoning, next from love and reverence, reasoning after believing. And thus she symbolizes to us, not only the faith of the unlearned, but of the doctors of the Church also, who have to investigate, and weigh, and define, as well as to profess the Gospel; to draw the line between truth and heresy; to anticipate or remedy the various aberrations of wrong reason; to combat pride and recklessness with their

own arms ; and thus to triumph over the sophist and the innovator.

4. If, then, on a Day dedicated to such high contemplations as the Feast which we are now celebrating, it is allowable to occupy the thoughts with a subject not of a devotional or practical nature, it will be some relief of the omission to select one in which St. Mary at least will be our example,—the use of Reason in investigating the doctrines of Faith ; a subject, indeed, far fitter for a volume than for the most extended notice which can here be given to it; but one which cannot be passed over altogether in silence, in any attempt at determining the relation of Faith to Reason.

5. The overthrow of the wisdom of the world was one of the earliest, as well as the noblest of the triumphs of the Church ; after the pattern of her Divine Master, who took His place among the doctors before He preached His new Kingdom, or opposed Himself to the world's power. St. Paul, the learned Pharisee, was the first fruits of that gifted company, in whom the pride of science is seen prostrated before the foolishness of preaching. From his day to this the Cross has enlisted under its banner all those great endowments of mind, which in former times had been expended on vanities, or dissipated in doubt and speculation. Nor was it long before the schools of heathenism took the alarm, and manifested an unavailing jealousy of the new doctrine, which was robbing them of their most hopeful disciples. They had hitherto taken for granted that the natural home of the Intellect was the Garden or

the Porch; and it reversed their very first principles to
be called on to confess, what yet they could not deny,
that a Superstition, as they considered it, was attracting
to itself all the energy, the keenness, the originality,
and the eloquence of the age. But these aggressions
upon heathenism were only the beginning of the
Church's conquests; in the course of time the whole
mind of the world, as I may say, was absorbed into the
philosophy of the Cross, as the element in which it
lived, and the form upon which it was moulded. And
how many centuries did this endure, and what vast
ruins still remain of its dominion! In the capitals of
Christendom the high cathedral and the perpetual
choir still witness to the victory of Faith over the
world's power. To see its triumph over the world's
wisdom, we must enter those solemn cemeteries in
which are stored the relics and the monuments of ancient
Faith—our libraries. Look along their shelves, and
every name you read there is, in one sense or other, a
trophy set up in record of the victories of Faith. How
many long lives, what high aims, what single-minded
devotion, what intense contemplation, what fervent
prayer, what deep erudition, what untiring diligence,
what toilsome conflicts has it taken to establish its
supremacy! This has been the object which has given
meaning to the life of Saints, and which is the subject-
matter of their history. For this they have given up
the comforts of earth and the charities of home, and
surrendered themselves to an austere rule, nay, even
to confessorship and persecution, if so be they could
make some small offering, or do some casual service, or

provide some additional safeguard towards the great
work which was in progress. This has been the origin
of controversies, long and various, yes, and the occasion
of much infirmity, the test of much hidden perverseness, and the subject of much bitterness and tumult.
The world has been moved in consequence of it,
populations excited, leagues and alliances formed,
kingdoms lost and won : and even zeal, when excessive,
evinced a sense of its preciousness ; nay, even rebellions
in some sort did homage to it, as insurgents imply the
actual sovereignty of the power which they are assail-
ing. Meanwhile the work went on, and at length a
large fabric of divinity was reared, irregular in its
structure, and diverse in its style, as beseemed the
slow growth of centuries ; nay, anomalous in its details,
from the peculiarities of individuals, or the interference
of strangers, but still, on the whole, the development
of an idea, and like itself, and unlike any thing else, its
most widely-separated parts having relations with each
other, and betokening a common origin.

6. Let us quit this survey of the general system, and
descend to the history of the formation of any Catholic
dogma. What a remarkable sight it is, as almost all
unprejudiced persons will admit, to trace the course of
the controversy, from its first disorders to its exact and
determinate issue. Full of deep interest, to see how
the great idea takes hold of a thousand minds by its
living force, and will not be ruled or stinted, but is
" like a burning fire," as the Prophet speaks, " shut
up " within them, till they are " weary of forbearing,
and cannot stay," and grows in them, and at length is

born through them, perhaps in a long course of years, and even successive generations; so that the doctrine may rather be said to use the minds of Christians, than to be used by them. Wonderful it is to see with what effort, hesitation, suspense, interruption,—with how many swayings to the right and to the left—with how many reverses, yet with what certainty of advance, with what precision in its march, and with what ultimate completeness, it has been evolved; till the whole truth "self-balanced on its centre hung," part answering to part, one, absolute, integral, indissoluble, while the world lasts! Wonderful, to see how heresy has but thrown that idea into fresh forms, and drawn out from it farther developments, with an exuberance which exceeded all questioning, and a harmony which baffled all criticism, like Him, its Divine Author, who, when put on trial by the Evil One, was but fortified by the assault, and is ever justified in His sayings, and overcomes when He is judged.

7. And this world of thought is the expansion of a few words, uttered, as if casually, by the fishermen of Galilee. Here is another topic which belongs more especially to that part of the subject to which I propose to confine myself. Reason has not only submitted, it has ministered to Faith; it has illustrated its documents; it has raised illiterate peasants into philosophers and divines; it has elicited a meaning from their words which their immediate hearers little suspected. Stranger surely is it that St. John should be a theologian, than that St. Peter should be a prince. This is a phenomenon proper to the Gospel, and a note

of divinity. Its half sentences, its overflowings of
language, admit of development[1]; they have a life in
them which shows itself in progress; a truth, which
has the token of consistency; a reality, which is fruit-
ful in resources; a depth, which extends into mystery:
for they are representations of what is actual, and has a
definite location and necessary bearings and a meaning in the great system of things, and a harmony in
what it is, and a compatibility in what it involves.
What form of Paganism can furnish a parallel? What
philosopher has left his words to posterity as a talent
which could be put to usury, as a mine which could be
wrought? Here, too, is the badge of heresy; its
dogmas are unfruitful; it has no theology; so far forth
as it is heresy, it has none. Deduct its remnant of
Catholic theology, and what remains? Polemics, explanations, protests. It turns to Biblical Criticism, or
to the Evidences of Religion, for want of a province.
Its *formulæ* end in themselves, without development,
because they are words; they are barren, because they
are dead. If they had life, they would increase and
multiply; or, if they do live and bear fruit, it is but as
"sin, when it is finished, bringeth forth death." It
developes into dissolution; but it creates nothing, it
tends to no system, its resultant dogma is but the
denial of all dogmas, any theology, under the Gospel.
No wonder it denies what it cannot attain.

8. Heresy denies to the Church what is wanting in
itself. Here, then, we are brought to the subject to
which I wish to give attention. It need not surely

[1] Vide Butler's Analogy, part ii. ch. iii.

formally be proved that this disparagement of doctrinal statements, and in particular of those relating to the Holy Trinity and Incarnation, is especially prevalent in our times. There is a suspicion widely abroad,—felt, too, perhaps, by many who are unwilling to confess it, —that the development of ideas and formation of dogmas is a mere abuse of Reason, which, when it attempted such sacred subjects, went beyond its powers, and could do nothing more than multiply words without meaning, and deductions which come to nothing. The conclusion follows, that such an attempt does but lead to mischievous controversy, from that discordance of doctrinal opinions, which is its immediate consequence; that there is, in truth, no necessary or proper connexion between inward religious belief and scientific expositions; and that charity, as well as good sense, is best consulted by reducing creeds to the number of private opinions, which, if individuals will hold for themselves, at least they have no right to impose upon others.

9. It is my purpose, then, in what follows, to investigate the connexion between Faith and Dogmatic Confession, as far as relates to the sacred doctrines which were just now mentioned, and to show the office of the Reason in reference to it; and, in doing so, I shall make as little allusion as may be to erroneous views on the subject, which have been mentioned only for the sake of perspicuity; following rather the course which the discussion may take, and pursuing those issues on which it naturally opens. Nor am I here in any way concerned with the question, who is the legi-

timate framer and judge of these dogmatic inferences
under the Gospel, or if there be any. Whether the
Church is infallible, or the individual, or the first ages,
or none of these, is not the point here, but the theory
of developments itself.

10. Theological dogmas are propositions expressive
of the judgments which the mind forms, or the impressions which it receives, of Revealed Truth. Revelation
sets before it certain supernatural facts and actions,
beings and principles; these make a certain impression
or image upon it; and this impression spontaneously,
or even necessarily, becomes the subject of reflection
on the part of the mind itself, which proceeds to investigate it, and to draw it forth in successive and distinct
sentences. Thus the Catholic doctrine of Original Sin,
or of Sin after Baptism, or of the Eucharist, or of
Justification, is but the expression of the inward belief
of Catholics on these several points, formed upon an
analysis of that belief[2]. Such, too, are the high doctrines with which I am especially concerned.

11. Now, here I observe, first of all, that, naturally
as the inward idea of divine truth, such as has been
described, passes into explicit form by the activity of
our reflective powers, still such an actual delineation is
not essential to its genuineness and perfection. A
peasant may have such a true impression, yet be unable

---

[2] The controversy between the English Church and the Church of
Rome lies, it is presumed, *in the matter of fact,* whether such and such
developments are true, (e. g. Purgatory a true development of the doctrine of sin after baptism,) not in the *principle* of development itself.

to give any intelligible account of it, as will easily be understood. But what is remarkable at first sight is this, that there is good reason for saying that the impression made upon the mind need not even be recognized by the parties possessing it. It is no proof that persons are not possessed, because they are not conscious, of an idea. Nothing is of more frequent occurrence, whether in things sensible or intellectual, than the existence of such unperceived impressions. What do we mean when we say, that certain persons do not know themselves, but that they are ruled by views, feelings, prejudices, objects which they do not recognize? How common is it to be exhilarated or depressed, we do not recollect why, though we are aware that something has been told us, or has happened, good or bad, which accounts for our feeling, could we recall it! What is memory itself, but a vast magazine of such dormant, but present and excitable ideas ? Or consider, when persons would trace the history of their own opinions in past years, how baffled they are in the attempt to fix the date of this or that conviction, their system of thought having been all the while in continual, gradual, tranquil expansion ; so that it were as easy to follow the growth of the fruit of the earth, " first the blade, then the ear, after that the full corn in the ear," as to chronicle changes, which involved no abrupt revolution, or reaction, or fickleness of mind, but have been the birth of an idea, the development, in explicit form, of what was already latent within it. Or, again, critical disquisitions are often written about the idea which this or that poet might have in his mind in certain of his compositions and characters; and we call such analysis the philosophy of poetry, not implying thereby of necessity that the author wrote upon a theory in his actual delineation, or knew what he was doing; but that, in matter of fact, he was possessed, ruled, guided by an unconscious idea. Moreover, it is a question whether that strange and painful feeling of unreality, which religious men experience from time to time, when nothing seems true, or good, or right, or profitable, when Faith seems a name, and duty a mockery, and all endeavours to do right, absurd and hopeless, and all things forlorn and dreary, as if religion were wiped out from the world, may not be the direct effect of the temporary obscuration of some master vision, which unconsciously supplies the mind with spiritual life and peace.

12. Or, to take another class of instances which are to the point so far as this, that at least they are real impressions, even though they be not influential. How common is what is called vacant vision, when objects meet the eye, without any effort of the judgment to measure or locate them; and that absence of mind, which recollects minutes afterwards the occurrence of some sound, the striking of the hour, or the question of a companion, which passed unheeded at the time it took place! How, again, happens it in dreams, that we suddenly pass from one state of feeling, or one assemblage of circumstances to another, without any surprise at the incongruity, except that, while we are impressed first in this way, then in that, we take no active cognizance of the impression? And this, perhaps, is the

life of inferior animals, a sort of continuous dream, impressions without reflections; such, too, seems to be the first life of infants; nay, in heaven itself, such may be the high existence of some exalted orders of blessed spirits, as the Seraphim, who are said to be, not Knowledge, but all Love.

13. Now, it is important to insist on this circumstance, because it suggests the reality and permanence of inward knowledge, as distinct from explicit confession. The absence, or partial absence, or incompleteness of dogmatic statements is no proof of the absence of impressions or implicit judgments, in the mind of the Church. Even centuries might pass without the formal expression of a truth, which had been all along the secret life of millions of faithful souls. Thus, not till the thirteenth century was there any direct and distinct avowal, on the part of the Church, of the numerical Unity of the Divine Nature, which the language of some of the principal Greek fathers, *primâ facie*, though not really, denies. Again, the doctrine of the Double Procession was no Catholic dogma in the first ages, though it was more or less clearly stated by individual Fathers; yet, if it is now to be received, as surely it must be, as part of the Creed, it was really held every where from the beginning, and therefore, in a measure, held as a mere religious impression, and perhaps an unconscious one.

14. But, further, if the ideas may be latent in the Christian mind, by which it is animated and formed, it is less wonderful that they should be difficult to elicit and define; and of this difficulty we have abundant

proof in the history whether of the Church, or of individuals. Surely it is not at all wonderful, that, when
individuals attempt to analyze their own belief, they
should find the task arduous in the extreme, if not
altogether beyond them ; or, again, a work of many
years; or, again, that they should shrink from the true
developments, if offered to them, as foreign to their
thoughts. This may be illustrated in a variety of ways.

15. It will often happen, perhaps from the nature of
things, that it is impossible to master and express an
idea in a short space of time. As to individuals, sometimes they find they cannot do so at all; at length,
perhaps, they recognize, in some writer they meet, with
the very account of their own thoughts, which they
desiderate ; and then they say, that " here is what they
have felt all along, and wanted to say, but could not,"
or " what they have ever maintained, only better expressed." Again, how many men are burdened with
an idea, which haunts them through a great part of
their lives, and of which only at length, with much
trouble, do they dispossess themselves? I suppose
most of us have felt at times the irritation, and that
for a long period, of thoughts and views which we felt,
and felt to be true, only dimly showing themselves, or
flitting before as ; which at length we understood must
not be forced, but must have their way, and would, if
it were so ordered, come to light in their own time.
The life of some men, and those not the least eminent
among divines and philosophers, has centred in the
development of one idea; nay, perhaps has been too
short for the process. Again, how frequently it hap-

pens, that, on first hearing a doctrine propounded, a man hesitates, first acknowledges, then disowns it; then says that he has always held it, but finds fault with the mode in which it is presented to him, accusing it of paradox or over-refinement; that is, he cannot at the moment analyze his own opinions, and does not know whether he holds the doctrine or not, from the difficulty of mastering his thoughts.

16. Another characteristic, as I have said, of dogmatic statements, is the difficulty of recognizing them, even when attained, as the true representation of our meaning. This happens for many reasons; sometimes, from the faint hold we have of the impression itself, whether its nature be good or bad, so that we shrink from principles in substance, which we acknowledge in influence. Many a man, for instance, is acting on utilitarian principles, who is shocked at them in set treatises, and disowns them. Again, in sacred subjects, the very circumstance that a dogma professes to be a direct contemplation, and, if so be, a definition of what is infinite and eternal, is painful to serious minds. Moreover, from the hypothesis, it is the representation of an idea in a medium not native to it, not as originally conceived, but, as it were, in projection; no wonder, then, that, though there be an intimate correspondence, part by part, between the impression and the dogma, yet there should be an harshness in the outline of the latter; as, for instance, a want of harmonious proportion; and yet this is unavoidable, from the infirmities of our intellectual powers.

17. Again, another similar peculiarity in developments

in general, is the great remoteness of the separate results of a common idea, or rather at first sight the absence of any connexion. Thus it often happens that party spirit is imputed to persons, merely because they agree with one another in certain points of opinion and conduct, which are thought too minute, distant, and various, in the large field of religious doctrine and discipline, to proceed from any but an external influence and a positive rule; whereas an insight into the wonderfully expansive power and penetrating virtue of theological or philosophical ideas would have shown, that what is apparently arbitrary in rival or in kindred schools of thought, is after all rigidly determined by the original hypothesis. The remark has been made, for instance, that rarely have persons maintained the sleep of the soul before the Resurrection, without falling into more grievous errors; again, those who deny the Lutheran doctrine of Justification, commonly have tendencies towards a ceremonial religion; again, it is a serious fact that Protestantism has at various times unexpectedly developed into an allowance or vindication of polygamy; and heretics in general, however opposed in tenets, are found to have an inexplicable sympathy for each other, and never wake up from their ordinary torpor, but to exchange courtesies and meditate coalitions. One other remark is in point here, and relates to the length to which statements run, though, before we attempted them, we fancied our idea could be expressed in one or two sentences. Explanations grow under our hands, in spite of our effort at compression. Such, too, is the contrast between conversation and epistolary correspondence. We speak our meaning with little trouble; our voice, manner, and half words completing it for us; but in writing, when details must be drawn out, and misapprehensions anticipated, we seem never to be rid of the responsibility of our task. This being the case, it is surprising that the Creeds are so short, not surprising that they need a comment.

18. The difficulty, then, and hazard of developing doctrines implicitly received, must be fully allowed; and this is often made a ground for inferring that they have no proper developments at all; that there is no natural connexion between certain dogmas and certain impressions; and that theological science is a matter of time, and place, and accident, though inward belief is ever and every where one and the same. But surely the instinct of every Christian revolts from such a position; for the very first impulse of his faith is to try to express itself about the "great sight" which is vouchsafed to it; and this seems to argue that a science there is, whether the mind is equal to its discovery or no. And, indeed, what science is open to every chance inquirer? which is not recondite in its principles? which requires not special gifts of mind for its just formation? All subject-matters admit of true theories and false, and the false are no prejudice to the true. Why should this class of ideas be different from all other? Principles of philosophy, physics, ethics, politics, taste, admit both of implicit reception and explicit statement; why should not the ideas, which are the secret life of the Christian, be recognized also as fixed and definite in

themselves, and as capable of scientific analysis? Why should not there be that real connexion between science and its subject-matter in religion, which exists in other departments of thought? No one would deny that the philosophy of Zeno or Pythagoras was the exponent of a certain mode of viewing things; or would affirm that Platonist and Epicurean acted on one and the same idea of nature, life, and duty, and meant the same thing, though they verbally differed, merely because a Plato or an Epicurus was needed to detect the abstruse elements of thought, out of which each philosophy was eventually constructed. A man surely may be a Peripatetic or an Academic in his feelings, views, aims, and acts, who never heard the names. Granting, then, extreme cases, when individuals who would analyze their views of religion are thrown entirely upon their own reason, and find that reason unequal to the task, this will be no argument against a general, natural, and ordinary correspondence between the dogma and the inward idea. Surely, if Almighty God is ever one and the same, and is revealed to us as one and the same, the true inward impression of Him, made on the recipient of the revelation, must be one and the same; and, since human nature proceeds upon fixed laws, the statement of that impression must be one and the same, so that we may as well say that there are two Gods as two Creeds. And considering the strong feelings and energetic acts and severe sufferings which age after age have been involved in the maintenance of the Catholic dogmas, it is surely a very shallow philosophy to account such maintenance a mere contest about words, and a very abject philosophy to attribute it to mere party spirit, or to personal rivalry, or to ambition, or to covetousness.

19. Reasonable, however, as is this view of doctrinal developments in general, it cannot be denied that those which relate to the Objects of Faith, of which I am particularly speaking, have a character of their own, and must be considered separately. Let us, then, consider how the case stands, as regards the sacred doctrines of the Trinity and the Incarnation.

20. The Apostle said to the Athenians, " Whom ye ignorantly worship, Him declare I unto you ;" and the mind which is habituated to the thought of God, of Christ, of the Holy Spirit, naturally turns, as I have said, with a devout curiosity to the contemplation of the Object of its adoration, and begins to form statements concerning Him before it knows whither, or how far, it will be carried. One proposition necessarily leads to another, and a second to a third ; then some limitation is required ; and the combination of these opposites occasions some fresh evolutions from the original idea, which indeed can never be said to be entirely exhausted. This process is its development, and results in a series, or rather body of dogmatic statements, till what was at first an impression on the Imagination has become a system or creed in the Reason.

21. Now such impressions are obviously individual and complete above other theological ideas, *because* they are the impressions of Objects. Ideas and their developments are commonly not identical, the develop-

ment being but the carrying out of the idea into its consequences. Thus the doctrine of Penance may be called a development of the doctrine of Baptism, yet still is a distinct doctrine; whereas the developments in the doctrines of the Holy Trinity and the Incarnation are mere portions of the original impression, and modes of representing it. As God is one, so the impression which He gives us of Himself is one; it is not a thing of parts; it is not a system; nor is it any thing imperfect, and needing a counterpart. It is the vision of an object. When we pray, we pray, not to an assemblage of notions, or to a creed, but to One Individual Being; and when we speak of Him we speak of a Person, not of a Law or a Manifestation. This being the case, all our attempts to delineate our impression of Him go to bring out one idea, not two or three or four; not a philosophy, but an individual idea in its separate aspects.

22. This may be fitly compared to the impressions made on us through the senses. Material objects are whole, and individual; and the impressions which they make on the mind, by means of the senses, are of a corresponding nature, complex and manifold in their relations and bearings, but considered in themselves integral and one. And in like manner the ideas which we are granted of Divine Objects under the Gospel, from the nature of the case and because they are ideas, answer to the Originals so far as this, that they are whole, indivisible, substantial, and may be called real, as being images of what is real. Objects which are conveyed to us through the senses, stand out in our

minds, as I may say, with dimensions and aspects and influences various, and all of these consistent with one another, and many of them beyond our memory or even knowledge, while we contemplate the objects themselves; thus forcing on us a persuasion of their reality from the spontaneous congruity and coincidence of these accompaniments, as if they could not be creations of our minds, but were the images of external and independent beings. This of course will take place in the case of the sacred ideas which are the objects of our faith. Religious men, according to their measure, have an idea or vision of the Blessed Trinity in Unity, of the Son Incarnate and of His Presence, not as a number of qualities, attributes, and actions, not as the subject of a number of propositions, but as one, and individual, and independent of words, as an impression conveyed through the senses.

23. Particular propositions, then, which are used to express portions of the great idea vouchsafed to us, can never really be confused with the idea itself, which all such propositions taken together can but reach, and cannot exceed. As definitions are not intended to go beyond their subject, but to be adequate to it, so the dogmatic statements of the Divine Nature used in our confessions, however multiplied, cannot say more than is implied in the original idea, considered in its completeness, without the risk of heresy. Creeds and dogmas live in the one idea which they are designed to express, and which alone is substantive; and are necessary only because the human mind cannot reflect upon it, except piecemeal, cannot use it in its oneness and

entireness, nor without resolving it into a series of aspects and relations. And in matter of fact these expressions are never equivalent to it; we are able, indeed, to define the creations of our own minds, for they are what we make them and nothing else; but it were as easy to create what is real as to define it; and thus the Catholic dogmas are, after all, but symbols of a Divine fact, which, far from being compassed by those very propositions, would not be exhausted, nor fathomed, by a thousand.

24. Now of such sacred ideas and their attendant expressions, I observe :—

(1.) First, that an impression of this intimate kind seems to be what Scripture means by "knowledge." "This is life eternal," says our Saviour, "that they might know Thee the only True God, and Jesus Christ whom Thou hast sent." In like manner St. Paul speaks of willingly losing all things, "for the excellency of the knowledge of Christ Jesus;" and St. Peter of "the knowledge of Him who hath called us to glory and virtue[3]." Knowledge is the possession of those living ideas of sacred things, from which alone change of heart or conduct can proceed. This awful vision is what Scripture seems to designate by the phrases "Christ in us," "Christ dwelling in us by faith," "Christ formed in us," and "Christ manifesting Himself unto us." And though it is faint and doubtful in some minds, and distinct in others, as some remote object in the twilight or in the day, this arises from the

---

[3] John xvii. 3.   Phil. iii. 8.   2 Pet. i. 3.

circumstances of the particular mind, and does not interfere with the perfection of the gift itself.

25. (2.) This leads me next, however, to observe, that these religious impressions differ from those of material objects, in the mode in which they are made. The senses are direct, immediate, and ordinary informants, and act spontaneously without any will or effort on our part; but no such faculties have been given us, as far as we know, for realizing the Objects of Faith. It is true that inspiration may be a gift of this kind to those who have been favoured with it; nor would it be safe to deny to the illuminating grace of Baptism a power, at least of putting the mind into a capacity for receiving impressions; but the former of these is not ordinary, and both are supernatural. The secondary and intelligible means by which we receive the impression of Divine Verities, are, for instance, the habitual and devout perusal of Scripture, which gradually acts upon the mind; again, the gradual influence of intercourse with those who are in themselves in possession of the sacred ideas; again, the study of Dogmatic Theology, which is our present subject; again, a continual round of devotion; or again, sometimes, in minds both fitly disposed and apprehensive, the almost instantaneous operation of a keen faith. This obvious distinction follows between sensible and religious ideas, that we put the latter into language in order to fix, teach, and transmit them, but not the former. No one defines a material object by way of conveying to us what we know so much better by the senses, but we form creeds as a chief mode of perpetuating the impression.

26. (3.) Further, I observe, that though the Christian mind reasons out a series of dogmatic statements, one from another, this it has ever done, and always must do, not from those statements taken in themselves, as logical propositions, but as being itself enlightened and (as if) inhabited by that sacred impression which is prior to them, which acts as a regulating principle, ever present, upon the reasoning, and without which no one has any warrant to reason at all. Such sentences as " the Word was God," or " the Only-begotten Son who is in the bosom of the Father," or " the Word was made flesh," or " the Holy Ghost which proceedeth from the Father," are not a mere letter which we may handle by the rules of art at our own will, but august tokens of most simple, ineffable, adorable facts, embraced, enshrined according to its measure in the believing mind. For though the development of an idea is a deduction of proposition from proposition, these propositions are ever formed in and round the idea itself (so to speak), and are in fact one and all only aspects of it. Moreover, this will account both for the mode of arguing from particular texts or single words of Scripture, practised by the early Fathers, and for their fearless decision in practising it; for the great Object of Faith on which they lived both enabled them to appropriate to itself particular passages of Scripture, and became to them a safeguard against heretical deductions from them. Also, it will account for the charge of weak reasoning, commonly brought against those Fathers; for never do we seem so illogical to others as when we are arguing under the continual

influence of impressions to which they are insensible.

27. (4.) Again, it must of course be remembered, as I have just implied, (though as being an historical matter it hardly concerns us here), that Revelation itself has provided in Scripture the main outlines and also large details of the dogmatic system. Inspiration has superseded the exercise of human Reason in great measure, and left it but the comparatively easy task of finishing the sacred work. The question, indeed, at first sight occurs, why such inspired statements are not enough without further developments; but in truth, when Reason has once been put on the investigation, it cannot stop till it has finished it; one dogma creates another, by the same right by which it was itself created; the Scripture statements are sanctions as well as informants in the inquiry; they begin and they do not exhaust.

28. (5.) Scripture, I say, begins a series of developments which it does not finish; that is to say, in other words, it is a mistake to look for every separate proposition of the Catholic doctrine in Scripture. This is plain from what has gone before. For instance, the Athanasian Creed professes to lay down the right faith, which we must hold on its most sacred subjects, in order to be saved. This must mean that there is one view concerning the Holy Trinity, or concerning the Incarnation, which is true, and distinct from all others; one definite, consistent, entire view, which cannot be mistaken, not contained in any certain number of propositions, but held as a view by the believing mind,

and not held, but denied by Arians, Sabellians, Tritheists, Nestorians, Monophysites, Socinians, and other heretics. That idea is not enlarged, if propositions are added, nor impaired if they are withdrawn: if they are added, this is with a view of conveying that one integral view, not of amplifying it. That view does not depend on such propositions: it does not consist in them; they are but specimens and indications of it. And they may be multiplied without limit. They are necessary, but not needful to it, being but portions or aspects of that previous impression which has at length come under the cognizance of Reason and the terminology of science. The question, then, is not whether this or that proposition of the Catholic doctrine is *in terminis* in Scripture, unless we would be slaves to the letter, but whether that one view of the Mystery, of which all such are the exponents, be not there; a view which would be some other view, and not itself, if any one of such propositions, if any one of a number of similar propositions, were not true. Those propositions imply each other, as being parts of one whole; so that to deny one is to deny all, and to invalidate one is to deface and destroy the view itself. One thing alone has to be impressed on us by Scripture, the Catholic idea, and in it they all are included. To object, then, to the number of propositions, upon which an anathema is placed, is altogether to mistake their use; for their multiplication is not intended to enforce many things, but to express one,—to form within us that one impression concerning Almighty God, as the ruling principle of our minds, and that, whether we can fully recognize our own possession of it or no. And surely it is no paradox to say that such ruling ideas may exert a most powerful influence, at least in their various aspects, on our moral character, and on the whole man : as no one would deny in the case of belief or disbelief of a Supreme Being.

29. (6.) And here we see the ordinary mistake of doctrinal innovators, viz. to go away with this or that proposition of the Creed, instead of embracing that one idea which all of them together are meant to convey ; it being almost a definition of heresy, that it fastens on some one statement as if the whole truth, to the denial of all others, and as the basis of a new faith ; erring rather in what it rejects, than in what it maintains : though, in truth, if the mind deliberately rejects any portion of the doctrine, this is a proof that it does not really hold even that very statement for the sake of which it rejects the others. Realizing is the very life of true developments ; it is peculiar to the Church, and the justification of her definitions.

30. Enough has now been said on the distinction, yet connexion, between the implicit knowledge and the explicit confession of the Divine Objects of Faith, as they are revealed to us under the Gospel. An objection, however, remains, which cannot be satisfactorily treated in a few words. And what is worse than prolixity, the discussion may bear with it some appearance of unnecessary or even wanton refinement ; unless, indeed, it is thrown into the form of controversy, a worse evil. Let it suffice to say, that my wish is, not

to discover difficulties in any subject, but to solve them.

31. It may be asked, then, whether the mistake of words and names for things is not incurred by orthodox as well as heretics, in dogmatizing at all about the " secret things which belong unto the Lord our God," inasmuch as the idea of a supernatural object must itself be supernatural, and since no such ideas are claimed by ordinary Christians, no knowledge of Divine Verities is possible to them. How should any thing of this world convey ideas which are beyond and above this world ? How can teaching and intercourse, how can human words, how can earthly images, convey to the mind an idea of the Invisible ? They cannot rise above themselves. They can suggest no idea but what is resolvable into ideas natural and earthly. The words " Person," " Substance," " Consubstantial," " Generation," " Procession," " Incarnation," " Taking of the manhood into God," and the like, have either a very abject and human meaning, or none at all. In other words, there is no such inward view of these doctrines, distinct from the dogmatic language used to express them, as was just now supposed. The metaphors by which they are signified are not mere symbols of ideas which exist independently of them, but their meaning is coincident and identical with the ideas. When, indeed, we have knowledge of a thing from other sources, then the metaphors we may apply to it are but accidental appendages to that knowledge ; whereas our ideas of Divine things are just coextensive with the figures by which we express them,

neither more nor less, and without them are not; and when we draw inferences from those figures, we are not illustrating one existing idea, but drawing mere logical inferences. We speak, indeed, of material objects freely, because our senses reveal them to us apart from our words; but as to these ideas about heavenly things, we learn them from words, yet (it seems) we are to say what we, without words, conceive of them, as if words could convey what they do not contain. It follows that our anathemas, our controversies, our struggles, our sufferings, are merely about the poor ideas conveyed to us in certain figures of speech.

32. Some obvious remarks suggest themselves in answer to this representation. First, it is difficult to determine what divine grace may not do for us, if not in immediately implanting new ideas, yet in refining and elevating those which we gain through natural informants. If, as we all acknowledge, grace renews our moral feelings, yet through outward means, if it opens upon us new ideas about virtue and goodness and heroism and heavenly peace, it does not appear why, in a certain sense, it may not impart ideas concerning the nature of God. Again, the various terms and figures which are used in the doctrine of the Holy Trinity or of the Incarnation, surely may by their combination create ideas which will be altogether new, though they are still of an earthly character. And further, when it is said that such figures convey no knowledge of the Divine Nature itself, beyond those figures, whatever they are, it should be considered whether our senses can be proved to suggest any real idea of matter. All

that we know, strictly speaking, is the existence of the impressions our senses make on us ; and yet we scruple not to speak as if they conveyed to us the knowledge of material substances.   Let, then, the Catholic dogmas, as such, be freely admitted to convey no true idea of Almighty God, but only an earthly one, gained from earthly figures, provided it be allowed, on the other hand, that the senses do not convey to us any true idea of matter, but only an idea commensurate with sensible impressions.

33. Nor is there any reason why this should not be fully granted.   Still there may be a certain correspondence between the idea, though earthly, and its heavenly archetype, such, that that idea belongs to the archetype, in a sense in which no other earthly idea belongs to it, as being the nearest approach to it which our present state allows.   Indeed Scripture itself intimates the earthly nature of our present ideas of Sacred Objects, when it speaks of our now " seeing in a glass *darkly,* ἐν αἰνίγματι, but then face to face ;" and it has ever been the doctrine of divines that the Beatific Vision, or true sight of Almighty God, is reserved for the world to come. Meanwhile we are allowed such an approximation to the truth as earthly images and figures may supply to us.

34. It must not be supposed that this is the only case in which we are obliged to receive information needful to us, through the medium of our existing ideas, and consequently with but a vague apprehension of its subject-matter.   Children, who are made our pattern in Scripture, are taught, by an accommodation, on the part of their teachers, to their immature faculties and their scanty vocabulary.   To answer their questions in

the language which we should use towards grown men, would be simply to mislead them, if they could construe it at all. We must dispense and " divide " the word of truth, if we would not have it changed, as far as they are concerned, into a word of falsehood; for what is short of truth in the letter may be to them the most perfect truth, that is, the nearest approach to truth, compatible with their condition [4]. The case is the same as regards those who have any natural defect or deprivation which cuts them off from the circle of ideas common to mankind in general. To speak to a blind man of light and colours, in terms proper to those phenomena, would be to mock him; we must use other media of information accommodated to his circumstances, according to the well-known instance in which his own account of scarlet was to liken it to the sound of a trumpet. And so again, as regards savages, or the ignorant, or weak, or narrow-minded, our representations and arguments must take a certain form, if they are to gain admission into their minds at all, and to reach them. Again, what impediments do the diversities of language place in the way of communicating ideas! Language is a sort of analysis of thought; and, since ideas are infinite, and infinitely combined, and infinitely modified, whereas language is a method definite and limited, and confined to an arbitrary selection of a certain number of these innumerable materials, it were idle

---

[4] Hence it is not more than an hyperbole to say that, in certain cases, a lie is the nearest approach to the truth. [Vide Hist. of Arians, p. 67, &c. Edit. 3.] We are told that " God is not the son of man, that He should repent;" yet " it repented the Lord that He had made man."

to expect that the courses of thought marked out in one language should, except in their great outlines and main centres, correspond to those of another. Multitudes of ideas expressed in the one do not even enter into the other, and can only be conveyed by some economy or accommodation, by circumlocutions, phrases, limiting words, figures, or some bold and happy expedient. And sometimes, from the continual demand, foreign words become naturalized. Again, the difficulty is extreme, as all persons know, of leading certain individuals (to use a familiar phrase) to understand one another; their habits of thought turning apparently on points of mutual repulsion. Now this is always in a measure traceable to moral diversities between the parties; still, in many cases, it arises mainly from difference in the principle on which they have divided and subdivided that world of ideas, which comes before them both. They seem ever to be dodging each other, and need a common measure or economy to mediate between them.

35. Fables, again, are economies or accommodations, being truths and principles cast into that form in which they will be most vividly recognized; as in the well-known instance attributed to Menenius Agrippa. Again, mythical representations, at least in their better form, may be considered facts or narratives, untrue, but like the truth, intended to bring out the action of some principle, point of character, and the like. For instance, the tradition that St. Ignatius was the child whom our Lord took in His arms, may be unfounded; but it realizes to us his special relation to Christ and His

Apostles, with a keenness peculiar to itself. The same remark may be made upon certain narratives of martyrdoms, or of the details of such narratives, or of certain alleged miracles, or heroic acts, or speeches, all which are the spontaneous produce of religious feeling under imperfect knowledge. If the alleged facts did not occur, they ought to have occurred (if I may so speak); they are such as might have occurred, and would have occurred, under circumstances; and they belong to the parties to whom they are attributed, potentially, if not actually; or the like of them did occur; or occurred to others similarly circumstanced, though not to those very persons. Many a theory or view of things, on which an institution is founded, or a party held together, is of the same kind. Many an argument, used by zealous and earnest men, has this economical character, being not the very ground on which they act, (for they continue in the same course, though it be refuted,) yet, in a certain sense, a representation of it, a proximate description of their feelings in the shape of argument, on which they can rest, to which they can recur when perplexed, and appeal when questioned. Now, in this reference to accommodation or economy in human affairs, I do not meddle with the question of casuistry, viz. which of such artifices, as they may be called, are innocent, or where the line is to be drawn. That some are immoral, common sense tells us; but it is enough for my purpose, if some are necessary, as the same common sense will allow; and then the very necessity of the use will account for the abuse and perversion.

36. Even between man and man, then, constituted, as

men are, alike, various distinct instruments, keys, or *cal-culi* of thought obtain, on which their ideas and arguments shape themselves respectively, and which we must use, if we would reach them. The cogitative method, as it may be called, of one man is notoriously very different from that of another; of the lawyer from that of the soldier, of the rich from that of the poor. The territory of thought is portioned out in a hundred different ways. Abstractions, generalizations, definitions, propositions, all are framed on distinct standards; and if this is found in matters of this world between man and man, surely much more must it exist between the ideas of men, and the thoughts, ways, and works of God.

37. One of the obvious instances of this contrariety is seen in the classifications we make of the subjects of the animal or vegetable kingdoms. Here a very intelligible order has been observed by the Creator Himself; still one of which we have not, after all, the key. We are obliged to frame one of our own; and when we apply it, we find that it will not exactly answer the Divine idea of arrangement, as it discovers itself to us; there being phenomena which we cannot locate, or which, upon our system of division, are anomalies in the general harmony of the Creation.

38. Mathematical science will afford us a more extended illustration of this distinction between supernatural and eternal laws, and our attempts to represent them, that is, our economies. Various methods or *calculi* have been adopted to embody those immutable principles and dispositions of which the science treats, which are really independent of any, yet cannot be

contemplated or pursued without one or other of them. The first of these instruments of investigation employs the medium of extension; the second, that of number; the third, that of motion; the fourth proceeds on a more subtle hypothesis, that of increase. These methods are very distinct from each other, at least the geometrical and the differential; yet they are, one and all, analyses, more or less perfect, of those same necessary truths, for which we have not a name, of which we have no idea, except in the terms of such economical representations. They are all developments of one and the same range of ideas; they are all instruments of discovery as to those ideas. They stand for real things, and we can reason with them, though they be but symbols, as if they were the things themselves, for which they stand. Yet none of them carries out the lines of truth to their limits; first, one stops in the analysis, then another; like some calculating tables which answer for a thousand times, and miss in the thousand and first. While they answer, we can use them just as if they were the realities which they represent, and without thinking of those realities; but at length our instrument of discovery issues in some great impossibility or contradiction, or what we call in religion, a mystery. It has run its length; and by its failure shows that all along it has been but an expedient for practical purposes, not a true analysis or adequate image of those recondite laws which are investigated by means of it. It has never fathomed their depth, because it now fails to measure their course. At the same time, no one, because it cannot do every thing, would refuse to use it within the range in which it will act; no one would say that it was a system of empty symbols, though it be but a shadow of the unseen. Though we use it with caution, still we use it, as being the nearest approximation to the truth which our condition admits.

39. Let us take another instance, of an outward and earthly form, or economy, under which great wonders unknown seem to be typified; I mean musical sounds, as they are exhibited most perfectly in instrumental harmony. There are seven notes in the scale; make them fourteen; yet what a slender outfit for so vast an enterprise! What science brings so much out of so little? Out of what poor elements does some great master in it create his new world! Shall we say that all this exuberant inventiveness is a mere ingenuity or trick of art, like some game or fashion of the day, without reality, without meaning? We may do so; and then, perhaps, we shall also account the science of theology to be a matter of words; yet, as there is a divinity in the theology of the Church, which those who feel cannot communicate, so is there also in the wonderful creation of sublimity and beauty of which I am speaking. To many men the very names which the science employs are utterly incomprehensible. To speak of an idea or a subject seems to be fanciful or trifling, to speak of the views which it opens upon us to be childish extravagance; yet is it possible that that inexhaustible evolution and disposition of notes, so rich yet so simple, so intricate yet so regulated, so various yet so majestic, should be a mere sound, which is gone and perishes? Can it be that those mysterious stirrings

of heart, and keen emotions, and strange yearnings
after we know not what, and awful impressions from
we know not whence, should be wrought in us by
what is unsubstantial, and comes and goes, and
begins and ends in itself? It is not so; it cannot
be. No; they have escaped from some higher sphere;
they are the outpourings of eternal harmony in the
medium of created sound; they are echoes from our
Home; they are the voice of Angels, or the Magnificat
of Saints, or the living laws of Divine Governance, or
the Divine Attributes; something are they besides themselves, which we cannot compass, which we cannot utter,
—though mortal man, and he perhaps not otherwise distinguished above his fellows, has the gift of eliciting them.

40. So much on the subject of musical sound; but
what if the whole series of impressions, made on us
through the senses, be, as I have already hinted, but a
Divine economy suited to our need, and the token of
realities distinct from themselves, and such as might be
revealed to us, nay, more perfectly, by other senses,
different from our existing ones as they from each other?
What if the properties of matter, as we conceive of
them, are merely relative to us, so that facts and events,
which seem impossible when predicated concerning it in
terms of those impressions, are impossible only in those
terms, not in themselves,—impossible only because of
the imperfection of the idea, which, in consequence of
those impressions, we have conceived of material substances? If so, it would follow that the laws of physics,
as we consider them, are themselves but generalizations
of economical exhibitions, inferences from figure and

shadow, and not more real than the phenomena from which they are drawn. Scripture, for instance, says that the sun moves and the earth is stationary; and science, that the earth moves, and the sun is comparatively at rest. How can we determine which of these opposite statements is the very truth, till we know what motion is? If our idea of motion be but an accidental result of our present senses, neither proposition is true, and both are true; neither true philosophically, both true for certain practical purposes in the system in which they are respectively found; and physical science will have no better meaning when it says that the earth moves, than plane astronomy when it says that the earth is still.

41. And should any one fear lest thoughts such as these should tend to a dreary and hopeless scepticism, let him take into account the Being and Providence of God, the Merciful and True; and he will at once be relieved of his anxiety. All is dreary till we believe, what our hearts tell us, that we are subjects of His Governance; nothing is dreary, all inspires hope and trust, directly we understand that we are under His hand, and that whatever comes to us is from Him, as a method of discipline and guidance. What is it to us whether the knowledge He gives us be greater or less, if it be He who gives it? What is it to us whether it be exact or vague, if He bids us trust it? What have we to care whether we are or are not given to divide substance from shadow, if He is training us heavenwards by means of either? Why should we vex ourselves to find whether our deductions are philosophical

or no, provided they are religious? If our senses supply the media by which we are put on trial, by which we are all brought together, and hold intercourse with each other, and are disciplined and are taught, and enabled to benefit others, it is enough. We have an instinct within us, impelling us, we have external necessity forcing us, to trust our senses, and we may leave the question of their substantial truth for another world, "till the day break, and the shadows flee away[5]." And what is true of reliance on our senses, is true of all the information which it has pleased God to vouchsafe to us, whether in nature or in grace.

42. Instances, then, such as these, will be found both to sober and to encourage us in our theological studies,—to impress us with a profound sense of our ignorance of Divine Verities, when we know most; yet to hinder us from relinquishing their contemplation, though we know so little. On the one hand, it would appear that even the most subtle questions of the schools may have a real meaning, as the most intricate *formulæ* in analytics; and, since we cannot tell how far our instrument of thought reaches in the process of investigation, and at what point it fails us, no ques-

---

[5] The senses convey to the mind "substantial truth," in so far as they bring home to us that certain things are, and *in confuso* what they are. But has a man born blind, by means of hearing, smelling, taste, and touch, such an idea of physical nature, as may be called *substantially* true, or, on the contrary, an idea which at best is but the *shadow* of the truth? for, in whichever respect, whether as in substance or by a shadow, the blind man knows the objects of sight, in the same are those things, in "which eye has not seen, nor ear heard," apprehended by us now, "in a glass darkly," *per speculum, in ænigmate.*]

tions may safely be despised. " Whether God was any where before creation ?" "whether He knows all creatures in Himself?" "whether the blessed see all things possible and future in Him ?" " whether relation is the form of the Divine Persons ?" " in what sense the Holy Spirit is Divine Love ?" these, and a multitude of others, far more minute and remote, are all sacred from their subject.

43. On the other hand, it must be recollected that not even the Catholic reasonings and conclusions, as contained in Confessions, and most thoroughly received by us, are worthy of the Divine Verities which they represent, but are the truth only in as full a measure as our minds can admit it; the truth as far as they go, and under the conditions of thought which human feebleness imposes. It is true that God is without beginning, if eternity may worthily be considered to imply succession; in every place, if He who is a Spirit can have relations with space. It is right to speak of His Being and Attributes, if He be not rather super-essential; it is true to say that He is wise or powerful, if we may consider Him as other than the most simple Unity. He is truly Three, if He is truly One; He is truly One, if the idea of Him falls under earthly number. He has a triple Personality, in the sense in which the Infinite can be understood to have Personality at all. If we know any thing of Him,—if we may speak of Him in any way,—if we may emerge from Atheism or Pantheism into religious faith,—if we would have any saving hope, any life of truth and holiness within us,—this only do we know, with this

only confession, we must begin and end our worship—
that the Father is the One God, the Son the One God,
and the Holy Ghost the One God; and that the Father
is not the Son, the Son not the Holy Ghost, and the
Holy Ghost not the Father.

44. The fault, then, which we must guard against in
receiving such Divine intimations, is the ambition of
being wiser than what is written; of employing the
Reason, not in carrying out what is told us, but in
impugning it; not in support, but in prejudice of
Faith. Brilliant as are such exhibitions of its powers,
they bear no fruit. Reason can but ascertain the
profound difficulties of our condition, it cannot remove them; it has no work, it makes no beginning, it
does but continually fall back, till it is content to be a
little child, and to follow where Faith guides it.

45. What remains, then, but to make our prayer to
the Gracious and Merciful God, the Father of Lights,
that in all our exercises of Reason, His gift, we may
thus use it,—as He would have us, in the obedience of
Faith, with a view to His glory, with an aim at His
Truth, in dutiful submission to His will, for the comfort of His elect, for the edification of Holy Jerusalem,
His Church, and in recollection of His own solemn
warning, " Every idle word that men shall speak, they
shall give account thereof in the day of judgment; for
by thy words thou shalt be justified, and by thy words
thou shalt be condemned."

LONDON:
PRINTED BY GILBERT AND RIVINGTON, LD.,
ST. JOHN'S HOUSE, CLERKENWELL ROAD, E.C.

CPSIA information can be obtained
at www.ICGtesting.com
Printed in the USA
LVHW051601191121
703844LV00013B/1048